At the Corner
of East and Now

ALSO BY FREDERICA MATHEWES-GREEN

Facing East: A Pilgrim's Journey into the Mysteries of Orthodoxy

Real Choices: Listening to Women, Looking for Alternatives to Abortion

At the Corner
of East and Now

A MODERN LIFE IN ANCIENT
CHRISTIAN ORTHODOXY

Frederica Mathewes-Green

JEREMY P. TARCHER/PUTNAM
a member of Penguin Putnam Inc.
New York

Most Tarcher/Putnam books are available at special quantity
discounts for bulk purchases for sales promotions, premiums,
fund-raising, and educational needs. Special books or book
excerpts also can be created to fit specific needs. For details,
write Putnam Special Markets, 375 Hudson Street,
New York, NY 10014.

JEREMY P. TARCHER/PUTNAM
a member of
Penguin Putnam Inc.
375 Hudson Street
New York, NY 10014
www.penguinputnam.com

First Trade Paperback Edition 2000

The Library of Congress has catalogued the hardback edition
as follows:
Mathewes-Green, Frederica.
    At the corner of east and now : a modern life in
ancient Christian Orthodoxy / Frederica Mathewes-Green.
        p.   cm.
    ISBN 0-87477-987-1
    I. Christian life—Orthodox Eastern authors. 2. Orthodox
Eastern Church—Doctrines. I. Title.
BX382.M38   1999   99-29731 CIP
281.9'73—dc21

ISBN 1-58542-044-1 (paperback edition)

Printed in the United States of America
10 9 8 7 6 5 4 3 2 1

Book design by Marysarah Quinn

With love to

MEGAN, DAVID, AND STEPHEN.

May God give you children as wonderful as mine.

CONTENTS

PROLOGUE: *Re-Scandalized*
AT THE CORNER OF MAPLE AND CAMP MEADE ROAD   1

1. *The Curse of the Law*
7:53 AM: KAIRON, VESTING PRAYERS,
AND PROSKOMEDIA   15

2. *Jesus of Santa Rosa*
AT A MEXICAN RESTAURANT IN SANTA ROSA   33

3. *Suffering*
8:31 AM: MATINS   49

4. *Dirty Words*
AT A RADIO STATION IN BALTIMORE   68

5. *The Virgin Theotokos*
9:36 AM: THE DIVINE LITURGY: OPENING ANTIPHONS
AND LITANIES   83

6. *Carolyn Writes an Icon*
AT A TOWNHOUSE IN ARBUTUS   98

7. *Holy Texts and Holy Doubt*
9:55 AM: THE LITTLE ENTRANCE, TRISAGION HYMN,
SCRIPTURES, SERMON   112

8. *Sad Santa*
AT A THRIFT SHOP IN GLEN BURNIE   127

9. *Not Seeker-Friendly*
10:12 AM: PRAYER FOR THE CATECHUMENS   146

10. *Twelve-Inch Mohawk*
AT A CAMPSITE IN BUSHNELL   156

11. *Something Specific*
10:15 AM: CHERUBIC HYMN, GREAT ENTRANCE,
KISS OF PEACE, CREED   175

12. *My Father*
IN A PLACE UNKNOWN   192

13. *Not Like Judas*
10:42 AM: THE EUCHARISTIC PRAYER   200

14. *Rachel Weeping*
AT A PRISON IN COLDWATER   215

15. *"This Is a Hard Saying"*
10:54 AM: RECEIVING COMMUNION   238

16. *Where Will You Spend Eternity?*
AT A BUFFET IN SELMA   250

17. *Lasagna*
11:11 AM: CONCLUDING PRAYERS AND DISMISSAL   266

APPENDIX A: *First Visit to an Orthodox Church—*
12 Things I Wish I'd Known   269

APPENDIX B: *For Further Reading*   276

Re-Scandalized

A little church on Sunday morning is a negligible thing. It may be the meekest, and least conspicuous, thing in America. Someone zipping between Baltimore's airport and beltway might pass this one, a little stone church drowsing like a hen at the corner of Maple and Camp Meade Road. At dawn, all is silent, except for the click every thirty seconds as the oblivious traffic light rotates through its cycle. The building's bell tower is out of proportion, too large and squat and short to match. Other than that, there's nothing much to catch the eye.

In a few hours, heaven will strike earth like lightning on this spot. The worshippers in this little building will be swept into a divine worship that proceeds eternally, grand with seraphim and incense and God enthroned, "high and lifted up, and his train filled the temple" (Isaiah 6:1). The foundations of that temple shake with the voice of angels calling "Holy" to each other, and we will be there, lifting fallible voices in the refrain, an outpost of eternity.

If this is true, it is the most astonishing thing that will happen in our city today.

I believe it is true. I didn't always. But I now believe it is the most important thing I will do in my life. When death strips away from me all the shreds of foolishness, self-indulgence, gossip, and greed, this will remain, one of the few things to remain. In the moment after Communion, I press my lips against the chalice, a kiss of surrender, veneration, and gratitude. It is the one true centering moment of my oblivious cycling days and weeks. On the chalice I see the face of Christ painted in enamel. I look at him and he looks at me. He has been looking at me a long, long time—long before I would look at him.

It is strange that I would be here. Back in my college days I was pretty dismissive of Christianity—to be more accurate, I was contemptuous and hostile. Though raised in a minimally Christian home, I had rejected the faith by my early teens. I remained spiritually curious, however, and spent the following years browsing the world's spiritual food court, gathering tasty delights. The core of my home-made belief system was "the life force"; the raw energy of life, I'd concluded, was the essence of God, and the various world religions were poetic attempts to express that truth. I selected among those scraps of poetry as they pleased me.

My senior college year I gained a startling insight: I realized that my selections were inevitably conditioned by my own tastes, prejudices, and blind spots. I was patching together a Frankenstein God in my own image, and it would never be taller than five foot one. If

I wanted to grow beyond my own meager wisdom, I would have to submit to a faith bigger than I was and accept its instruction.

At that point I chose Hinduism. I can't say it was a mature decision. Frankly, there weren't a lot of Hindus attending the University of South Carolina in the 1970s, and I chose it in part because I thought it would look really cool on me. I enjoyed the vivid poetry and mythology of the faith, but can't say I engaged it deeply.

When all the world's religions were coquetting to be my choice, Christianity didn't even make the lineup. I considered it an infantile and inadequate religion. I found it embarrassing, childish—probably because I associated it with my own naïve childhood. A rhetorician could have told me which logical fallacy this was, to presume that since I was immature when I was a preteen Christian, the faith itself was immature.

Now I stand in front of the chalice and meet Jesus' steady gaze. I have been fasting from all food and drink since last night, and standing up in this swirl of incense and chant for almost ninety minutes. I'm hungry and my feet ache. Yet all I want is more of him. To see the beauty of your face, Lord Christ, this is all I want.

I didn't become a Christian because somebody with a Bible badgered me till I was worn down. I wasn't persuaded by the logic of Christian theology or its creeds. I met Christ. This was, at the time, a big surprise, and pretty disconcerting.

It happened not long after my wedding. Gary and I were married out in the woods, me wearing sandals and unbleached muslin with flowers in my hair. You can picture it: the women in tie-dyed dresses and floating batik scarves, the jovial black lab with a red bandanna around his neck, the vegetarian reception under the trees. When archaeologists discover my wedding photos hundreds of years from now, they'll be able to place the date within five years.

We'd saved up enough funds to stretch our European honeymoon to three months, as long as we traveled by hitchhiking and discount train seats, lived on bread and cheese, and stayed in the cheapest hotels. (In one northern Italian town we figured out why it was so cheap: all afternoon we sat on the little balcony and watched women go in and out with different men.) On June 20, 1974, we took the ferry from Wales to the Irish coast and hitchhiked up to Dublin. We found a hotel, dropped our bags, and went out in the late afternoon to see what we could sightsee.

In a block of business buildings we came upon a church and decided to go inside for a look: even declared Hindus can't travel Europe without being exposed to some church architecture. I strolled around the dimly lit building, admiring stained-glass windows and stonework. Eventually I came upon a small side altar. Above it there was a white marble statue of Jesus with his arms held low and open, and his heart exposed on his chest, twined with thorns and springing with flames. This depicts an apparition to a French nun in 1675; she heard Jesus say, "Behold the heart which has so loved mankind."

I can't really explain what happened next. I was standing there looking at the statue, and then I discovered I was on my knees. I could hear an interior voice speaking to me. Not with my ears—it was more like a radio inside suddenly clicked on. The voice was both intimate and authoritative, and it filled me.

It said, "I am your life. You think that your life is your name, your personality, your history. But that is not your life. I am your life." It went on, naming that "life force" notion I admired: "Beyond that, you think that your life is the fact that you are alive, that your breath goes in and out, that energy courses in your veins. But even that is not your life. I am your life.

"I am the foundation of everything else in your life."

I stood up feeling pretty shaky. It was like sitting quietly in your living room and having the roof blown off. I didn't have any doubt who the "I" was that was speaking to me, and it wasn't someone I was eager to get to know. If someone had asked me a half hour earlier, I would have said I was not sure the fellow had ever lived. Yet here he was, and though I didn't know him, it seemed he already knew me, from the deepest inside out.

I kept quiet about this for a week, trying to figure it out. I didn't even tell Gary, though he must have wondered why my eyebrows kept hovering up near my hairline.

This wasn't one of those woo-woo spiritual experiences where everything goes misty and the next day you wonder if it really happened. It was shockingly *real*, as if I'd encountered a dimension of reality I'd never known existed before. Years later I read C. S. Lewis's novella *The Great Divorce*, which begins with the charming idea that every day a bus crosses the great divide from hell to heaven. Anyone who wants can go, and anyone who wants can stay. The thing is, heaven hurts. It's too real. The visitors from hell can't walk on the grass, because the blades pierce their feet like knives. It takes time to grow real enough to endure heaven, a process of unflinching self-discovery and repentance that few are willing to take. At the end of the day, most of the tourists get back on the bus to hell.

This experience in the church was real like that, like grass that pierces your feet. In that explosive moment, I found that Jesus was realer than anything I'd ever encountered, the touchstone of reality. It left me with a great hunger for more, so that my whole life is leaning toward him, questing for him, striving to break down the walls inside that shelter me from his gaze. I am looking for him all my life, an addict.

———————

What we do in this little stone church is pretty strange: what's strange is that it should seem so unremarkable. The whole Christian story is strange. Frederick Buechner describes the Incarnation as "a kind of vast joke whereby the creator of the ends of the earth comes among us in diapers." He concludes, "Until we too have taken the idea of the God-man seriously enough to be scandalized by it, we have not taken it as seriously as it demands to be taken."

But we have taken the idea as seriously as a child can. America is far from spiritually monolithic, but the vast backdrop of our culture is Christian, and for most of us it is the earliest faith we know. The "idea of the God-man" is not strange or scandalous, because it first swam in milk and butter on the top of our oatmeal decades ago. At that age, many things were strange, though most were more immediately palpable. A God-filled baby in a pile of straw was a pleasant image but somewhat theoretical compared with the heartstopping exhilaration of a visit from Santa Claus. The way a thunderstorm ripped the night sky, the hurtling power of the automobile Daddy drove so bravely, the rapture of ice cream—how could the distant Incarnation compete with those? We grew up with the Jesus story, until we outgrew it. The last day we walked out of Sunday School may be the last day we seriously engaged this faith. Thus the average person's conception of the Christian faith is a child's conception, still hobbled by a child's perspective and presumptions. We were fed the oatmeal version of Christianity, boiled down to what a child could comprehend, and to many it never occurs that there might be something more to know. The other great faiths of the world we encounter as adults and can perceive their depth and complexity. We cease thinking about Christianity when we are children, and so fail to glimpse the power and passion that has inspired poets and martyrs and theologians for millennia. There is ample material here to ponder for a lifetime. The problem is we think we already know it all.

Eastern Orthodoxy gives us a chance to see it new again, because the form is unfamiliar, while the Lord at its heart is the same. Many people don't even realize that there is an Eastern Christian Church; check the bookstores where shelves are tidily labeled "Eastern Religions" and "Western Religions." But Christianity began in the Middle East, and spread in both directions at once; it is not an exclusively western possession.

Christian faith begins not with a teaching or insight but with a geographically rooted event: a crucifixion on a hill outside Jerusalem. From there, one branch of the faith moved westward, to Rome and through Europe, while another reached south into Egypt and Ethiopia, north and east to Greece, Finland, Persia, India, and Russia. Soon five main cities emerged as centers of the faith: Jerusalem, Rome, Antioch, Constantinople, and Alexandria in Egypt.

This united faith endured a division roughly every five hundred years. In the fifth and sixth centuries some of the churches of the south and east separated over issues of the divinity of Christ. These churches—for example, the Armenian Orthodox and the Egyptian Copts—share with Eastern Orthodoxy a great many elements of faith and practice, such as icons, incense, and chant. Full Communion, however, has not been restored.

More significant in western history was the Great Schism between what would become Eastern Orthodoxy and Roman Catholicism, usually dated to 1054 A.D. For some time tempers had been flaring over the role of the pope: was he the supreme head of all Christians, empowered to rule over local churches everywhere? Or was his role mostly honorary, that of "first among [self-governing] equals"? Could he hand down doctrine single-handedly, or were points of faith to be determined by consensus, as leaders deliberated in council and the laity either received or rejected their conclusions? In one of those pinpoints of history, this conflict between top-down and bottom-up church leadership came to a head over the pope's authority to add a single word to the Nicene Creed. Rome went one way and the four other cities—Constantinople, Antioch, Alexandria, and Jerusalem—went the other. Those four have continued united to this day, sharing a faith indistinguishable from that of the first century. In the West, however, another split took place five hundred years after the break between East and West, and the Protestant Reformation began peeling new denominations off of Rome.

Though westerners tend to think of Protestant and Roman Catholic as the two opposite poles of Christian faith, in eastern eyes this quarreling mother and daughter bear a strong family resemblance. The two circle around questions of common obsession, questions which often do not arise in the East: works versus faith, Scripture versus Tradition, papacy versus individualism. This very context of habitual argument creates a climate of nitpicking, and every theological topic that can be defined, and some which are beyond definition, gets scrutinized in turn. As a result, the East sees in the West an unhelpful tendency to plow up the roots of mystery.

While the initial schism between East and West led to further divisions in the West, as new Protestant denominations continue to emerge, the Orthodox Church remained intact. The Church is kept from significant change by its characteristic governing principle:

conciliarity. Unlike religious bodies where a single powerful leader dispenses the faith, in Orthodoxy it is believed that the Holy Spirit guides the whole community of believers into the truth (as Jesus promised in John 16:13). Faith is a treasure jointly possessed by all believers, not one guarded by a powerful few; it accumulates over the centuries, never contradicting what has been previously held. Thus there is continuity from first-century Jerusalem, to fourth-century Egypt, to seventh-century Constantinople, to eleventh-century Russia, to nineteenth-century Alaska. What diverges from this shared faith would automatically disprove itself, even if it was urged by high ecclesiastical authority. No authority is greater than the common faith.

Since there is no locus of power where the faith may be tailored to fit current fashion, it doesn't change in any significant way—not over long centuries or across great geographical distances. The faith of the first century is the faith of Orthodox today. When we meet in this little stone church outside Baltimore, we celebrate a Liturgy that is for the most part over fifteen hundred years old. We join in prayers that are being said in dozens of languages by Orthodox all over the world, prayers unchanged for dozens of generations.

I'm a recent convert, so I have to check a tendency to gush. The history of this Church is not spotless. When people criticize Christianity, they usually point to two incidents in western history, the Spanish Inquisition and the Crusades. While Orthodoxy is not implicated in either of these—Greek Orthodox were among the *victims* of the Crusades—Orthodox must confess their own sins. The pogroms that occurred against the Jews of Russia, for example, were executed by mobs which included Orthodox believers. Sadly,

many clergy were less than vehement in condemning these persecu-
tions, though some clergy risked their lives to defend their Jewish
neighbors. There has been a general tendency of the Orthodox
Church to reflexively support the state rather than criticize it; Serbian Patriarch Pavle's brave denunciations of Slobodan Milosevic
stand as a welcome exception.

Of course, when I became Orthodox I didn't become Russian,
Finnish, or Serbian. I'm here for the faith, not the pierogis; I don't
know how to do Greek dancing or paint Ukrainian eggs. My ethnic background remains that of the quirky Southern tribe known
as "Charlestonian." I am not responsible for the sins of Orthodox
of other lands through the ages, but I more than make up for that
with sins of my own.

Yet Orthodox sing on Sunday, "We have seen the true light! We
have found the true faith!" It's the faith that's true, not us; even the
most beloved saints of history weren't perfect. The problem is that
this radiant faith is handled by sinful people, who are only partially
transformed by it during our earthly lives. The faith is like a hospital, and we come to it sick with sin. The more we receive it, the
more we are changed; not ever to be perfect on this earth, but to be,
at least, better than we otherwise would have been. Examples of the
flaws of the earthly institution of Orthodoxy are easy to find, and,
sad to say, there is no guarantee that all such failings are in the past.
Not everyone in the hospital takes his medicine.

Though I've been a Christian for twenty-five years, I came to
this hospital only a few years ago. Soon after my conversion in the
Dublin church, my husband made his own journey from atheism to
faith, and when he went to seminary I attended as well. He was ordained, and we served in a mainline Protestant denomination for
fifteen years. I counseled and taught at the church, had a daughter

and two sons, taught natural childbirth classes, and helped out at some home births. More recently I started doing some writing, and, because I've been on both sides of the abortion issue, got involved with "common ground" dialogues between representatives of the opposing sides. Our national group ranges from abortion clinic owners to sidewalk protest leaders, and it has been a fruitful environment to see "love your enemies" (Luke 6:27) put healingly into practice.

In the midst of this busy time my husband began to develop a hunger for more ancient Christian roots. Gary wanted to be part of a church that was immersed in the unchanging faith of the ages, rather than one which had an active history of only a few hundred years, or which was eagerly jettisoning its history in favor of transitory relevance. Neither of us had heard much about Orthodoxy, but as soon as he discovered it, he loved it.

I didn't. Orthodoxy initially struck me as strange and off-putting: beautiful but rigorous, and focused much more on God than on me. Western Christianity of many stripes has tended in recent decades to become somewhat soft and emotional—in a sense, consumer-focused. Orthodoxy has missed that bandwagon and still stubbornly addresses its energy toward worshipping God; every believer's primary need, Orthodox would say, is to come further into union with God, and the whole work of the faith is to enable this.

It didn't take long for me to be won over, as I found this God-focus was what I'd hungered for all along. My husband was ordained and we founded a small parish outside Baltimore, which has grown to number about a hundred. There were many strange new things to learn about this unfamiliar Church, but learning them was a delight. Immersed in a continuous, centuries-old faith, at last we feel at home.

This continuity has become the hidden thread that runs through my life. I live at the corner of East and Now. The blaring, immediate Real Life we all share chugs from one vivid episode to another, events which are overstuffed but mostly inexplicable, like a chain of sausages. I drive carpool, write e-mail, read the paper, go to the mall, pop a tape in the VCR. None of this matters; all of it could blow away overnight. What matters is this slim golden thread: the Liturgy that begins each Sunday morning in a little stone church and reaches its fulfillment in the moment I receive Communion. Prayer spills backward and forward from that moment, wrapping me into union with God. It's the work of a lifetime that stretches on beyond my earthly life.

This perspective is backward from the usual. What happens in the meek stone church is the most important thing; what happens in the rest of my life is transient and contingent. The Liturgy is whole and beautiful; the rest of my life seems random and bumpy. In this book I alternate between chapters describing times of worship and chapters describing points of encounter with ordinary life. Ones that trace the Liturgy on a typical Sunday morning roll smoothly from one to the next; ones displaying how that ancient faith might be lived in slice-of-life moments are as oddly matched as shoes on a thrift shop shelf.

The point of this book, however, is not Orthodoxy, because Orthodoxy is not about itself but about Jesus. Everything I say here must be under that steady gaze, because he is the beginning and the end, and the foundation of my life. Those whose Christian education halted at the elementary-school level should be warned that there is more to Jesus than the consoling Good Shepherd they tell children about. His words are frequently challenging and sometimes disturbing.

For example, Jesus warned that following him would be difficult, and that his disciples would be hated: "The hour is coming when whoever kills you will think he is offering service to God" (John 16:2). He called his followers to standards of behavior even higher than those of the era's religious professionals: "Unless your righteousness exceeds that of the scribes and Pharisees, you will never enter the kingdom of Heaven" (Matthew 5:20). Now, not only deeds but even thoughts would be examined: "You must be perfect, as your heavenly Father is perfect" (Matthew 5:48).

Finally, Jesus expected that most people would not accept this challenge: "Enter by the narrow gate: for the gate is wide and the way is easy, that leads to destruction, and those who enter by it are many. For the gate is narrow and the way is hard, that leads to life, and those who find it are few" (Matthew 7:13–14).

Unlike faiths that teach one has only to go within to find truth, Christianity presumes that each human is a mixed bag, with some impulses pulling us toward selfishness and egocentricity, while others yearn toward oneness with God, and resulting self-sacrificial love for others. It's not a matter of bad people versus good people but of a tumultuous blend within each human heart. The person who resolves to pursue the hard path toward reconciliation with God must treat his inner impulses with careful discernment, and resolve to put aside anything that hinders.

Thus, this is not a faith of broad self-affirmation, but one which explicitly calls for self-denial. "If anyone would come after me, let him deny himself and take up his cross and follow me" (Matthew 16:24). The life we clutch greedily close will rot in our arms, and only transformed life in Christ can save us: "Whoever would save his life will lose it; and whoever loses his life for my sake will save it" (Luke 9:24).

Reading over such a series of statements by Jesus feels something like being repeatedly punched in the nose. Good Lord, who would *want* to do such a thing? Why sign on for such a grueling experience?

I look into his thin face, that strong and battered face, in enamel on the side of the chalice. My heart feels like a rock falling down a well. It is for love of him. Not mere admiration for his teachings—to think of him as a mere "good teacher" at such a moment is preposterous. He is Lord, the Christ, the Son of God—like he said. If he is a teacher, he taught disturbing things about himself. And those are the teachings that sting; those are the teachings that were so scandalous they eventually got him killed. When a woman poured out on his feet a jar of fragrant ointment worth a year's wages, it was Judas who protested (reasonably, it would seem) that the money should have been given instead to the poor. It was Jesus who accepted the extravagant honor as his due: "The poor you have with you always, but you do not always have me" (John 12:8). A mere "good teacher" doesn't make such audacious claims. Either this man is a monstrous egoist and a charlatan, or he is telling the truth. Who is this strange and compelling man?

He turned the question on his apostles: "But who do *you* say that I am?" (Matthew 16:15). Peter had the lucky, bell-ringing right answer, the answer that got him crucified as well, a weary old man in a strange city, hanging upside down like mutton from a spike through his feet. Only powerful love can enable such sacrifice, love greater than death. And that may be the most scandalous assertion of all: that Jesus proved who he is by destroying death, that Jesus *is* still alive.

CHAPTER 1

The Curse of the Law

Early Sunday morning the small stone church is quiet and empty, except for my husband, the priest. (At church he's Father Gregory, but at home I call him Gary.) He moves from icon to icon praying, and the old pine floor creaks a bit underfoot. "Blessed is our God always, now and ever and unto ages of ages," he chants. This opening verse sets God's majesty in the context of time; God is blessed in the intimate now, and in all eternity. This first service of the day is called the "Kairon," from the Greek word for time. Not *chronos*, orderly measured time, but *kairos*, the right time, the moment-in-time, the time of fulfillment. Worship lifts us out of ordinary time into the eternal now. At the beginning of the Divine Liturgy, the deacon says to the priest, "It is time for the Lord to act."

But it is sequential time, chronos-time, week after week, Sunday after Sunday, that brings out the patina in a soul—or in a building. These old walls have seen a lot of worship. The church was built in 1911, initially for a Methodist congregation. The interior is tidy, foursquare, with dark beams bracing the vaulted ceiling, and a half-shell dome over the altar. Small but perfectly proportioned, it fits a hundred worshippers like a tailored spring jacket.

The original tenants went in for dark paneling and lots of organ pipes, which appear in an old photo to be the majestic central focus of attention, soaring above the small altar. My husband calls this arrangement "praying to the organ." At the opposite end of the building, a large stained-glass rendition of the Good Shepherd looks out on the street. A small coterie of sheep huddles next to Jesus, one of which is looking directly at the viewer and inexplicably sticking out its tongue. At the top of this window, there is a broad patch of silver duct tape, which covers a fractured indentation suspiciously corresponding to the size and shape of a basketball. The window is dedicated to founding couple Sweetser and Laura Ellen Linthicum, the family for which this town, nestled at Baltimore's southern border, is named. A recent newspaper story chronicled the family's history and ran an antique photo of Sweetser with his progeny. He wore a drooping moustache and an expression that suggested no one called him Sweetser to his face.

The Methodists sold the church to Baptists, who put in plumbing and a baptismal pool at the site of the altar. The Baptists sold it to Episcopalians, who had differing ideas of church decor, and raised a platform over the pool so that the altar lay up a flight of four steps. When we bought it, the congregation was Korean Pentecostal, with a pastor who spoke almost no English. On our first day here, and their last, he shook my husband's hand and found the words to say, "Your church many grow."

The Koreans, though Eastern Christians, worshipped in an enthusiastically western manner; we are the reverse, having somehow passed them completely on the liturgical beltway of life. When we first walked through the building, there were big speakers in the dark-wood ceiling beams, while electronic instruments, guitars, keyboards, and two full drum sets stood in clusters on the floor. All the original dark-wood appointments were gone, replaced with mismatched blond oak. At the back, below the Good Shepherd, a cubicle had been built to house amps and taping equipment. The padded pews were fitted with speakers for simultaneous translation.

We took it down to the bones. Even the pews were carted away, to furnish the Koreans' new church. We don't use pews; Orthodox traditionally stand for worship, though those who find this too difficult are welcome to use the chairs along the sidewalls. The amps and speakers were hauled away, too. We don't use electronic instruments; in fact we don't use instruments at all, just a cappella singing and chanting.

One summer Saturday a crew of parishioners scrubbed the church down. We are several dozen families, mostly recent converts, and still have a convert's enthusiasm. My teenaged sons, David and Stephen, helped pull dozens of screws out of the wooden cubicle and hauled the boards outside. Basil sat on a crate nearby, supervising and sipping coffee. "I tell you *one* thing," he said emphatically, his habitual tone for any topic from politics to pizza. "When we're through with this place, it's going to look like an Orthodox temple!" Downstairs, Basil's eighty-something mother, Lillian, was scrubbing the insides of kitchen drawers, shaking her head at a level of cleanliness far below what she'd tolerated in decades of running a restaurant. Rose was setting up books and icons in a corner of the parish hall, staking out a permanent space for her miniature bookstore. For the previous four years, ever since the parish was founded, she'd had to pack up these items every Sunday after church, relinquishing the space to weekday tenants.

Andy, who had faithfully mopped the green linoleum floor of our rental worship home each week before church, was on hands and knees with a putty knife, scraping the residue of foam-backed carpet off the pine church floor. My sons' buddy, Mary Catherine, sat with my buddy Colleen on the window ledge and carefully washed the Good Shepherd and his rude sheep.

At the altar end of the church, Mitchell and a team of guys were dismantling the multiple platforms put in over the years, to create a broader space of more reasonable elevation. Mitchell is a convert like most of us, but unlike anyone else, came over from Orthodox Judaism. The rest of us were Episcopalians, agnostics, Pentecostals, Catholics, and all sorts of Protestants; only a few, like Basil and Lillian, are "cradle" Orthodox.

A year ago we baptized Mitchell in a brown Rubbermaid horse trough in the middle of Basil's dining room. My husband had been trying to figure out how to accomplish an immersion baptism, which is what the Church expects; previously, we'd set an old steel tub, the Falstaff beer stencil draped with sheets, out on the linoleum floor and poured water over the baptismal candidate. His Internet appeal for immersion-font ideas brought a consensus from other priests of small missions: you gotta get a horse trough. He enjoyed getting it, going to the feed and seed store in his cassock and raising eyebrows around the goat chow bin.

That Saturday evening we couldn't use the rental space, so we fell back as usual on Basil's home. We moved out the dining table and set the trough on the orange shag rug, filling it with water warmed in pots on Lillian's stove. Mitchell went under the water with his usual tranquil smile, his long, tangled black ponytail floating behind him. Mitchell drives a puttering old blue car with his children's handprints and "Work in Progress" painted on it. Abundant bumperstickers come and go, including "Friends Don't Let Friends Vote Republican." Mitchell had asked Basil to be his sponsor, though their styles contrast profoundly. Mitchell is a dreamy soul; Basil is a noisy character with views several blocks farther to the right. Many in the church were surprised at the quirky friendship that sprung up between the gentle younger man and the vehement older one. It was a match made in heaven; it certainly didn't make sense anywhere else.

I washed windows, scraped the floor, and took pictures. The walls hadn't seen fresh paint for decades, it seemed, but the job was too big for one afternoon. I settled for rollering on a new coat over the most visibly shopworn part, all around the room from shoulder height to the floor.

Late that afternoon our exhausted crew looked it over. The space had a harmony that I hadn't recognized before, when it was full of pews and electronics. The wooden floor lies open, broad and appealingly worn, now topped with a few oriental rugs. The white walls are set with vertical round-arched windows in pairs, which swing inward at the top, rotating on a bar through their centers.

When all are open, it looks like rows of swords saluting at a royal wedding. It is not large, this church, but the proportions are peaceful, and it is full of light.

Now in the silent church Father Gregory moves from icon to icon, praying before each one. It will be a long day. He prays to be strengthened for the worship ahead, then bows three times before the altar, saying under his breath, "O God, be gracious unto me, a sinner, and have mercy upon me." The Orthodox priest is not thought of as a shaman or even, necessarily, a holy man. He is a sinner like everyone else. Though set apart to handle holy things, he does this in humility and without presuming on his own worthiness.

For the Vesting service he moves to the sacristy. This little room is tacked on the side of the building, and served as the Korean pastor's study. We have so many changes of vestments and appointments for the rotating liturgical seasons that there's no room for a desk, and my husband's study is in our home. Our church is emptier than theirs was, but our storage room is more crowded. Here, one by one, my husband takes the vestments for the day and makes the sign of the cross over them, then kisses them before putting them on.

As he pulls on the long white robe, called an alb, he prays, "My soul shall rejoice in the Lord, for he hath clothed me with the garment of salvation."

Laying the stole about his neck: "Blessed is God, who poureth out his grace upon his priests." He ties a belt of brocade about his waist, saying, "Blessed is God, who girdeth me with strength, and hath made my path blameless."

A brocade cuff is tied around each wrist. With the right he prays, "Thy right hand, O Lord, is glorified with strength," and with the left, "Thy hands hath made and fashioned me; teach me, and I shall learn thy commandments."

With the donning of each of these garments, there is a symbolic association. Every moment of our lives, even the most private, lies open before the eyes of God. What do they mean? Can we slow down and examine each step, in the light of eternity? Can we make it an offering? Our mortal lives hurtle toward extinction, that vast Time's Up! surprise of the moment everything stops, and something timeless and uncontrollable begins. In between we rush, blather, numb, avoid, consume; we kill time with a chainsaw, burn it like trash, anything to club down the fear that there is no meaning.

Father Gregory lifts a piece of cloth, blesses it, kisses it, and speaks aloud its meaning.

The meaning may seem arbitrary. That doesn't matter. It is the meaning given by the community, by the broader body of believers seen and unseen, in Jerusalem and Africa and Moscow and Alaska, now and through tumbling centuries. The little stone church stands empty in the morning mist, crowded with the multitude of believers through time.

Such an assertion might well annoy Christians of other traditions. How can we claim that Orthodox observances like these are authoritative? In fact, many theological doctrines more significant than these vesting prayers divide Christians; who can say which way is right?

In the fifth century St. Vincent of Lerins grappled with this problem. "I have given the greatest pains and diligence to inquiring, from the greatest possible number of those outstanding in holiness and in doctrine, how I can secure a fixed and guiding principle for distinguishing the true faith from falsehoods," he wrote. He concluded that a twofold guide was needed: Scripture, and the consistent witness of the Christian community as to what the various Scriptures mean.

Protestants will protest: why not *sola Scriptura*, the Bible alone? "Someone will ask, since Scripture is complete and sufficient, why join to it the interpretation of the Church?" St. Vincent wrote. "The answer is that because of the very depth of Scripture all do not place one identical interpretation upon it. The statements of the same writer are explained in different ways, so that it seems possible to extract from it as many opinions as there are interpreters."

This explains why *sola Scriptura* leads to thousands of Protestant denominations, each sincerely following the Bible alone. But if the truth is one, this discord is a sign that somebody—in fact, lots of somebodies—must be getting it wrong. A single truth logically requires a common faith, which would produce a united Church. The rule devised by St. Vincent, called the Vincentian Canon, then, is this: we should believe "that which has been believed everywhere, always, and by all." The faith consensus of the gathered community is our guide, and the Bible is the core document generated by, and consulted by, that community. Orthodox claim that our prayers and practices are the most ancient, continuous, and geographically widespread, and therefore represent the Holy Spirit's leading over time: as Jesus said, "When the Spirit of truth comes, he will guide you into all the truth" (John 16:13).

To the objection that "these prayers aren't found in Scripture!" one could note that these prayers are literally quotations from

Scripture, and that the practice of ceremonial, symbolic clothing goes back to the priest's vestments in the tabernacle of Moses' day. These prayers are not meant to be pressed too far; Orthodox don't believe that they turn priests' vestments into magic clothes. They are just one more element serving to deepen the reverence and beauty of worship.

Here may lie the deeper reason for discomfort: unfamiliarity with the ancient church's expectation of the necessity of beauty. Beauty is that which opens our eyes to the majesty of God and moves us to desire him. Worship is not just an intellectual grasping of truths but a process of falling in love. Beauty opens us to adoration, and a craving for God begins to take root. Without this, our love for him may be polite, respectful, and theologically accurate, but it lacks the headlong abandonment that should characterize a relationship between lover and beloved.

"I want creation to penetrate you with so much admiration that wherever you go, the least plant may bring a clear remembrance of the Creator," wrote the fourth-century archbishop St. Basil the Great. "One blade of grass or one speck of dust is enough to occupy your entire mind in beholding the art with which it has been made."

Modern church architecture seldom shows such a regard for beauty; in fact, contemporary "worship spaces" often look like they've been designed to be lecture or entertainment spaces. Other important activities, like fellowship and education, have somehow invaded the time that should be set aside for falling down in awe before God. In contrast, Orthodox worship is quite elaborate, though it feels very different from western "high church" style. In the West, fancy worship is associated with formality and reserve, with coolly precise choreography and chant. Orthodox worship is instead voluptuous with beauty. Extravagant but not formal, fancy but not fussy, our worship is like a big family Christmas dinner, with the best linens and finest dishes and everyone having a hearty time.

Worship was always meant to be gloriously, delightfully beautiful. This was true even in the time of Moses; though his people were wandering the desert in tents, God commanded them to construct a tabernacle for worship that was staggeringly elaborate. The directions given in Exodus require gold, silver, precious stones, blue and purple cloth, embroidery, incense, bells, and anointing oil. The pattern continues in the visions of the prophets, where God appears in glorious settings. Isaiah sees him "high and lifted up," wearing a robe with a voluminous train, while soaring angels chant a hymn and the smoke of incense fills the temple (Isaiah 6). Daniel pictures the entrance of the Son of Man into the heavenly throne room of the Ancient of Days (Daniel 7:9–14). In the last book of the Bible, St. John has a vision of heavenly worship that includes precious stones, gold, thrones, crowns, white robes, crystal, and incense (Revelation 4). From the beginning to the end of Scripture, worship is accompanied with great beauty.

Beauty is not to become an end in itself; mere ceremonialism would be a circular exercise and ultimately dead. But when entered with expectant joy, nothing opens the heart to deeper worship like beauty. In his *Confessions*, St. Augustine wrote of the passage through beauty into passionate love for God:

"Late it was that I loved you, beauty so ancient and so new, late I loved you! And, look, you were within me and I was outside, and there I sought for you and in my ugliness I plunged into the beauties you had made. You were with me, and I was not with you.

Those outer beauties kept me far from you, yet if they had not been in you they would not have existed at all.

"You called, you cried out, you shattered my deafness; you flashed, you shone, you scattered my blindness; you breathed perfume, and I drew in my breath and I pant for you; I tasted, and I am hungry and thirsty; you touched me, and I burned for your peace."

Father Gregory comes back to the altar for the Proskomedia, the third of these short preliminary services. On a small side table are five round loaves of bread, each about ten inches in diameter, which were baked by a parishioner; we rotate this duty each week. The top of each was pressed with a round seal while rising, and the various marks will guide him in cutting and dividing the loaf.

Bowing before the table he prays, "Thou hast redeemed us from the curse of the Law, by thy precious Blood."

Those who presume Christianity is mostly about obeying rules and regulations might be surprised to hear the Law—the Ten Commandments and all supporting moral and religious laws—labeled a curse. Yet this is one of the most basic points of Christian theology, one on which Protestants, Roman Catholics, and Orthodox all agree. The Law, the commandments and moral code, the Christian Scriptures say, is good in itself: it reveals the mind of God and shows the purity necessary to be one with him. But it presents us with a hopeless task, because nobody can do it. The standard is too high.

St. Paul explains that in fact we have within us *two* laws. One is this radiant but impossible standard conveying the mind of God; the other is the more frankly human law of self-aggrandizement, the law of me-first and look-out-for-number-one. The latter is a law written in our bones, and has a quality of compulsion; the former is a law written mysteriously in our hearts, stirring us with restless dissatisfaction at our failure to reach it.

These two laws, as we all know from blushing personal experience, are frequently in conflict. An inner voice can urge a man to dive into an icy river and save a victim of drowning. Another inner voice can urge a man to pocket a bracelet from a jewelry box when visiting a forgetful elderly aunt. Learning to tell these voices apart is the work of a lifetime, because the selfish voice can wheedle a very convincing imitation of the other when the will is disposed to be deceived.

But why "the curse of the Law"? If the Law is good, beautiful, and just, and reflects the mind of God, how can it be a curse? Because the Law can no more help us *keep* the Law than a ladder can give you a boost to the first rung. The Law can only show us how we fail. A perfect good in theory, it becomes in practice a curse and futility.

St. Paul described his personal struggle with the two laws: "I do not understand my own actions. I can will what is right, but I cannot do it. For I do not do the good that I want, but the evil I do not want is what I do. For I delight in the Law of God in my inmost self, but I see in my members another law at war with the Law of my mind and making me captive.

"Wretched man that I am! Who will deliver me from this body of death? Thanks be to God through Jesus Christ our Lord!" (Romans 7:15, 18–19, 22–25).

The essence of the Christian faith, then, is that Jesus frees us from "the curse of the Law." We are forgiven and accepted just as we are, no longer burdened by an impossible weight of duty. But since we have been loved at such great cost ("God so loved the world that he gave his only-begotten son, that all who believe in him should not perish but have everlasting life," John 3:16), we respond with grateful love in turn. Now we do our best to keep God's law, because we are irresistibly drawn nearer his beauty and perfection.

This brings us to one of the more awkward things to explain about Orthodoxy. Anyone attending an Orthodox service will soon become aware of the frequent references to sin and repentance. We don't live in an age that is big on repentance; the word usually conjures images of haranguing, fire-and-brimstone preachers, judgementalism, and hate. It's an unfortunate confusion because the ancient Christian approach is subtly different, though utilizing some of the same vocabulary. For us Orthodox, repentance is the key to joy. The more you repent, the more you see God's love.

To start with the human condition, our basic problem is guilt. No matter how we deny it, we continually harbor a gummy wad of guilt because we know deep inside that we behave pretty badly on a regular basis. Though we've always been this way, we never get used to it; we keep thinking we should be doing better.

It's that two-laws problem again. The holy and just Law of God is somehow planted inside us, alongside the body-law of me-first, and the echo of its beauty provokes a primal longing. We feel restless and unhappy that we fall so far short. We are like sick children looking out the window at a beautiful spring day, and longing to be well.

What can you do with this lingering guilt? Much contemporary theology suggests that because God is love, he just doesn't care about our sins. We might cope, then, by imagining he'll weigh our good and bad deeds and decide on balance that we deserve a passing grade. As popular as this notion is, it has no basis in Christian theology.

Nor does God compare us with anyone else in the world; it's us and him alone. Yet it's almost impossible for us to avoid the temptation of making comparisons. When we discover people who are unquestionably more evil than we are—for example, racists—the guilt momentarily eases and we experience a surge of relief that is delicious and gratifying. We can discover how much fun it is to hate and judge others, and award ourselves the laurel of virtue. I think this is one of the appeals of afternoon tabloid TV: it provides a cavalcade of characters the viewer feels free to hold in contempt.

Alternatively, we can try to numb ourselves by buying things to entertain or satiate, though this becomes a junkie's endless quest. If we're more sophisticated, we'll buy more sophisticated things, and display how enlightened, egalitarian, or tasteful we are. Yet highbrow or low-brow, the self-medicating dynamic is the same. I call it the Frosting Cycle: we feel bad so we open up a can of chocolate frosting and start eating it with a spoon. It tastes gratifyingly yummy and we are soothed—for a while, anyway. But pretty soon, oh, we feel *bad*. How can we console ourselves? Quick, more frosting!

None of these methods succeeds; what we know of ourselves deep inside continually undermines the trembling self-esteem all this reassurance and comfort are trying to prop up. Self-esteem is just a shiny-happy word for self-respect, and a million self-concessions add up to a person you can't respect very much.

The approach of ancient Christian spirituality is utterly different. We believe God cares deeply about our helpless immersion in sin. He doesn't ignore it, recalculate it, or rationalize it; he forgives it, at immense cost to himself. We were sick, and he came to heal us. When we were still ungrateful and ugly he died for us. That having been done, what more could he ever withhold?

When we grasp this, we are flooded by his love. Sorrow for sin, sorrow for wounding him, becomes the ground of exuberant joy. The fifth-century abbot St. John Climacus coined a word for it, "charmylopi," which means "joyful sorrow." This experience of merged repenting and rejoicing is the basis of all Orthodox spirituality.

Contrary to Jesus' sweetie-pie reputation, throughout the Gospels his most constant exhortation is "Repent." Only bracing honesty with ourselves is able to open us to receive this enormous love. People who think they have only a little dinky bit of sin can only visualize a little dinky cross. Those who are forgiven much, as the Gospel says, love much.

They not only love God but show a gracious and forgiving love toward others. This is not the same as pretending others don't sin—everybody does, and everybody needs to repent and receive this joy. But that is a lifelong ongoing project between them and God, and our only part is to show kindness. We are to behave at all times like people whose primary thought is "I have been forgiven a great deal."

Now Father Gregory takes up a pointed implement, called "the spear." In the story of Jesus' crucifixion, in order to test whether he was really dead, a soldier pierced his side with a spear, "and immediately there came forth blood and water." This is what would happen if you pierced the pericardium of a man who'd died of congestive heart failure, such as would be caused by hanging for hours from one's nailed arms. Early Christians insisted on this as proof that Jesus really died; he didn't merely faint to be revived later, as contemporary skeptics suggested. The priest takes the loaf of bread and begins to cut with the spear along the right side of the square in the middle of the seal. This area is embossed with the Greek letters "IC XC NIKA," which means "Jesus Christ Conquers."

"He was led as a sheep to the slaughter," he says. Then, cutting along the left side, "As a spotless lamb is dumb before his shearer, so opened he not his mouth." Across the top, "In his humiliation his judgment was taken away," and along the bottom, "And for his generation, who shall declare it?" The entire cube of bread bearing the seal, known as "the Lamb," is now cut free, and Father Gregory lifts it out with the spear, saying, "For his life is taken away from the earth."

These lines are drawn from Isaiah 53, a powerful passage describing the death of a mysterious figure known as the Suffering Servant. He is described as "despised and rejected by men, a man of sorrows and acquainted with grief." Though he dies abjectly and is considered by humans "stricken by God and afflicted," yet his death is revealed to be redemptive for all: "Surely he hath borne our griefs and carried our sorrows . . . he was wounded for our transgressions, he was bruised for our iniquities, upon him was the chastisement that made us whole, and by his stripes we are healed."

The Bible passage concludes with promise of the Servant's reward and victory. "He shall see the fruit of the travail of his soul and be satisfied." Christians take this passage as a prophecy of Christ's crucifixion and resurrection.

Father Gregory continues to cut out pieces from the seal, laying them next to the Lamb on a pedestaled gold dish called the diskarion. Each piece has a symbolic meaning, representing the Virgin, saints, angels, clergy, or Orthodox living and dead. The last is for himself, and he prays, "Remember, O Lord, my unworthiness, and forgive all my offenses, both voluntary and involuntary."

He takes the asterisk, or star-cover, a golden four-legged piece that fits over the diskarion, and sets it in place, saying, "And the star came and stood over the place where the young child was." He covers the asterisk with a gold brocade cloth with the words "The Lord hath reigned, he hath clothed himself with majesty." After covering the chalice, he takes the aer, a square fringed garment of brocade about the size of a scarf, and lays it over both chalice and diskarion. "Shelter us in the shelter of thy wings; drive away from us every enemy and foe; make our life peaceful; O Lord, have mercy on us and on thy world, and save our souls, for thou art good and lovest mankind." This closing reminder of God's unwearied love is the conclusion of many Orthodox prayers. Father Gregory swings the golden censer, and smoke billows around the preparation table while the tiny bells on the chain chime.

As with the Vesting prayers, many of these prayers make symbolic connections that are not mystically rarefied. Father Gregory places a triangular piece of bread next to the square one, and describes the queen standing at the king's right hand; he places the golden asterisk over the Lamb, and recalls the star standing over the Bethlehem manger. There is something broad, trusting, even affectionate in these typological references, so simple a child could grasp them. They are rooted in a premodern age, where childlike faith could dwell unmolested.

This is the kind of faith that took a beating under the Enlightenment, when man took the measure of God and found him amusing but vague. Rationalism is now taking the beating, getting beaten to pieces, and a fragmentary curiosity is scenting the air: maybe something exists that we can't see, maybe there is healing and reason to hope, maybe I should invest a buck in a guardian angel lapel pin. We don't live in a coherent age. Walking through the culture is like walking through the surf after a battering storm, stepping through shards of insatiable consumerism, gaudy FunTime noise, self-indulgent weepiness, toilet humor, posturing nihilism. Things keep saying they're important, but they turn out to be more loud than deep. Stepping around the shards of the shipwreck, we begin to wonder if anything might be important, anything might last or have meaning. Could bread mean a Body? Could wine mean Blood? Could a body broken and blood spilled two thousand years ago restore my own damaged life?

It is that simple, and yet the simplicity we gratefully embrace is only the shadow of a reality blasting beyond the boundaries of our comprehension. Father Gregory censes around the altar and concludes with a final prayer, recognizing the limitless mystery: "In the grave with the body, but in Hades with the soul, as God, in Paradise with the Thief, and on the Throne with the Father and the Spirit, wast thou, O Christ, filling all things, thyself uncircumscribed."

CHAPTER 2

Jesus of Santa Rosa

AT A MEXICAN RESTAURANT
IN SANTA ROSA

A half-dozen years of flying around has at last won me five frequent-flyer tickets, so the family takes the Big Vacation we've always wanted: fly to the West coast, rent a car, drive around for two weeks, from Vancouver to Monterey. On the first day, we putter around San Francisco in our minivan, feeling clumsy and obvious. "But there are some places you want to look like a tourist," says Megan, the oldest, who is twenty-enough to be superior to California Cool. "I wouldn't want to look like I belonged here," she says with the hauteur of a life-long eastcoaster.

"How about lunch?" Gary asks. "There's a Thai restaurant. Does everybody like Thai?"

I put my foot down. "I didn't fly all this way to have food I could have had at home. I want to have distinctive local food, whatever San Francisco is known for."

David says, "Rice-A-Roni?"

An hour later we settle the debate by buying cheese, salami, fruit, and bread from a guy who's vending from the back of a battered truck on the twisting coastline highway. His hand-lettered sign promises that this will be "Fun to Eat" and indeed it is, so we do not have to circle back later and beat him up. We stop at the beach so the kids can put their toes in the Pacific, which they do quickly and then take them out again because it is very cold. The water is cold, the wind is fierce, the sand is gray, and overall we prefer our usual vacation beach outside Charleston, South Carolina, where Gary and I grew up. This looks very dramatic and wild, but it's not very enjoyable. At Folly Beach, we would set out low canvas chairs, nestle a beer in the sand, and bake in a basting of lotion and sweat while reading paperback novels. This beach is better suited to Heathcliff and Catherine.

The next day we spend weaving along the California coast, then turn inland. At a tourist stop, Megan comes out of the souvenir shop saying disdainfully, "There sure are a lot of alternative-looking people in there." She's wearing ragged plaid pants resembling pajama bottoms, a t-shirt with sleeves and collar cut off, scuffed blue nail polish, and lots of rings. There's something I'm not getting here. It reminds me of our old family joke about "alternative" rock: "Alternative to what?" "Alternative to *good* music."

By evening we're in Santa Rosa, a beautifully proportioned old town in the lush, low hills. Here I see my favorite bumpersticker of the trip: "Isis! Isis! Ra! Ra! Ra!"

My husband, however, is preoccupied with spotting the Santa Rosa Mountains. He is sure that there is a chain by that name centered here, though none of the rest of us can confirm this. As we drive into town he keeps peering down the cross-streets, as if to spot the snowcapped peaks crouched in hiding.

"Doesn't that sound familiar to you?" he asks. "The Santa Rosa Mountains? The famous, beautiful Santa Rosa Mountains?"

It sounds nice, we agree, but not familiar. However, these invisible mountains do gradually acquire substance in our imagination, and provide fodder for commentary for the rest of the trip. When driving past Mount Saint Helens, we point out a formerly majestic peak in the Santa Rosa chain. Megan remembers that her college in Virginia, situated on the Shenandoah River, stands in the shadow of the Eastern Santa Rosa Mountains. We think we recall old ballads from the Gold Rush era, like "It was just a shack, but I'd gladly have it back, my home in the Santa Rosa hills." Gary takes this needling pretty well, but he does try to change the subject.

I wanted to come to Santa Rosa, not for the mountains ("I was misinformed"), but because there's a coffeehouse here run by monks who put out a zine called *Death to the World* for street kids. This story began in 1993, when a young punk-rock musician named John Marler arrived at the St. Paisius Abbey in Platina, California. Though only nineteen, he had already been guitarist in two successful bands, Sleep and Paxton Quiggly. When he came to faith in Christ and found his home in Orthodox spirituality, the new monk wanted to bring the same hope to the punk subculture he had just escaped, which he saw as crippled by nihilism and despair.

The St. Herman of Alaska Brotherhood (which sponsors the Platina abbey as well as several other monasteries for women and men) had already begun attracting some kids in the nearby town of

Chico, and Mother Neonilla—previously a "serious punker" her-self—encouraged young Father John to reach out to them. He and another former musician took to calling themselves "punks turned monks."

The first idea called for fellow-monk Father Damascene Chris-tensen to write an article for *Maximum Rock and Roll*, described as "the most hardcore" of all punk-rock magazines. He intended to write a piece drawing on his biography of an American monk who died in 1982, "Not of This World: The Life and Teaching of Fr. Seraphim Rose." "But as I read over the magazine, I realized there was no way they'd publish something like this," Father Damascene told me.

Next, they decided to try to place an ad, but the editor's re-sponse—"What the blankety-blank is a Brotherhood?" is how Fa-ther Damascene relayed his comment to me—tipped them off that this wasn't going to fly either. The editor told them, "We only run ads for music and zines." (A zine is a rough, homemade-looking magazine, offered cheap or free on the streets.)

"We need a zine," the monks decided, and thus appeared one of the oddest of the punk-style publications, *Death to the World.*

The cover of the first issue shows a white-bearded monk hold-ing a skull, and the inaugural essay begins, "The last true rebellion is death to the world. To be crucified to the world and the world to us." The back cover shows the figure on the Shroud of Turin, with this biblical caption: THEY HATED ME WITHOUT A CAUSE.

"These kids are sick of themselves," said Father Damascene, "and they feel out of place in this world. We try to open up to them the beauty of God's creation, and invite them to put to death 'the passions,' which is what we mean by 'the world.' God takes despair and turns it around to something positive. Selfish passions can then be redirected into love for God, as Mary Magdalene did. We talk about the idea of suffering, because that is what the kids feel most strongly. We show that there can be meaning in suffering."

"Putting to death the passions" was a concept that concerned me when I first became Orthodox. And I wasn't sure about hating the world either, since, as we all know, God so loved the world that he gave his only-begotten Son. I gradually came to understand that this was shorthand for putting to death the inner tumult of self-serving emotion and greed, which is tickled by the seductive materialism of the world. It is, in short, death to the body-law of selfishness, in order to make room for the gradual blooming of the presence of God.

A common fallacy, dating back to the gnostics and probably before, divides spiritual from physical realms. The physical is seen as inferior, and we readily recognize the stereotype of a scolding religious leader urging his followers to shun bodily pleasures as dangerous and dirty. A less-recognized variation of this philosophy, however, teaches that the physical is simply irrelevant, so it doesn't matter how you indulge it. Divorced from transcendent meaning, physical pleasures become compulsory, banal, and exhausted, curiously deprived of the charge of healthy, joyful passion. Thus we develop a culture saturated in the erotic yet bereft of eros, deprived of the classic lover's unswerving ardor and self-sacrificing fidelity.

In Orthodoxy, believers are called to asceticism—to discipline the body to self-control, cleansing the eye so that it may better see the rich beauty of this physical world, God's good gift. We fast, restrain, and temper the appetites, to reunite body and soul as they are meant to be, in harmony; then we love the world as we see it with God's eyes—beautiful, good, and filled with people whom he loved into being and saved by his death. At this point, the passions are transformed, and their energy redirected into zeal for truth, for loving others, and for humility.

Ascetic disciplines like these make many Protestants wary, because they suspect such deeds aim to pay off the debt of sin and win salvation by works. This charge is worth examining, since it represents the biggest single controversy in western Christendom, and the root of the Protestant Reformation.

The essential question was: Does human effort to do good aid in our salvation, or is it gained solely by God's doing? Do we have a free will that allows us to choose good, or are we hopelessly bound in sin and rescued only by grace? As western writers wrestled with the problem, stark and intolerable alternatives emerged.

On the one hand, popular Roman Catholicism of the Middle Ages supposed that Christians have free will and are able to choose to do good. The good deeds done through the ages accumulate like money in a bank, erasing the debt of sin and winning access to salvation. Some, like the greatest saints, store up more savings than they need, and this excess remains in the treasury for other, needier Christians to use. A custom grew up that one could acquire these "indulgences" by buying them from the church. Official teaching was more subtle than this, but in this form, or even more crudely, a divine transaction was popularly imagined.

Protestant Reformers countered that this was hogwash; God is utterly sovereign and has no need for the good deeds we do. So high is his majesty, and so tainted by fallibility is any effort we expend, that our works are useless. From this point, a leading theologian of the Reformation, John Calvin, developed his doctrine of double predestination: God chooses to damn some and to save others for private reasons which no human can discern. No one deserves salvation, since all are sick with sin, Calvin taught. "[T]hose only recover health to whom the Lord is pleased to put forth his healing hand. The others whom, in just judgment, he passes over, pine and rot away till they are consumed."

In addition to its dismaying harshness, the doctrine presents a practical problem. If our good works have no bearing on our salvation, if no effort is required or even possible, why should we bother to follow the moral Law? Why not just give up, and live it up?

Much earlier this dilemma was explored by St. Augustine, whose fourth-century writings were a major source for Calvin. St. Augustine is widely viewed in the West as the greatest of the Church Fathers. His status is not as high in the East: his devotional works are beloved, but his theological writings are viewed with skepticism. St. Augustine was a western figure, formed by Rome, and the fact that he was one of the few of his era who wrote in Latin made him disproportionately influential in the West.

St. Augustine's writings on grace and free will stirred controversy even at the time they were published, and at the end of the fourth century St. John Cassian recorded a conversation on the subject between the monk Germanus and the wise Abbot Paphnutius, who lived in the Egyptian desert. Germanus asked the question in simplest form: "Where then is there room for free will . . . if God both begins and ends everything in us which concerns our salvation?"

Abbot Paphnutius replied, "This would fairly influence us, if in every work and practice the beginning and the end were everything, and there were no middle in between."

Anyone who has attempted to live the spiritual life, in fact, knows this; we don't dwell in a theoretical world where it is either all grace or all laborious will, but in a middle-in-between where vigilant effort repeatedly discovers that enabling grace has already gone before. "[A]s we know that God creates opportunities of salvation in various ways, it is in our power to make use of the opportunities granted to us by heaven more or less earnestly," Abbot Paphnutius went on. Far from trusting in our sporadic ability to choose good, our fallibility puts us on guard. "We ought every moment to pray . . . that he who is the unseen ruler of the human heart may vouchsafe to turn to the desire of virtue that will of ours, which is more readily inclined to vice . . . [T]he Lord's help is always joined to [our effort], that we may not be altogether destroyed by our free will, [and] when he sees that we have stumbled, he sustains and supports us, as it were by stretching out his hand."

The kindness of God is the notable thing in the abbot's explanation, and runs all through Orthodox writing on this subject. An analogy used by the early church was that of a mother and child. As St. Isaac of Syria wrote in the seventh century: "It is like a mother teaching her little son to walk, moving away and calling him; and when he comes towards his mother and starts to shake, and to fall over because his feet and legs are soft and tender, his mother runs and picks him up in her arms. This is how God's grace carries and teaches men."

Such analogies reveal the squirrel in the attic of western theology, the insidious and irrelevant concept of "merit." The Reformers opposed any role for human good works in the scheme of salvation because they thought such works inevitably meant boasting of one's accumulated merits, and viewing God as contractually obligated to save. But this obviously false idea is not the only way to view good works. No one could look at that mother and child and imagine that the child struggles to walk in order to earn points that will obligate the mother's love. No such external scale of obligations and payments exists in a relationship of love. The entire exercise is more simple than that. The child works hard to learn to walk *so he can learn to walk.* He wants to move toward his mother's arms; that is reward enough.

When I have a sore throat, I gargle, and nobody gives me a medal. When I drive under the speed limit, the Department of Motor Vehicles doesn't send me a fruitcake. When I follow the practices that the community has found, through trial and error over long centuries, are helpful in drawing closer to God, I get the only reward I want: I get closer to God.

The first issue of Death to the World, published in December 1994, was advertised in *Maximum Rock and Roll,* and brought letters from "all over the world—Japan, Lithuania, Ireland," Father Damascene said. Copies of that issue were mailed to an ever-growing list, distributed at punk shows, and photocopied and passed along by others. Over fifty thousand copies are now in circulation.

"Kids were writing to us, and we realized they needed more personal contact," said Father Damascene, so the Brotherhood began turning bookstores and restaurants into coffeehouses, or as they call them, "mystical hangouts." There are now fourteen of these across the country and in Europe and Australia.

A typical flier, handed out to street kids, reads: "Desert Wisdom Kaffe House, Kansas City's most mystical hangout. Drink Ethiopian coffee & espresso. Hear ancient otherworldly chants. Smell rare middle-eastern incense. Discover the ancient African & Eastern superheroes." Of course the chants are Orthodox Christian hymns, the incense is borrowed from liturgical use, and the "superheroes" are saints of the Bible and Church history. A poster used at some coffeehouses shows a young monk holding open a wooden box of bones and a skull, the remains of another monk. The sober remembrance of death is a classic element of monastic spirituality. The poster's caption reads "Death to the tyranny of fashion!"

Pretty sophisticated marketing strategy; I can well imagine this reaching kids who will tune out anything less as manipulative and sugar-coated. But like any good evangelism, it gets its power from love for the lost. Father Paisius, also at the monastery, explained, "This subculture is raucous and deeply disturbed because of their own pain. It's demonic; they're living in hell, overdosing on drugs or maybe going into a rage and killing someone. They see life as worthless. We want to show them an ideal that is worth their life. These are marginalized youth who are wounded, and *Death to the World* is meant to touch with a healing hand that wound."

A successful zine and chain of coffeehouses is an especially impressive accomplishment, considering how simply the monks live. The mountaintop monastery of St. Herman of Alaska, farther north, has no electricity, phone, or running water, and according to an issue of *Death to the World*, "the monks live in the midst of rattlesnakes, scorpions, and peacocks, translating and publishing wisdom from the holy fathers and mothers of ages past." Twelve miles farther up the mountain is a sister monastery for women, St. Xenia Skete, also without phone, water, or electricity. The St. Xenia nuns live in log cells they construct themselves; they "till the garden, chop wood, and also work on publishing." When I spoke to Father Damascene, I learned that getting a quote from Father John wouldn't be as easy: he was then living in a similar monastery on an island off the Alaska coast, where getting to a phone requires prior notice by mail.

When we walk into Santa Rosa's Not of This World bookstore I'm a little disappointed. I was expecting a dark and smoky coffee-house that would fit the description "mystical hangout," but this is a small, cheerful bookstore with white walls and tidy cases of icons, books, tapes, and magazines. The coffee component is represented by a small square table holding a thermos carafe and a few mugs, with chairs pulled up around. Our kindly, beaming host is Brother Maximos, who explains that he belongs to the community that runs the coffeehouse. He is sixty, with a gray ponytail and a Santa Claus white beard, and he does nothing with undue haste. Each of my questions is pondered carefully.

Brother Maximos explains that the community tries to reach street people, especially kids, in various ways. They hand out zines and booklets, and I look over several examples; in addition to *Death to the World* there is one called *Sunrise of the East* with an American Indian on the cover, and one titled *The Mission of Bob Marley*. A booklet titled *Christ the Eternal Tao* offers the Gospel message in the cadences of Lao-tzu. Father Damascene, who wrote this one, says that he "discovered the depth of ancient, unadulterated Christianity, and . . . found it to be the fullness of what [I] had been probing for in Lao-tzu." Father Damascene was a student of Father Seraphim Rose, who was in turn a student of the scholar Gi-ming Shein and assisted him in translating the *Tao Teh Ching*.

"While Lao-tzu's *Tao Teh Ching* represents the highest a person can know through intuition," Father Damascene writes, "St. John's Gospel represents the highest a person can know through revelation." He reminds the reader that in ancient Greek and Romanian monasteries there are paintings of the philosophers of ancient

Greece, "who are thus honored as seekers of Truth before the coming of Christ." He quotes the second-century apologist St. Justin Martyr: "Those who lived in accordance with the Logos are Christians, even though they were called godless, such as, among the Greeks, Socrates, and Heraclitus and others like them."

My mind is on more earthly things, and I buy a black t-shirt that shows an aged monk holding a skull and says "Death to the World" in large red letters, figuring it will be just the thing to wear when I'm called up for jury duty. The bookstore offers a "carefully chosen" movie every Friday night, and this week it is the classic in which Ingrid Bergman portrays a missionary to China, *The Inn of the Sixth Happiness.* Wednesdays there is a lecture, and Brother Maximos shows me the ad they're posting around town for this week's event. It displays the crumpled figure of an old woman with her cheek pressed against a pillow. The lecture's title is "Beloved Sufferer," and it concerns Schema-nun (the most spiritually advanced rank of nun) Macaria, a profoundly disabled Russian woman of the earlier part of this century, revered for her generosity of spirit and wisdom. I wonder if a lecture like this attracts street people. Of course, these are *California* street people.

Stephen is staring out the open door of the store. "Do you know him?" he asks Brother Maximos.

I look over to see a man in his thirties wearing a white bedsheet and Teva sandals, making his way vigorously up the street. He begins shouting, "God is good! Yes! God is good!" as if he were in a lively Pentecostal church packed with happy worshippers.

Brother Maximos gazes at him like you'd look at a toddler who's pulled all the toilet paper off the roll and draped it around the dog. "Yes, I know him. He thinks he's Jesus. He says, 'I'm back! I'm back!," and Brother Maximos imitates a little wave. "He knows he can't come in here and go on shouting, so he doesn't come in much anymore. It's hard to have a conversation with him; he's so excited all the time. Mostly, he just wants attention."

I look at the solitary figure moving up the street and wonder about the difference between being an unpredictable divine witness, and being simply mentally ill. Orthodoxy reveres as saints some who are called "Fools for Christ," who might have been classed elsewhere merely as fools. St. Xenia of St. Petersburg, for example, would wear only the military uniform of her deceased husband; she was a street person given to cryptic sayings and occasional clairvoyance. She is a greatly beloved saint, and when Gary and I were about to become Orthodox and pondering which saints to adopt as our patrons and name-saints, Gary said, "I think you should take Xenia Fool-for-Christ, and I'm only half joking." He said this many times, exactly this way, even after I stopped smiling when he said it.

Is this Jesus coming up the sidewalk a Fool for Christ? I know that the category allows for a good deal of originality but must presume that claiming to actually *be* Christ would be a disqualifier, a case of mistaken identity at least.

Then there's a third category, that of possession by evil spirits. There's a whole lot of exorcism in the New Testament, but it rarely comes up today, and I can't imagine that that's because most demons have been eliminated, like Science Marching On defeating smallpox. I don't think about evil spirits very often. Maybe I don't take them as seriously as I should.

"Does Orthodoxy believe in exorcism?" I ask, and Brother Maximos reminds me that exorcism is a part of the baptismal Liturgy. The priest begins the rite with a prayer that the Lord will expel from the candidate every operation of the devil. The candidate re-nounces the devil three times, then spits on him, or in his presumed general direction (that is, west).

I point at the now-silent Jesus loping up the sidewalk. "Do you think he has an evil spirit?" I ask.

Brother Maximos considers this question seriously. "I leave a judgment like that up to priests. But I think in general that people who have some involvement with evil spirits are much more sly. They have a dark quality. I've dealt with some of them," he says meaningfully, and I guess he has.

I recognize what he means by "a dark quality." I've occasionally encountered people who seemed to emanate a sinister miasma, something that felt unearthly, inhuman; not just ordinary human-nature sneakiness, but a loathsome fog that was actively repellent and induced a desire to flee. I've felt this not only with people, but with places: I know a lovely, quaint town in a valley that, as I drive into it, conveys an increasing sense of cold, clammy dread with each foot I descend. Occasionally other people have volunteered to me they've had the same reaction to this town—a place that, on a post-card, would be irresistible. One day I walked the mile-long main street attempting to comprehend this feeling. At foot-level I no-ticed details I didn't see from my car: shop after shop of palm read-ers, astrologers, "magic crystals," and tarot dealers.

Are these just manifestations of an ancient pagan religion, one older than Christianity? No doubt about it. And apparently what-ever spirit they share, it's one that conflicts with the spirit of Christ, provoking a visceral disturbance even below awareness. Not all spir-itual forces happily co-exist.

Maybe such things don't exist. Maybe it's foolish to declare con-fidently that they don't, since such a theory cannot be proved, and most people in most cultures in most times have been convinced they do. It might be well to keep an open mind in such matters and "[give] votes to the most obscure of all classes, our ancestors," as G. K. Chesterton said.

But this Jesus doesn't seem particularly dark. Brother Maximos says that he gets some quite strange people in here, some of whom are beyond his powers of communication. "What I try to do is, if I can, just get close enough to give 'em a hug," he says.

The family repairs to a Mexican restaurant, where we amuse the staff by being incompetent to differentiate between enchiladas, burritos, tacos, and tostadas (being lifelong eastcoasters has its limitations). Apparently these are all composed of piles of very hearty food wrapped in different manners. The only one that we've ever prepared at home is tacos, but that meager expertise makes us more sophisticated than my mother-in-law, who had her first taco in our kitchen a few years ago. She took a few gingerly bites, then declared, "This needs mayonnaise," and pulled the jar of Hellmann's from the refrigerator. Tacos, with that unforgettable South Carolina touch.

As I look across the table over Megan's shoulder, however, I realize that the sidewalk Jesus is here. He is sitting alone in a booth munching the complimentary tortilla chips and salsa, his feet crossed at the ankles and toga-draped bedsheet falling casually open around his narrow shins. He is not a big man. The exposed patch of chest hair shows a bloom of gray at the center. His face is lined like someone who has spent a lot of time in the sun, and his brown hair and beard are not very long. Perhaps he only started being Jesus a little while ago.

He leans his elbows on the tabletop and studies an open Bible, a floppy white-leather edition that has the Lord's words printed in red. The page he is looking at is almost all in red, an extended passage of Jesus' teaching, perhaps the Sermon on the Mount. I'm glad he's looking down when we bow our heads and say grace; I'm afraid that if he notices he'll come over like a waitress and say, "Sure thing, and is there anything else I can do for you now?"

What must it be like to be Jesus in there? What warring words and images inside his head? He eats chips, dipping them in salsa, then sips a glass of water. He is quiet but intent, studying these red-letter words. Is he trying to remember when he said them, why, comprehend their meaning? Does he have brilliant technicolor memories of teaching beside the Sea of Galilee, changing water into wine under his mom's admiring gaze? Did he begin with a hunger for God, yearning to know and understand more and more, until one day he was sucked up into his obsession and turned inside out, transformed into its embodiment? How can he get out again?

He never does order a meal, and the staff pays him little heed. When the chips are gone, he lays two dollars on the table and walks out the back, passing our table without a glance. He is slight and vulnerable. This is just someone's boy, someone's dreamer, who grabbed a sheet out of the linen closet and walked out of the suburbs, a nice young man breaking someone's heart, lost and gliding over the beautiful Santa Rosa Mountains in a private plane of bliss.

CHAPTER 3

Suffering

Out in the narthex Basil is swinging the heavy rope down, ringing the bell in the tower. Not very comfortably; he

missed the rack when he was hanging up his bar-
bells the other day, and the weight dropped directly on his chest. "How old do you think you
are?" my husband teased when he phoned with the
news. I think he's about sixty-five, and speckled
decades they have been, marked a decade ago by a
vehement conversion that led him to repaint the
windows of his Main Street grill in huge letters:
"Praise Jesus! World's Number One Chili Dog!"
Basil greets every visitor to Holy Cross, and when
Basil greets somebody, they stay greeted.

Basil and his tiny mother, Lillian, are among
the only "cradle Orthodox" at our church, two of
the few who aren't converts. Lillian looks like a
small wintry bird and has the grip of a longshore-
man, thanks to decades of wrestling kitchen plat-

ters. She's quieter than Basil—*everyone* is quieter than Basil—and that very quietness makes her reliably perceptive. She's sitting in one of the chairs up front on the right, near the icon of the Crucifixion. Next to her is her neighbor, Joan, recently widowed, as usual dressed impeccably. I wish I could have that stylish taste and trim figure when I'm seventy, but it seems doubtful since I've never had them yet.

Only a few others are in the church: choir director Margo sits in the back until the choir arrives for the Liturgy proper in an hour, and new members Sylvia and John are a few rows behind Lillian and Joan. Three chanters stand at the lectern at the front: our sixteen-year-old son Stephen, Margo's husband David, and Zenaida. Sylvia and Zenaida were nuns together at the Episcopal convent near here, twenty-five years ago. I have a photo of them then standing side by side under a tree in their full habits, and they look not a bit older today.

Father Gregory stands facing the altar while our eighteen-year-old, David, waits near him in his acolyte robes. Between the congregation and altar there is an arched mahogany screen, called the iconostasis or icon-stand. On either side of the central opening (the "Holy Doors") there are icons: the Virgin Mary on the left and Christ on the right, as in every Orthodox church. Our iconostasis is being gradually built by parishioners, the master carpenter and guitar-builder Ross, and his teenaged assistant Luke. It's a work in progress. We hope to actually have doors in our Holy Doors someday, and they will hold a diptych icon of the Annunciation, as is the usual custom.

On an Orthodox iconostasis the images of Jesus and Mary are usually flanked by other saints and biblical scenes, including one representing the patron or title of the parish. Since our church is named Holy Cross, we see on the other side of Mary two ornately clad and crowned figures holding up a slim cross between them: the Emperor St. Constantine and his mother. St. Helena is honored for having discovered the remains of the Cross, after it had lain buried beneath the rubble of Jerusalem for three centuries. She is also said to have been an English princess, the daughter of Coel of Caercolvin (Colchester), a personage elsewhere known as "Old King Cole."

The altar itself is a square mahogany table, also made by Ross and Luke, with bars underneath connecting the legs diagonally, and a small wooden cross standing upright at the intersection. The top of the cross was drilled with a hole. On the day of our building's consecration, Bishop Basil and a crew of local priests ceremonially washed the altar with warm water and some mysterious squarish white objects, which looked to me like bars of Ivory soap. Turned out they were bars of Ivory soap. Then the altar was wiped again with red wine and rosewater, then consecrated oil (called "chrism"). The process can be messy, and for it the bishop wears over his robes a white cotton garment that ties in the back, like a long-sleeved hospital gown. When this washing and anointing is over, the bishop takes off this garment, the "savanon," and it is immediately cut up into squares, which are distributed to worshippers as they leave. When I told my son David that this surprising event would be part of the consecration service, he responded emphatically, "Orthodoxy *rules.*"

The bishop also got on his knees and leaned under the altar, to reach the standing cross with the hole in the top. Into the hole he put a scroll listing the names of all the members of the parish, and small foil-wrapped packets of saints' relics, tiny chips of bone mixed with beeswax. Though I've never been comfortable imagining the processing of relics, I understand the idea behind them. Relics often are taken from the bodies of saints that did not decay after death, and this incorruption is evidence that the person was thoroughly transformed by the Holy Spirit, body as well as soul. As a contemporary monk of Mt. Athos, Metropolitan Hierotheos Vlachos, writes, "[H]oly relics are the token that through the *nous* [the eye of the soul] the grace of God transfigured the body also." Orthodoxy does not exalt the soul and despise the body; both are to be transformed. "The primary work of the Church is to lead man to *theosis*, to communion and union with God," Bishop Hierotheos goes on. "Given this, in a sense we can say that the work of the Church is to 'produce relics.'"

Once he'd placed these items inside the cross, the bishop poured melted beeswax into the hole and sealed it. He warned us that from then on an angel would stand beside the altar day and night, offering praise to God and intercession for all of us. No more joking around or chatting in the church after services; no more sitting in the back sipping coffee on a weekday. This would be a place of worship, even when none of us was here; we would enter in order to join something already going on.

At the church's consecration, David and Stephen were among those who knelt before the bishop to be tonsured as acolytes; the bishop not only prayed over them but clipped wisps of their hair as a sign of service. In the past when my husband tonsured newly baptized people he had dutifully followed the tradition of placing the clipped hair in the censer, though worried about the awful burnt-hair smell and trying to compensate with extra incense. Before this service he asked the bishop if the boys' hair should likewise go into the censer. "No! It smells awful!" the bishop said.

Now, as Matins begins, Father Gregory bows three times, crossing himself, and under his breath says, "God be merciful to me, a
sinner." As he kisses the altar, all stand.

The three chanters, Zenaida, our sixteen-year-old Stephen, and
Margo's husband David, stand behind a blocky blond-oak lectern
that was the previous congregation's pulpit. Matins (also called Orthros) is the most variable of Orthodox services, and open before
the chanters are the various books of proper prayers and hymns, il-
luminated by a, hey, wait a minute, I know that lamp. I thought that
lamp was on the desk in my living room. Now that I think of it, last
time I passed by I thought, "Gee, that desk doesn't look as cluttered
as usual."

This happens to me all the time. Pieces of my home keep popping up in the church, squirreled away here by my husband. He
loves trying out and rearranging things, and since we got a church
building it's provided him with a whole new venue for this hobby.
The appearance of these wandering tokens of domesticity is always
a surprise to me. Like the ladies' magazines say, you have to keep the
mystery in your marriage.

The three chanters take turns with the opening hymns, or
troparia. Each of these is a prayer about a paragraph long, and there
is no printed music indicating which notes to sing, nor any organ or
other accompaniment. Each chanter in his own way fits the words
of the hymn to its proper melody, or "tone"; another chanter might
have sung it slightly differently. There are eight tones in the Byzantine style, and eight corresponding tones in the Russian style, and
most Orthodox hymnody is variation on these basic tones. The

Byzantine style has the flavor westerners think of as Middle Eastern, a haunting minor-key plaint. Middle Eastern music can be quite vigorous, and newcomers sometimes find the only thing they know that sounds like this is "Hava Nagilah." Russian tones sound more familiarly western, and readily adapt to harmony. In either case, Byzantine or Russian, people in the congregation sing along spontaneously with the chanter as much as they want; some just hum, some pick up and drop out of the melody quietly below the chanter's lead, and some sing or hum on a single low note called the "ison," rather like a bagpipe's drone. Besides these solo-chanted prayers there are congregational hymns, such as our parish "fight song," the Troparion of the Holy Cross, and these we all sing out with gusto.

Stephen has been going to the chanter's workshop Zenaida teaches every week for months now and is getting the feel of the tones. But his first hymn today, the Theotokion, or hymn to Mary the Theotokos (God-bearer), throws him. "Oh Champion dread, who canst not be put to confusion, despise not our petitions, O Good and all-praised Theotokos," he sings, chasing after the tone like a tardy commuter chasing a train. It's in there somewhere, but he gets to the end of the paragraph before catching it. Stephen is a sturdy guy, though, and not particularly dismayed or embarrassed. There'll be another troparion pulling up to the station any minute.

Early in the Matins service is the reading of six psalms, each one read by a different member of the congregation. These are said to be the psalms that will be read at the Last Judgment, so all stand and listen in attentive silence. Basil reads Psalm 3 loudly, standing smack in the middle of the church with his feet apart, declaiming toward the iconostasis. Stephen reads Psalm 38, and I can't think of the Last Judgment. It is my own dear son this tender morning, and

I hate this, his fresh teenaged voice reciting, "My wounds stink and are corrupt . . . There is no soundness in my flesh. I am feeble and sore broken . . . My heart panteth, my strength faileth me." Oh, not my son, Lord, please, let it never be my son. But it was somebody's child who wrote this. It has to be somebody it happens to.

"As for the light of mine eyes, it is also gone from me. My lovers and friends stand aloof from my sore . . . I am ready to halt, and my sorrow is continually before me." Oh Lord, not my son, please. This is the pain of being a parent, knowing that your child could be hurt someday, crying out words like these, and you would not be able to fix it.

It's the big stupid, stupid prize question of all spiritual life—how can bad things happen to good people—and no matter how many words are poured over it the problem remains, mocking us: good people still get clobbered by bad things. This, finally, is the problem. We don't want so much to know *why* it happens as to know how to stop it from happening, as if understanding what triggers such catastrophe might help us avoid it. Our quest is for prevention, yet the cruel centuries keep rolling and no one's yet found a way to prevent it.

The term for this, the "problem of evil," is "theodicy" and the alternatives have been cleverly summarized: "Either God is God and he is not good, or God is good and he is not God." That is, either God is not all-loving in the way we think, and tolerates our pain because his goals don't require our happiness, or God suffers with us helplessly but is unable to stop our suffering, is not all-powerful. Neither alternative works. A God who is not good would violate the definition and violate what we know of his overwhelming goodness running through most of our lives. A God who is not all-powerful would likewise void the meaning of the word. The retired Episcopal bishop of South Carolina, Fitzsimmons Allison, explained that accepting this confounding mystery is the only way to resolve it: "I've got the 'I don't know' theodicy. God is God, and God is good, and I don't know."

A number of different suggestions have been made through the ages to work out the dilemma. Maybe it is the devil wreaking his anger on the faithful. Maybe it is random effects from the initial fall of Adam and Eve, which sent a wave of disorder rolling obliviously forward through time. Maybe God won't stop bad people from hurting others, because then he'd have to stop everyone from doing even small bad things, and human history would become mere puppetry.

Archimandrite Sophrony Sakharov recounts hearing this discussion between two monks: "I cannot understand why the Lord does not grant peace to the world even if only a single person implored him to do so." "And how could there be complete peace in the world if but a single malicious man remained?" A world of free creatures requires the possibility that they will freely choose evil. Since the flood of Noah, God has declined to fix things by wiping out all the troublemakers. The only solution that remains is for each of us to realize that we are ourselves junior troublemakers to one extent or another, and do our part to clean up our own corners.

This is why Jesus was always telling people to repent. He gave no other explanation of suffering. When an atrocity was reported to him—worshippers murdered in the Temple itself—he rejected the idea that they suffered this because they were worse sinners than anyone else. Yet he concluded, "Unless you repent, you will all likewise perish." This is a hard word, one that doesn't get preached on very often, nor written up in curly script on Bible refrigerator magnets.

We keep asking why, but we don't need to know why something

happened; we can't use that knowledge to go back in time and stop it. And the terrifying truth is that we can't gather enough clues to know how to prevent it happening the next time. Theodicy nettles us, but the bottom line is that it's irrelevant. The only useful question in such a time is not "Why?" but "What next?" What should I do next? What should be my response to this ugly event? How can I bring the best out of it? How can God bring Resurrection out of it?

That is, of course, what he did when his own Son was bleeding and crying out in agony. He did not prevent the suffering and did not cut it short, but he completed it with Resurrection. If this is true, it changes everything; if it is not true, Christians are pathetic fools, because it is on this that we have staked all our hopes. "If Christ is not raised, your faith is futile and you are still in your sins . . . If for this life only we have hoped in Christ, we are of all people most to be pitied" (I Corinthians 15:17, 19).

So, there you are. All we can do is persevere and trust that if Jesus was raised we, too, will be raised, and all our suffering will be made right. In light of this, we forgive those who hurt us; in light of this, we live at peace. Stephen concludes the psalm, repeating three times a cry of faith that I hope he would make at such an awful time: "Forsake me not, O Lord: O my God, be not far from me. Make haste to help me, O Lord of my salvation."

As the service continues, more parishioners are gradually coming in: Carolyn, our iconographer; Emelia, a catechumen; Tom and Rose, who carries their toddler, Nicole, while one of Dr. Pat's twins (Krissy, I think) carries Rose's new baby, Nathaniel. Seeing how diligent Krissy and Cece are at finding opportunities to hold babies reminds me again of the raw animal programming of puberty; it sticks teenaged girls to any available babies with a force akin to gravity.

I usually describe our church as a "convert parish," but with the enthusiastic reproductive rate of its members we're rapidly creating a whole new subset of cradle Orthodox, cradle-ready. By the time Liturgy begins, the broad oriental rugs in the center of the church will be dotted with toddlers and babies, as parents stand around forming loose corrals.

Subdeacon Gregory (my sons call him "SDG") brings his vestment to my husband to be blessed, before donning it and joining him behind the iconostasis. Our new subdeacon is also named Gregory, but my boys call him "Subdeacon Sting" because of his resemblance to the rock star. (He says, "You should have seen me when I used to bleach my hair platinum.") He and his pregnant wife, Chris, station themselves near me, with their blond preschooler Chloe and irrepressible two-year-old Nicholas. Nicholas lies flat out on the floor, rolls, crawls, gets up and bolts for the door, and never stops grinning. I can't wait till he starts talking and can tell us what's so funny; I imagine he'll still be telling jokes when he's an old guy with hair coming out of his ears. I'm probably a bad influence on Nicholas, because I think he's adorable, even after Chris told me he lies on the floor so he can look up skirts.

We chant through intercessions and more hymns as the light through the alabaster south-facing windows grows stronger. When the doors open to admit more worshippers, I can hear the birds outside peeping. Against the right wall, up front, there is an icon of the crucifixion between two golden windows, and before it stands a box of sand into which worshippers put lighted taper candles. The amber-colored candles are made of pure beeswax by our friend Father John in New Mexico, and the drowsy scent of honey hangs over the yellow flames. Four years ago Father John sat with us one spring evening drinking beer and mourning the problems that hindered him from leaving his Protestant pastorate for Orthodoxy. Somehow these turned out to be more resolvable than he thought they would be, and he was able to make the trip across the Bosphorus a surprisingly short time later.

I went to Father John for bee advice not long ago. The first piece of furniture my husband and I ever owned was "Big Brown," a 1920s-era brown velvet armchair. During a party last spring we set it on the side porch to spare its wobbly frame, and when we remembered to bring it in again a few weeks later it had become a mansion for bees. (Perhaps this is one way of understanding the Monty Python sketch in which a torturer threatens his victims with "Ah-HA! The Comfy Chair!") I discovered this late one evening as I carried Big Brown to my station wagon and wedged it in the back, preparatory to delivering it to Luke (the teenaged iconostasis-builder) for frame repair. I noticed that as I ducked my head down near the underside of the chair, I could hear a sort of a strange hum, vaguely familiar but unidentifiable. Then I identified it and ran lickety-split for the kitchen door, slamming it behind me.

Stephen, sitting at the kitchen table, looked up from his history book. He asked, "Mom? What's the matter?"

I said, "I think there are bees in Big Brown." Or was it all my imagination? We crept to the bathroom window and opened it a crack to shine a flashlight on the bottom of the chair, which was still partly hanging out of the station-wagon door.

And then I pictured the neighbors, looking out their side windows at *us*. What do they think we're doing? "And once a year every Orthodox family has to cluster in the smallest bathroom in the house and shine a flashlight out the window onto the bottom of a chair in a station wagon." Yeah, they'd buy it.

I sent Father John an e-mail asking advice on how to encourage the bees to relocate; I didn't want to merely poison them and then have a chair full of *dead* bees. I didn't get a response for weeks; as he explained apologetically, he thought any e-mail with a subject line like "Bees in a chair" must be just one of those circulating Internet jokes. Some judicious combination of spraying and chair jostling was successful, and Big Brown is back in our midst, as sweet, or sweeter, than ever.

As the hymns and appointed prayers roll by, more parishioners arrive. Andy comes in with Annette leaning heavily on his arm. She had hip surgery a couple of weeks ago, the latest in a series of procedures that never quite resolves the problem. She's a widow whose son attends church elsewhere, and Andy drives twenty miles out of his way to pick her up.

Her Jamaican accent is so thick that I can't always understand her. We've enjoyed some aspects of her heritage—gifts of spices, tea, and barbecued goat—but had to discourage others, such as her desire to hire a "conjure man" to help a relative get a job. Annette appreciates Andy's assistance, as she's told me many times. "If it wasn't for him, I couldn't come to church, because I need somebody I can lean on to help me walk," she told me one day after church as they were making their way to Andy's car. "Andy promised my son he would take care of me, God bless him."

"I keep telling her she has to do her exercises," Andy said. He held out his hand, palm down, about chest high. "Here, kick your foot up here."

Annette glanced at the gray sky, which had been drizzling earlier when we'd had a procession around the exterior of the church. "I owe Father one of these," she said, making a fist and punching the air, "for ruining my new hairdo."

This morning as they come in they are making slow progress toward Annette's usual front-row seat. Andy lets her move at her own pace, and she clings to his arm with both hands. He wears a red v-necked pullover with a white shirt, and his brown hair is short. He's a dependable guy, not garrulous, who for years has faithfully cleaned the floor every week before church. Since Annette needs both hands to lean all her weight on Andy's arm, her shiny black pocketbook dangles from Andy's other hand.

The focus of Matins is the Resurrection, and the prayers and hymns return to the topic over and over. At the hymn known as the Evlogetaria, the choir and whole congregation sing out the refrain boldly, in a Byzantine minor key with a thumping beat: Blessed art thou, O Lord; teach me thy statutes!

Margo's David sings the first verse in his sterling tenor. He is tall and slim, good-natured and easygoing, a more lenient choir leader than his exacting wife. However, Margo's perfectionism has crafted a choir that's pretty near perfect, astonishing many newcomers.

"The company of the angels was amazed," he sings, "when they beheld thee numbered among the dead, yet thyself, O Savior, destroying the power of death, and with thee raising up Adam and releasing all men from Hell."

We sing gladly: Blessed art thou, O Lord; teach me thy statutes!

Stephen and Zenaida flank David, coming up to his shoulders. Stephen takes the next verse in a firm, deep voice: "Wherefore, oh

Women Disciples, do ye mingle sweet-smelling spices with your tears of pity? The radiant Angel within the sepulchre cried unto the Myrrh-bearing Women: Behold the grave and understand; for the Savior is risen from the tomb." He spins each of the last three words with a confident trill. Caught the train that time.

Blessed art thou, O Lord; teach me thy statutes!

Zenaida leans over the book, and her black lace veil falls forward around her face. "Very early in the morning did the Myrrh-bearing Women run lamenting unto thy tomb; but an Angel came toward them, saying: the time for lamentation is passed; weep not; but announce unto the Apostles the Resurrection."

The "Myrrh-bearing Women" were the handful who came early on Sunday morning, following the crucifixion, to give Jesus' body the customary anointing for burial; time had run out on Friday, since the Sabbath began at sunset and such work was forbidden on that holy day. There had been only enough time to lay the body hastily in a tomb. When the women arrived that morning to discover the body missing, an angel told them to spread the news that Jesus had risen. The "Myrrh-bearing women," these first witnesses of the Resurrection and the first announcers of the good news, are praised regularly as champions of the faith. St. Mary Magdalene is even honored with the title "Equal to the Apostles."

There are a few more verses, interspersed with responses, and my husband is standing at the right side of the altar singing along. Not long ago a visitor's three-year-old pointed at him after church and said to her mom, "There's the one that was singing with the angels." She seemed more surprised to see the priest again than the angels, whom perhaps she'd seen before.

Zenaida sings a concluding verse addressed to the Theotokos: "In that thou didst bear the Giver of Life, O Virgin, thou didst redeem Adam from sin, and didst give to Eve joy in place of sadness; and He who was incarnate of thee, both God and man, hath restored to life . . . "

And here everyone joins in, vigorously: " . . . those who had fallen therefrom!"

In the same melody we chant three times, "Alleluia, alleluia, alleluia; Glory to thee, O God," and each time cross ourselves and brush our right hands to the floor. This low bow is called a *metania;* when we get down on our knees and put our foreheads to the floor, it's a prostration. Even without the bowing, the emphatic beat would get our hearts pumping.

This is followed by more hymns, psalms, prayers, and a Gospel reading, after which everyone lines up to kiss the Gospel book. Vince and Hardworking Jeannie arrive with their four daughters, and take a stand toward the front. They are the last line of defense to catch toddlers making a dash toward the iconostasis (Nicole likes to go gaze at the acolytes, especially Luke, or "Wookie," on whom she has a pint-sized crush). Jonathan wheels his chair up front near Lillian, and Victor the plumber stations himself against the back wall. Adam the exterminator settles his dramatically dark-haired Greek family on the left side of the church. ("One day a week I worship God, and the other six I kill things," he told me in his Cypriot accent, grinning.)

Nobody had a cup of coffee when they got up this morning. Nobody who plans on receiving Communion, that is. Part of preparing for Communion is fasting, abstaining from all food and drink from midnight Saturday. After the Liturgy, we have an ample brunch, provided by a different team of families each week. The amount of fasting in Orthodoxy takes inquirers by surprise: no meat, fish, dairy, wine, or olive oil on Wednesdays or Fridays, nor during Lent or several other seasons during the liturgical cycle. Without tuna or macaroni and cheese to fall back on, we're pretty much confined to spaghetti with tomato sauce and peanut butter sandwiches. All in all, we're adhering to this regimen of abstaining from these foods (a discipline we call fasting, even though it's not a total fast) about half the days of the year.

Fasting is essential to Orthodox spirituality; unlike some of the other more titillating sins, misuse of food is an equal-opportunity temptation available three times a day to everyone from nine to ninety. Those who overcome this most basic temptation gain spiritual strength to battle all the rest. Of course, almost no one does. St. Gregory of Sinai wrote in the fourteenth century, "What shall we say of the belly, the queen of passions? If you can slay it or half kill it, keep a tight hold. It has mastered me, beloved, and I serve it as a slave and a vassal."

Overeating does more than make you plump and cuddly; it limits your spiritual perception. These words by the nineteenth-century Russian Bishop Ignatius Brianchaninov build to an alarming crescendo: "Wise temperance of the stomach is a door to all the virtues. Restrain the stomach, and you will enter Paradise. But if you please and pamper your stomach, you will hurl yourself over the precipice of bodily impurity, into the fire of wrath and fury, you will coarsen and darken your mind, and in this way you will ruin your powers of attention and self-control, your sobriety and vigilance." If that doesn't make you take a second look at your second helpings, nothing will.

Another part of preparing for Communion is the holy mystery, or sacrament, of confession. On a regular basis, Orthodox are expected to go privately to their parish priest and confess the sins they are currently struggling with. Typically, the two stand before an icon of Christ, and the priest listens and gives counsel. Confession is made to Christ in the presence of the priest, not to the priest himself, and the focus is less on punishment for past misdeeds than on self-examination equipping one to do better in the future.

As with fasting, the discipline is meant to make one stronger, like an athlete's regimen of exercise. The priest functions as a personal trainer might, helping the parishioner determine how to apply the Church's spiritual resources for best effect. While only priests (or higher ranks of clergy) can hear confessions, Orthodox may have a separate relationship with a spiritual father or mother, usually a monk or nun, who supplies this intensive spiritual counseling.

At the end, the priest places his stole over the penitent's head and pronounces the Lord's forgiveness. Preparing to go to confession can be stressful; one feels awkward and embarrassed to say some things aloud. But saying them, and then hearing them forgiven, turns out to be surprisingly liberating. It's freeing to have no secrets and to know that one's most shameful moments are seen, known, and forgiven by God. Receiving this forgiveness through the priest, hearing the words aloud, contributes to a sense of permanency and reliability; it's not just you talking to the bedroom ceiling. As my husband says, on the way in people say, "I hate confession!" On the way out they say, "I love confession!"

The choir files into place, and Mimi takes the lone chair on the platform so she won't have to lean on her metal crutches for the whole service. The rest will stand for the next hour and a half.

It strikes me that there is a lot of fodder for theodicy right in this room. Annette's hip, Joan's widowhood, Mimi's crutches,

Jonathan's wheelchair, others with sorrows that are obvious to everyone, or known only to my husband and me, or known only to my husband, or known only to God. Everyone has a wound, and some have many. People keep showing up anyway.

Years ago, long before we became Orthodox, I was standing at the back of our Protestant church in Virginia watching people go forward to Communion. They would file up the three steps, kneel at the altar rail, receive Communion, then go back to their pews, a continuous stream of worshippers. And as if my eyes were opened, I suddenly saw the suffering each one carried: this one whose son was killed, this one with cancer, that one with an alcoholic spouse, that one whom no one had ever wanted to marry. As my eyes lingered over each one, I could see past these obvious injuries through other, hidden layers of murky pain, and I wondered that anyone had the strength to climb those stairs; wondered that every broken person didn't crawl up them with tears, bitter at the God who failed to prevent this suffering but bereft of any other hope than that distant, stony entity.

"Why do you allow this?" I demanded of God in my heart, blinking back hot tears. "Why do you let this happen? Look at how these people love you. Look at how they serve you. If you love them, why do you let them get so hurt?"

Then it seemed as if the picture reversed itself. I became aware, first, of the mildness of the air. It was early spring and the fresh scent of daffodils was drifting in. The very air seemed a patient blessing. Next I became aware of the light filling the building, sunlight coming in the clear bottle-glass windows. Light is good. I saw the colors and realized what an extravagance it was to fill the world with an infinite range of hues and shades; these very people I saw as so wounded were clothed in a festival of colors, as if refuting my bitterness by wrapping themselves in glorious shades.

And I saw that life is good, and God pours down goodness on us, in air and light and color, and that it is good to be here, even when it is hard. That the sheer gift of life in the first place is so overflowingly rich that sufferings dwindle in comparison; they are the hurts that can be borne only by people who are already alive, who feel the air and stand in the light this Sunday morning. And God is with us in our hurts, and they are transitory, and the Judge will one day make all things right, and "he will wipe every tear from their eyes" (Revelation 21:4).

I worry that I am saying this badly, that it sounds sappy. Words are flimsy tools. Maybe you had to be there; I had to be there myself for a dozen years or so before I saw this, a dozen years trying to unfold the heart of Christ and understand what following him meant. Maybe another couple of dozen and I'll find a way to say it.

It's getting toward the end of Matins, and Basil moves back to the bell rope to ring in the beginning of the Divine Liturgy. As he passes me, he grunts, "I tell you what, it feels like my ribs are being squeezed in a vise!" It is one more little, temporary suffering. Basil looks jaunty today in a black vest and bright green shirt. He tentatively stretches one arm up and winces. "Thank you, Jesus," he says with determination, and heads out toward the rope.

CHAPTER 4

Dirty Words

The doorway gives off beeps as I pass through, on my way down the short hallway to Robert's cave. This interior room is windowless, dim, and, in my opinion, gloomy. It doesn't matter much; a radio station rarely has cause to worry about visuals, and besides, Robert is blind.

The station manager of the Radio Reading Network is a large black man with hair just going gray at the temples. When I come in, he greets me, leaning back expansively in his rolling desk chair, a v-shaped smile beneath his aviator-framed dark glasses. Robert asks about my family and tells me about his growing church in a silky voice.

First I go to the gray metal filing cabinet and fish around in the top drawer, standing on tiptoe, looking for my videotape. Of course, there's no video recording on it; Robert uses VHS tapes for audio recording because, at six hours, they offer the longest continuous recording available. I hand the cassette to Robert and tell him, "I'm going in the little studio now." I like the smaller of the two studios, with its dinged brown metal fluorescent lamp and desktop covered with a muffling sheet of old carpet. On the underside of the desk, about as far over as my arm can reach, is the cough button. In a fancy studio, this would halt the tape, but this one merely substitutes silence for those seconds I need to sneeze or clear my throat. The blind, I've learned, are more sensitive to these random sounds than I am.

"It used to be that radio and television announcers had a high standard of professionalism," Robert complained to me one day. "Not anymore. Now you hear them cough and clear their throats on the air. Next I expect you'll hear one of them burp."

What I and others read here is broadcast across the state to citizens who are blind or otherwise unable to read. They pick up the closed-circuit signal on a special receiver, made of blond oak with a large gold-tone metal grille. It looks like a high-school shop project, circa 1955. We don't know exactly how many of these are out there; probably in the neighborhood of four thousand.

Twenty-four hours a day, something is being broadcast. In the morning and afternoon, readers present the Baltimore and Washington newspapers. In between, it's magazines and poetry, television listings, gardening news, and grocery store advertisements. I read novels. Each week I put on tape another hour, and when the whole book is recorded, Robert airs it over the course of a week or two.

Reading aloud, I become aware of how hard it is to be dependent on the spoken word for information. Sight allows you to take in a whole landscape at once, everything in proper perspective and standing in relation to everything else. But when you can only hear, the world comes to you sequentially, one element at a time, a narrow thread approaching inch by inch. Information mumbled by the reader or forgotten by the listener is irretrievably lost. If between yesterday's chapter of the novel and today's you forgot who Jim is, there is no way for you to go back and look him up. If this author likes to sail off into a patch of dialogue and only get to " . . . said Jim" at the end of the sentence, you can spend a lot of time wondering who's saying all this. If the reader spontaneously decides to present Jim's voice in an agitated falsetto, then arrives at an authorial direction like "Jim said in a deep, husky voice," you, the listener, are once again at the mercy of incompetents.

As I read, I think of how difficult it can be to keep characters straight, and try imperfectly to give them different voices. A group conversation among several characters can be an impenetrable tangle, and I insert more landmarks than the author did: "Sam said" or "Doris went on." My voice goes stealing into homes across the state, and I can only see far enough to imagine that yellow wooden box and a hand resting upon it. Where I sit, I can see the paperback in my hands, the battered desk lamp, the window to the control booth, and Robert through there, listening. He can't see me.

Christian faith is broader than the individual journey to oneness with God. In fact, we are assured that we do not see Jesus at all if we do not see him in those in need. In a cautionary parable at the end of the 25th chapter of Matthew, Jesus describes the Day of Judgment. He tells how he will recognize those who belong to him: "I was hungry and you gave me food, I was thirsty and you gave me drink, I was a stranger and you welcomed me, I was naked and you clothed me, I was sick and you visited me, I was in prison and you came to me." To those who did not do these things, Jesus says, "Depart from me, you cursed, into the eternal fire prepared for the devil and his angels . . . Truly, I say to you, as you did it not to one of the least of these, you did it not to me." This command to care for others gave rise to hospitals, orphanages, leprosariums, schools, hostels, and hospices wherever Christians went, from the Church's earliest days. We believe that our eternal destiny is bound up with that of all who surround us, and that we are particularly obligated to help those in need.

Care of the needy is logically a theme in many religions, but I always wondered about India—obviously one of the most religious cultures in the world, but one where Mother Teresa found widespread neglect of the suffering. The presumptions she brought with her, that the dying poor deserve love, were not ones that arose naturally in that context. My friend Mark, who grew up in Japan, offered a partial explanation: if the cycle of reincarnation provides us with an opportunity to suffer for sins in past lives, intervention to relieve suffering hinders the process of spiritual growth.

"When those philosophies are actually lived out," he says, "it tends to produce people who are indifferent to human suffering. They conclude that sufferers probably deserve it for sins in past lives, and that pain is to be endured rather than relieved." Opportunities to suffer are meant to be embraced. For example, Mark says, his dentist in Japan would only give him the minimum amount of Novocaine. "When I complained, he was loath to give me more, urging me to 'gaman' or 'bear the pain.'" Likewise, he says, the Kobe earthquake did not inspire the reaction it would have over here. "Television images of their countrymen suffering after the quake did not produce the type of outpouring of donations that would have been routine in the U.S. Those sufferers, too, were supposed to 'gaman.'"

In Christian faith there is no belief in reincarnation, or that believers must pay for their own sins; the death of Christ on the cross covers all. Our response to this divine compassion is compassion toward others. The view of suffering Mother Teresa brought to Calcutta was very different from the one prevalent there. She got it from Matthew 25.

Care of the sick can be taxing and unpleasant work, as we see in some stories from the early history of the Church. In the fourth and fifth centuries, men and women went out to the deserts of the Middle East and Egypt to devote their lives to prayer and spiritual struggle. Hundreds of anecdotes and sayings remain from those Desert Mothers and Fathers, who bear the titles "Amma" or "Abba" (roughly corresponding to "Mommy" and "Daddy").

A disciple once asked a Desert Father to declare whose work was more pleasing to God: a brother who fasts six days at a time in continuous prayer and penance, or a brother who takes care of the sick. The Abba replied, "If that brother who fasts six days at a time were to hang himself up by the nose, he could not equal the one who takes care of the sick."

Several stories about care of the sick concern Abba Agathon. When he found a sick man lying in a city square, he rented a cell and nursed the man there for four months till he was healed, working with his hands to pay for the sick man's needs. He may well have agreed with Mother Teresa's statement that in the dying poor she saw "Jesus in his distressing disguise." Abba Agathon also had a near-literal experience along these lines. One day when he was going to market to sell some wares, he met a paralyzed man by the road, who demanded to be carried to the town. Once there, the man ordered Abba Agathon to use the proceeds from each sale to buy him cake or a gift. Last, he told the Abba to carry him back to his original spot. There the cripple announced, "Agathon, you are filled with divine blessings, in heaven and on earth," and disappeared.

Among the Orthodox saints are several called "unmercenaries," that is, physicians who refused to take money for their work. Physician-saints of the early church include St. Panteleimon, the companion saints Cyrus and John, and the twin brothers Cosmas and Damian. The latter were so dedicated to the principle of free service that when Damian accepted three eggs from a grateful patient, the infuriated Cosmas announced he refused to be buried next to his brother. The patient insisted that she offered the eggs not as payment but to fulfill a vow she had made, and the pair was reconciled.

Overall, the Christian and Orthodox view is that the world is full of genuine suffering. We cannot deny it, dismiss it, ignore it; we cannot pretend that it's an illusion, or that people get what they deserve for deeds in previous lives. Instead, we are compelled to take positive action, bringing healing wherever we can and comfort where we cannot.

Likewise, in this mutable world, we ourselves may face suffering someday; indeed, it's very likely. Being able-bodied is a temporary condition. Bearing suffering well is a spiritual gift. When other kind faces bend over ours, wiping our brow or changing our diapers, we can receive that gift with patience, humility, and peace. "If I could meet a leper, give him my body and take his, I should be very happy," said Abba Agathon. The Desert Mother Amma Syncletica taught, "If illness weighs us down, let us not be sorrowful as though we could not sing, for all things work for our good."

The devout Catholic novelist Flannery O'Connor died young of systemic lupus, a miserable disease. Like Amma Syncletica, she could sing. "I have never been anywhere but sick. In a sense sickness is a place, more instructive than a long trip to Europe, and it's always a place where there's no company, where nobody can follow. Sickness before death is a very appropriate thing and I think those who don't have it miss one of God's mercies." There is a mystery here I can barely grasp, but I hope to learn it by the time I need it.

I am still able-bodied and want to give to those who are not as long as I can. Ever since the kids were small I've enjoyed reading aloud, and people tell me I have a comforting voice, so I began looking for an opportunity to read to the blind. Since beginning at the Radio Reading Network, I've completed three novels.

I'm reading this one cold and occasionally run across passages I don't like. Dirty words are one example. I've found, somewhat to my surprise, that I feel different about profanity (cursing based on holy names) and obscenity (cursing based on body parts and functions). Obscene words are crude, but in a sense innocent; it's not the syllables themselves that are "dirty," but the hostility of the user and the hurt he intends through inappropriateness (more flatteringly, "daring"). As I'm reading a novel, if such language suits the character, I don't object much.

The only thing that gives me pause is that, for reasons I don't understand, the radio signal also sometimes shows up on the educational television station. One day after church, Subdeacon Sting said to me, "The other day when Chloe was watching *Sesame Street* the audio went away, and instead we heard what sounded like somebody reading a book. I *swear*, it sounded just like your voice." I thought, Uh oh. I could remember an argument the main character had with her boyfriend that was rather explicit, and however I was picturing my audience then it wasn't little Chloe listening to those words during *Sesame Street.*

Other than the possibility that I'm providing unscripted voiceover for Bert and Ernie, obscenity doesn't bother me. Profanity does. This is the name of the one I love, my own Lord Jesus. It hurts when I have to read a character's "God dammit" or angry "Jesus Christ!" I feel almost a physical wound, as if someone had struck me or someone I love. I find it painful to say these words, and so I don't. If I spot them coming in time, I substitute an equivalent—perhaps an obscenity.

Ancient belief holds that there is power wrapped in a name, and the speaking of a holy name calls forth the presence of the Holy One. The Hebrew scriptures treated the name of God with such reverence that it was never written or spoken. Early Christian contemplative prayer began with the simple invocation of the name of Jesus and the plea for mercy; this prayer gradually expanded to "Lord Jesus Christ, Son of God, have mercy on me, a sinner." Those who practice this, the "Jesus Prayer," form the habit of saying it over and over again, perhaps using a knotted cord of black wool (a "prayer rope") to count the repetitions and keep mind and hand occupied. By God's grace, some find that the prayer "descends into the heart." It then may become self-activating; the heart seems to be speaking the prayer while the mind listens in peaceful attentiveness.

"The heart" here doesn't mean just the seat of human emotions; it means both the center of the whole being, and the physical heart itself. According to the anonymous nineteenth-century work *The Way of a Pilgrim,* one should visualize the heart beating with each word of the prayer. (This is the book poor Franny was reading in

Salinger's short story.) Eyes should be closed, and attention should be paid to the words of the prayer. Any other thoughts—even lofty spiritual insights—should be dismissed.

This is not a nifty technique by which a person can reach enlightenment. It's a prayer directed to someone, naming his name—the Lord Jesus Christ. If you're not ready to ask him for mercy, don't pray this prayer. His name, like his presence, is powerful.

"The Jesus Prayer is not a talisman," St. Theophan the Recluse wrote. "Its power comes from faith in the Lord, and from a deep union of the mind and heart with him. With such a disposition, the invocation of the Lord's name becomes very effective in many ways. But a mere repetition of the words does not signify anything."

I soon began to find that the moment in this prayer when the name of Jesus rings forth had a physical effect. My heart would ache, or reel as if from a blow; his name sounded in me like a gong. Shortening the prayer to "Jesus, mercy" was almost too intense to endure; using the longer form couched that jewel of piercing light in a setting that provided more of a shield.

I gradually began to feel that the center of my heart, where that prayer goes on, is the real center of me, and the nattering, flighty, worried, show-offy person that flaps around it like a spooked chicken is not. The problem is that Chicken Person is the one who's in control of operations. She's got the keys, she's got her hands on the steering wheel, she's the one who talks and writes and shows up places when you were expecting me. This is a real shame, because she's pretty clueless. (That's why the second half of the prayer is "have mercy on me.") But the real me is there in the center of my heart, where there is certainty and peace, and where all the air is filled with the vibrating hum of the name of Jesus.

This heart sometimes seems like foreign territory, a chunk of golden heaven, being carried around in this body that is too full of self-indulgence, hurt pride, and chocolate. Not a worthy temple, most of the time, not the way the Chicken Person runs it. According to the Macarian Homilies, written in Syria in the late fourth century, "There are unfathomable depths within the heart . . . God is there with the angels, light and life are there, the kingdom and the apostles, the heavenly cities and the treasures of grace: all things are there."

The name is what does this; it's the tuning fork that sets the whole world in harmony. It is what enables us to separate from the golden heart the garbage and dross of selfishness that are always trying to assert control. I read novels into a microphone, and I don't mind talking about body parts or functions. But I cannot misuse the name.

Robert is a Christian, too. His congregation is brand-new and small and has just bought a huge warehouse to make over into their church. They are evangelizing vigorously to fill it. He updates me on this most weeks and turns his head from side to side as he talks. I wonder if this is a gesture that aids orientation. Robert, blind from birth, depends a great deal on ambient sound, and noises that interfere with that—like a window unit air conditioner—cause trouble. Once we had a fire drill while I was reading, and finding the path outside was difficult for Robert because the blaring alarm interfered with his ability to hear where the doorways were.

My son Stephen is somewhat in awe of Robert, because he has a B.A. in Percussion from the Peabody Institute of Music. Stephen went into debt to buy a drum kit before he'd ever played a lick and has been trying to teach himself ever since, sitting in the attic beating out rhythms to his favorite rock tunes. Fortunately, the neighbors like to hear him. At least, that's what they *say*. The young doctors on the left say they get up and dance; the elderly black couple on the right claim to enjoy it, too, though they've had a soft spot for Stephen since that day, years ago, they watched him in our driveway practicing a standing jump into an empty garbage can.

Robert came over one afternoon to give Stephen a little coaching, then sat at the beginner's set and scorched the skins. "It was awesome, Mom, because of course he never looked down at the drums," Stephen said. "He just kept his head up, turning it a little bit, like Stevie Wonder."

Robert told me once about boarding at the school for the blind when he was a child. They played tricks on each other, like kids do everywhere. A new kid might be taken out for a picnic by the older kids, the group settling on a blanket in the middle of a field. The older kids would then tell him: "This blanket is on the edge of a cliff, don't step off it!" and run away, stopping at a distance to enjoy the new kid's noisy plight.

Robert grew up on the rough side of Baltimore. "I wanted money, a fine sound system, to have a good meal, nice cologne. I grew up around gangs, and I heard people get their throat cut, heard 'em burned, heard 'em crying for their mother. I learned so much about God, and I learned to pray."

He came to love God but developed some skepticism about the church. "Black people talk a lot about God, but when I was thirteen or fourteen I began to understand the way it is. You see a pastor digging in the dirt, you say, Can I get dirty too? A pastor who's over ninety, and there's one woman in the congregation he makes sure gets a house, a car, a salary—you know that years ago, something took place. Pastor asks for a special collection for the building fund, takes up thousands of dollars, and nobody sees it again. White churches don't do that." He's told me a couple of times that I act different from the pastors' wives he knows. "The average lady married to a pastor is arrogant. She walks around like she's on a mattress of air."

It's not just the church that is corrupt. "God is tired of this world, and if it wasn't for Jesus Christ, he'd blow it up. Why doesn't he avenge with his two-edged sword? Because the Devil is the prince of the air. The Devil has this world sewn up, and the angels fight for us every day. If we didn't have that, what would happen? If God took time off for a moment, just to wipe the sweat from his brow, think of how many people would go to destruction."

I enjoy reading books for the Radio Reading Network, but it seems kind of like cheating as a volunteer activity, because I don't actually get face-to-face with anyone except Robert. So when I can, I go with my friend Jean to visit the AIDS patients at a nursing home downtown; we offer them fresh fruit and pray with them. The home is not elegant, and patients are mostly poor and black.

Jean is gorgeous, in a monumental way. She's my age but tall and amply proportioned, with a headful of glossy black braids, large eyes, and—strange to say, but true—remarkably beautiful teeth. "My, doesn't she have beautiful teeth!" was the first comment we heard on meeting one new patient. "If I wasn't gay, her husband would have to watch out!" I think her beauty is due to the quality of radiance and joy about her, which carries her forward with winning grace. Her porcelain teeth are often on display, because she laughs frequently and smiles so much.

We go down the hallways, a tall black Baptist woman and a short white Orthodox woman, side by side, carrying blue plastic grocery bags. Jean takes the lead, knocking on doors and calling out, "How are you doing today? Would you like a piece of fruit?" Some like the bananas because their teeth are too wobbly for apples; some want apples because they aren't hard to peel like oranges; everybody likes grapes. After some chatting, Jean asks, "Would you like to have prayer today?" Most say yes. We link hands or lay an arm around a frail shoulder, and either Jean or I pray aloud. Jean may do a little catechesis: "Do you understand what it means to be saved? You know you can't be saved just by being a good person. You're not saved by your works, only by Jesus' death on the cross. Have you taken Jesus Christ as your personal savior?"

In a more upscale AIDS ward I can imagine this approach might be unwelcome. Here, most of the patients come from a background with deep Christian roots. They have spent long hours here, thinking about death, and about what their grandma used to tell them about the Lord's watching over them. They want reconciliation with God in the familiar terms of their spiritual tradition. AIDS doesn't have anything to do with it; Jean starts with the assumption that everyone is a sinner, and everyone needs Jesus.

I don't ask close questions about basic faith; I'm too shy, and Orthodox would phrase things differently. My eastern faith is foreign territory in this Southern Protestant context, so I don't refer to its specifics much. I did once, at our annual Christmas dinner; it seemed like a great idea at the time. Every Christmas we put on a dinner for the patients, with turkey and yams and decorations. Af-

terward we sit and sing carols till we're all sung out. One year, inspired by the Christmas spirit, I leapt to my feet and announced
that I wanted to sing for them one of the Christmas songs from my
church. I started in on this ancient free-verse hymn, said to have
been miraculously given to the fifth-century hymnographer St. Romanus the Melodist. It is set to a lilting, sinuous melody:

> The Virgin brings forth today the Omnipotent,
> And the earth offers a cave to the Unapproachable.
> Angels give glory with shepherds
> and the Magi journey with the stars,
> When for our sakes was born
> As a new babe
> He who is from eternity, God.

By the end of the second line, I realized that this train was not
going to make it all the way to the station. I was receiving quizzical,
studied attention, but not much comprehension. At the end, the
patients tendered polite applause, a testimony to their good manners.

So I don't try to imitate Jean's style in talking with patients. I do
try to figure out what the person's central spiritual concern is. How
to cope with pain? Desperate wishes to be healed? Making peace
with an estranged child or parent? I try to fit my prayer to their
needs.

Once I went ahead to the next room while Jean was remaining
with a patient. I found a young, plump white man lying in a fetal
position, apparently dazed. I'd seen him once previously, stumbling
naked in his room while an aide hollered at him to come back to
bed. Today his eyes were open but apparently unseeing.

I covered his hand with mine and prayed aloud—that he would be freed from pain, that God would give him light, that his sins would be forgiven, that he would know peace. I wondered if he could hear me at all. When I said, "Amen," he lifted my hand to his lips and kissed it.

Jean's right, none of this volunteering, no good works, will save me. The Chicken Person gets some things right and some things wrong, but mostly she needs grace, fresh showers of it every day. This good news of God's love and forgiveness is both the message we have to bring and what empowers us to bring it. It would be a shame to conceal it; apples and conversation alone are not enough. As Robert says, "You can feed the poor all you want, but what really counts is to tell them about God. We have to keep asking God for his mercy. If he was to stop for a moment just to blow his nose, what would happen to me?"

CHAPTER 5

The Virgin Theotokos

As the last notes of the Matins service die away, Subdeacon Gregory says to my husband, "In the name of the Lord, Father, bless."

"Blessed is the Kingdom of the Father, and of the Son, and of the Holy Spirit," he sings out in reply, marking the opening of the Divine Liturgy. This service has two parts: the Liturgy of the Catechumens (or of the Word) and the Liturgy of the Faithful (or of the Eucharist). The first roughly follows the pattern of first-century Jewish synagogue worship, with prayer, readings from Scripture, hymns or psalms, a sermon, and concluding prayers. "Catechumens" are those taking instruction to become members of the Church, and in the early centuries they would be welcome to attend this first segment. Only those who had made a commitment to the faith were permitted to receive Communion, though, so only "the Faithful" were allowed to stay for the rest.

Near that turning point in the Divine Liturgy the priest or deacon still cries out, "The doors! The doors!" This was a reminder to shut the doors behind the departing catechumens so that the sacrament of Communion—what Orthodox call the Sacred Mysteries—could be observed in appropriate privacy. So notable is this moment in the service that my young nephew Thomas, on seeing a bumpersticker commemorating the rock band The Doors, remarked, "That guy must be Orthodox!"

The movement from the end of Matins to the beginning of the Divine Liturgy is a seamless slide, a division not strongly noticeable to the congregation. Though the sign outside says, "Matins 8:30, Divine Liturgy 9:30," the starting time for the latter service is only approximate—it begins when Matins ends. As a result, parishioners' arrival time is similarly approximate. No matter when you get there, worship will be already going on.

Unfortunately, this makes for less than conscientious punctuality. "Get Me to the Church on Time" is not a song from an Orthodox culture. All during the opening hymns, worshippers will continue to trickle in, and most go up to the front of the church to stand and pray before the iconostasis or the icon of the crucifixion on the side wall, and place candles before them. There is a feeling of quiet, intent bustle. Private and corporate prayer are going on simultaneously, and worshippers move up and back through the length of the church. Everyone is not lined up in their places with bright, shiny faces.

This can be disconcerting to visitors from other denominations. A friend of mine who went to Romania as a Protestant missionary wrote me of the negative rumors she'd heard about Orthodox worship: "People don't come on time, and when they get there they don't sit down, and they wander all around the church." I regretfully agree that they might not come on time. But they might not be sitting down because they stand for worship, like we do; they might be "wandering around" in order to go up to the front and pray and light a candle, which we do even though worship is already going on. I know there are more organized ways to have church, and punctuality would be a blessing. My friend Father Dan says, "I don't believe in organized religion. I'm Orthodox."

This service is called the Liturgy of St. John Chrysostom, after a famed fourth-century preacher whose surname means "Golden Mouth." Thanks to his eloquence, he was made bishop of Constantinople. The Liturgy is indeed very beautiful, but Chrysostom's explanatory writings—commentaries on the Scriptures, exhortatory sermons, and so forth—are blunt, clear, and energetic, far from purple prose. I note that he's Golden Mouth, not Golden Pen, so I imagine he had a vigorous presence to fit these instructive essays.

Perhaps St. John Chrysostom's best-known piece of short writing is his Paschal Sermon, which is still delivered by the celebrant in every Orthodox congregation on Pascha (Easter) each year. It welcomes all to the feast, whether or not they have kept the strenuous Lenten fast. It recalls Jesus' parable of the laborers in the vineyard, who were each paid by their employer a day's wage, no matter how late in the day they began to work (Matthew 20:1–16).

> If any man be devout and love God, let him enjoy this fair and radiant triumphal feast.
> If any man be a wise servant, let him enter rejoicing into the joy of his Lord.

If any have labored long in fasting, let him now receive his recompense.

If any have wrought from the first hour, let him today receive his just reward.

If any have come at the third hour, let him with thankfulness keep the feast.

If any have arrived at the sixth hour, let him have no misgivings, because he shall in no wise be deprived.

If any have delayed until the ninth hour, let him draw near, fearing nothing.

If any have tarried even until the eleventh hour, let him also be not alarmed at his tardiness; for the Lord, who is jealous of his honor, will accept the last even as the first; he gives rest unto him who comes at the eleventh hour, even as unto him who has worked from the first hour.

And he shows mercy upon the last, and cares for the first; and to the one he gives, and upon the other he bestows gifts.

And he both accepts the deeds, and welcomes the intention, and honors the acts and praises the offering.

Wherefore, enter ye all into the joy of your Lord, and receive your reward, both the first and likewise the second.

You rich and poor together, hold high festival. You sober and you heedless, honor the day.

Rejoice today, both you who have fasted and you who have disregarded the fast.

The table is fully laden; feast sumptuously. The calf is fatted; let no one go hungry away. Enjoy the feast of faith; receive all the riches of loving-kindness.

Let no one bewail his poverty, for the universal kingdom has
been revealed.

Let no one weep for his iniquities, for pardon has shone forth
from the grave.

Let no one fear death, for the Savior's death has set us free: he
that was held prisoner of it has annihilated it.

By descending into hell, he made hell captive. He embittered it
when it tasted of his flesh. And Isaiah, foretelling this,
cried: "Hell was embittered when it encountered thee in the
lower regions."

It was embittered, for it was abolished. It was embittered, for it
was mocked.

It was embittered, for it was slain. It was embittered, for it was
overthrown.

It was embittered, for it was fettered in chains.

It took a body, and met God face to face. It took earth, and
encountered heaven.

It took that which was seen, and fell upon the unseen.

O Death, where is your sting? O Hell, where is your victory?

Christ is risen, and you are overthrown. Christ is risen, and the
demons are fallen.

Christ is risen, and the angels rejoice. Christ is risen, and life
reigns.

Christ is risen, and not one dead remains in the grave.

For Christ, being risen from the dead, is become the first-fruits
of those who have fallen asleep. To him be glory and do-
minion unto ages of ages. Amen.

John Chrysostom did not write the Divine Liturgy as a wholly original composition but edited and amended a version already in use. That longer version had been produced by St. Basil the Great, a bishop of Cappadocia who lived earlier in the fourth century, and it is still used for several great feasts during the liturgical year. St. Basil, in turn, had assembled and composed his Liturgy from ancient elements in use before him. Our Liturgy bears the imprint of many hands, and proof of specific authorship is rare. Though credited to St. John Chrysostom, it is the fruit of a common faith rather than the work of a single author. The Liturgy was not set in stone when St. John Chrysostom died, either. The basic structure gained some additions over the next few centuries, a process which gradually slowed and came to rest with the Liturgy in its present form by the fourteenth century.

Today's Liturgy begins with the "Litany of Peace," which asks peace and salvation for us, as well as civil peace, healthful seasons and crops, and safety for travelers. We respond each time, "Lord, have mercy," the usual response to intercessory petitions. The frequent repetition of this phrase can sound a little craven to newcomers, as if we think God will be wrathful instead if we don't remind him to be nice. But it's more like an acknowledgment of the way things already are, a reminder to ourselves. God already is bestowing mercy, whether we notice it or not, as he sends the sun to shine on just and unjust alike. "He who did not spare his own Son but gave him up for us all, will he not also give us all things with him?" (Romans 8:32). His job is to give, but ours is to *ask* him to give; the act of asking changes us, makes us open and humble. The Greek word for "mercy" recalls the root for "oil," and thus has the association of balm and healing. We are inviting God to bless us with his kindness, and open our hearts to receive that gift.

As we sing, worshippers keep arriving a little late for church, and make their way to the front to stand, pray, and kiss icons. They have to part like the Red Sea around little Nicole, who is sitting in the middle of the rug with her legs straight out in front of her, admiring her little white shoes and tapping her toes together. These are special shoes covered with sparkles, as she likes to show me.

The whole congregation sings the first antiphon, "Through the prayers of the Theotokos, O Savior, save us." This is our title for the Virgin Mary, which proclaims that the child she bore was God himself; "Theotokos" means "God-bearer." Orthodox sing to Mary a lot, and in this as in other things I find less softness and sentiment than in the West. She is our Champion Dread, as Stephen sang during Matins; elsewhere she's hailed as Captain Leader, and even Queen of War. My daughter Megan comes home from her Roman Catholic college with prayer cards spilling out of her textbooks: dreamy Marys gazing tenderly, fresh-faced virgin saints, roses and clouds and blushes. Even the soldier saints look like adolescent boys with dewy expressions. I hope those rough old soldiers, now bivouacked upstairs, get a good laugh out of these cards.

Western and Eastern Christianity have so much overtly in common that the underlying differences in approach are easy to miss. To use archetypal terms, the eastern interest in challenge and rigor could be described as masculine. In Orthodoxy, Mary is a strong figure, not a helpless or vapid one. She's our Captain because she is first in the pack, the leader of all Christians, and it is her example we all follow, men as well as women. We strive like athletes, as St. Paul said (I Corinthians 9:24–27), to overcome the petty self-defeating behaviors that distract us from union with God.

Western Christianity, I find, has a comparatively feminine flavor. The emphasis is on nurturing and comfort; reunion with God occurs as he heals our inner wounds. In the West, we want God to console and reassure us; in the East, we want God to help us grow up and stop acting like jerks.

This situation in the West has been heightened in recent years by pervasive consumerism, which encourages self-focus and self-indulgence. Yet western Christian faith has long been considered women's business. Forty years ago Norman Rockwell captured the idea with his "Easter Morning": Dad slouches in his pajamas, awash in newspapers, while Mom and the kids march past him in their Sunday best. A hundred years before that clergy were already being stigmatized as prissy and effeminate, and in the seventeenth century Cotton Mather complained that only women came to church.

Author Leon Podles traces this situation all the way back to the thirteenth century and the writings of St. Bernard of Clairvaux. St. Bernard's mysticism was based on imagining oneself the Bride of Christ, which made it immensely popular with women though less accessible to men. As this emotional, individualized, and self-focused spirituality spread, there arose in reaction the dry and deliberate Scholastic theology epitomized by St. Thomas Aquinas. The outcome was an enduring and unfortunate split in the West between heart and head. In annoying confirmation of stereotypes, women generally preferred and patronized heart-based spirituality, while men went for the head.

As far as popular practice is concerned, heart won. Podles cites church growth expert Lyle Schaller as finding a 1986 average of 60 percent women to 40 percent men in American churches, a split that has since widened. The inner circle of laity who actually run the parish is even more likely to be populated by females, even when ordained leadership is all-male. Podles quotes Jesuit theologian Patrick Arnold as finding the female-to-male balance in churches he's visited ranging from 2:1 to 7:1, and "some liberal Presbyterian or Methodist congregations are practically bereft of men." Sociologist Edward H. Thompson states that "throughout all varieties of black religious activity, women represent from 75 to 90 percent of the participants."

For hundreds of years now it's been assumed that being religious is women's work. Men stay out of that kitchen. They still hunger for transcendence and meaning, of course, but seek these through alternative means that do not include felt banners, balloons, or hugs: career power, competitive sports, or, when particularly belittled or hopeless, through violence, drugs, and danger.

It's not religion that's feminine, but specifically western Christianity of recent centuries. Islam and Judaism, rigorous and demanding faiths, are balanced the other way, with more active men than women. Eastern Orthodoxy, likewise, is strongly attractive to men, and church attendance is more gender balanced. As Podles points out, among Christians only the Orthodox write basso profundo church music.

But while there is rigor in Orthodox spirituality, there is passion as well, and strict categories of masculine and feminine don't consistently apply. When you're used to a culture that presumes a division between head and heart, coming into one that doesn't is a little disorienting. Orthodox women as well as men fast and adhere to spiritual disciplines, led by our Champion Leader; men as well as women offer prayers of startling vulnerability, and cultivate humility, gentleness, and peace.

The image of the Church as the Bride of Christ was not invented by St. Bernard, but is just as much a part of Scripture as the image of the athlete; both, in fact, come from the pen of St. Paul. Some have said that ultimately all creation is feminine in response to the Creator's masculine. I recently heard my Bishop Basil expanding on this theme. "Imagine what heaven will be like! The Scripture calls it a wedding feast, and we know what happens on a wedding night, that two become one flesh. St. Paul says of married love that it represents Christ and his Church. Somehow, that is our destiny. We are all going to be the bride of God," said this hearty, bearded forty-nine-year-old, without hesitation or blush.

His comfort with this idea, which might in another context be called "genderbending," startled me, but I saw that it was strange only if you think that religion is really about sex. The reverse is more likely true: that sex is about religion, that God invented sex to teach us something about eternal reality. How could we understand what it's like for two to become one, union without annihilation? God came up with a human experience that would be universal, common, and enjoyable, and said, "Here, this is what it's like. This is where you're going." Likewise, eating food helps us to understand union in the Eucharist, and parenting teaches us what the Father's love is like. Sex, eating, parenting are all good things in themselves, but are also handy object lessons, available to give us ready, simple, intimate analogies for what heavenly reality will be like. In light of this, I think heaven is going to be not so bad.

Contrary to popular belief, the Church is not anti-sex. In speaking of the union of the Church with Christ, St. John Chrysostom draws a frank parallel to marital union; the sexual bonding of husband and wife, he says, is like the uniting of fragrance and ointment in the making of perfume. He rebukes those who were shocked at his words: "You call my words immodest, because I speak of the nature of marriage, which is honorable . . . By calling my words immodest you condemn God, who is the author of marriage." Chrysostom affirms St. Paul's image of the Church as the Bride of Christ: "Shall I also tell you how marriage is a mystery of the Church?" he writes. "The Church was made from the side of Christ, and He united Himself to her in a spiritual intercourse."

So which is it? Are Christians archetypally feminine, vessels of grace, nurturing the wounded of the world, rapt in intimate communion with the divine? Or are we archetypally masculine, athletes, warriors, leaving all behind for Christ's sake, taking up our crosses, valiantly shedding blood in martyrdom?

Gender has a certain fluidity when we enter the spiritual world; both males and females can wear attributes of the opposite sex, and both sexes are necessary for glorious completion. It might be observed that in these examples the individual Christian bears masculine traits, but the assembled body, the Church, takes on the feminine role of Bride. No analogy should be pressed too far. Ideally, these gender roles are intriguing and even delightful in their playful contrasts but not rigidly assigned. The reality they reflect is appealing but will someday be shown to be not ultimate. "For as many of you as were baptized into Christ have put on Christ. . . . There is neither male nor female, for you are all one in Christ Jesus" (Galatians 3:27–28).

The Liturgy continues with alternating hymns and litanies, which in the earliest centuries were sung by worshippers as they made their way to the central church. There are three antiphons, or prayers sung responsively by choir and congregation, and between the second and third we sing the "Monogenes" ("Only-begotten").

This brief hymn was incorporated into the Liturgy in 528 A.D. by the Emperor Justinian, who built the church of Hagia Sophia. It is an apostrophe to Christ:

> Only begotten Son and immortal Word of God,
> Who for our salvation willed to be incarnate
> Of the holy Theotokos and ever-virgin Mary,
> Who without change became man and was crucified,
> O Christ our God,
> Trampling down death by death,
> Who are one of the Holy Trinity,
> Glorified with the Father and the Holy Spirit:
> Save us.

The petition at the end of this hymn, "Save us," is tiny compared to the mountain of descriptives that precede it. This might be taken as an example of Oriental courtly style, heaping phrases of salutation on a sovereign before making a request. But it is more likely a mirror of the contentious time in which it was written, when the claim that Jesus was the only-begotten Son of God had been the subject of debate for several centuries already. The Docetists denied that Jesus had an actual, fleshly body; they believed all matter to be evil, so his body was an illusion, and the Crucifixion an apparition. Theodore of Mopsuestia (a wonderfully satisfying name to say) taught that the Son of God resided in Jesus' body side by side with the human Jesus, like a bicycle built for two. Mary was the mother only of the latter; she could not be called "Theotokos" or "God-bearer."

Arius, who died in 336 A.D., came nearest to persuading the

Church to follow his views. He declared that the Word of God was a creation of God the Father, not eternal and not one with the Godhead. Though it's hard to imagine today, a debate like this was not the sole province of sniping theologians but was truly a popular concern; these teachings of Arius were set to the tunes of contemporary songs, and carried around the Mediterranean basin by sailors. (Imagine the doctrine of double predestination made more appealing by setting it to the tune of "My Sharona.") St. Gregory of Nyssa complained: "The whole city is full of it, the squares, the market places, the cross-roads, the alleyways; old-clothes men, money changers, food sellers: they are all busy arguing. If you ask someone to give you change, he philosophizes about the Begotten and the Unbegotten; if you inquire about the price of a loaf, you are told by way of reply that the Father is greater and the Son inferior; if you ask, 'Is my bath ready?' the attendant answers that the Son was made out of nothing."

Arius nearly succeeded; though the Church council decided against his views, he weaseled a meeting with the Emperor Constantine and, fudging on his beliefs, won the opportunity to resume receiving Communion the next day. He went out boasting about this "and talked very wildly," St. Athanasius reports. Then, "urged by the necessities of nature, he withdrew" to the nearest toilet. There his friends found him dead, his bowels exploded. This event was taken as God's opinion on the matter.

This morning worshippers stand and sing this hymn without feeling very contentious about it; yes, Christ was incarnate in a real body; yes, his mother gave birth to a child who was God; yes, he was really immortal, really became human, really died on the Cross. If there is any line that resonates more strongly for us than the others,

it is "trampling down death by death." On Pascha and for weeks afterward we sing the exclamation, "Christ is risen from the dead,
trampling down death by death, and upon those in the tomb bestowing life!" It is from this, ultimately, that we ask him to "Save
us"; all evils are sprouts of the ultimate evil, death.

Being "saved" isn't a deathbed event. Eternal life begins now, if
it's eternal; death must be defeated in our lives every day. A story
from the Desert Fathers concerns Abba Joseph of Panephysis, who
was approached by Abba Lot with a question. "Father, as far as I
can I say my Little Office, I fast a little, I pray and meditate, I live
in peace and as much as I am able I purify my thoughts. What else
can I do?"

Abba Joseph, the story goes, then stood and spread out his
hands toward heaven, in the prayer stance called the "orans" position. Each of his fingertips was lit with flame. He said to Abba Lot,
"If you will, you can become totally fire."

This is one of my favorite stories because it illustrates so well
the concept of "theosis," the goal of Orthodox life. All the spiritual disciplines are tools to help us get self-will out of the way so
that we can gradually become totally filled with the light of God.
We are to catch fire from God's fire and shine with it, until the
"theos" himself animates us.

This doesn't mean that we are going to become independent
mini-gods. We remain beloved but humble creatures, simple as a
lump of coal. But coal has this essential attribute: it can receive fire.
One could even say that accepting fire, being consumed by it, is the
"telos" or destiny of coal—the thing it was made for. Dusty, dark,
cold, and hard, coal has no beauty of its own, but when it is con-
summated by fire it is beautiful and becomes what it was designed
to be.

It has been two hours since the first prayers were said in this building this morning and we have over an hour to go. Our task here is not limited to either head or heart, neither emotional nor intellectual, but ontological: we seek intimate transformation by the light himself. We are waiting to become totally fire.

CHAPTER 6

Carolyn Writes an Icon

At Carolyn's screen door, fluffy little black Max throws back his head in a howl of warning. His emotions on my arrival must divide near his midsection: the front part is barking with menace and the rear is wagging in eager friendship. Carolyn arrives to shoo him to the side and welcome me in. She is a soprano in the choir, and our church's chief iconographer. Carolyn is younger than I am, slim with large green eyes, and clad in casual denim for an evening with her paints.

Her icon studio is upstairs in a front bedroom, and we enter to find a large table laden with tubes of paint, compass, ruler, brushes, and a white board about the size of a coffee-table book. This board, Carolyn tells me, was prepared by sanding, laying down a coat of white gesso, then a layer of fabric, then more gesso, then sanding again until smooth as skin. Nearby are pencil sketches on tracing paper of the icon this will be. They show a man standing near a striding angel, who is pushing a scroll into his mouth. Another scroll—or, in the time-lapse logic of icons, the same one—tumbles open from his hand, bearing the words of a hymn. Above them, in a semi-circular niche, the Virgin Mary lifts her hands in prayer. On her torso there is a disk representing her womb, and in it we see her unborn Son offering a blessing.

Carolyn tells me, "This is going to be an icon of St. Romanus the Melodist, for Margo and David," our choir director and her husband. Carolyn goes on, "The story is that he wasn't very musical, and other monks made fun of him." One Christmas Eve, tone-deaf Romanus fell asleep weeping for shame, and the Theotokos appeared to him in a dream. She offered him a scroll saying, "Take this and eat it." The next morning he stood before the congregation and spontaneously sang out the hymn beginning, "The Virgin brings forth today the Omnipotent." This has been ever since our kontakion (hymn) of the feast of the Nativity. St. Romanus went on to write a thousand other hymns before his death in 530 A.D.

This is a complicated icon, featuring four faces—the more faces, the more difficulty. Carolyn shows me how she first gets a sketch the way she likes it on tracing paper, then transfers the image to the white board by penciling over it with a sheet of carbon paper underneath. Then she begins applying the darkest colors that will appear on the icon and gradually works up to the lightest. Where merely adding white to a pigment would result in milkiness, she goes back and forth between light and dark paints, keeping all thin as water to retain the luminosity of the white gesso underneath. The final strokes, dashes of brightness called "enliveners," appear almost as sparkles. Carolyn has to paint on a flat surface to keep these thin paints from running, and the process takes a long time. A "rush job" for an icon might take a month, whenever she can make time after work at her t-shirt shop nearby. Sometimes she'll take an icon in with her to the shop and work on it between silk screenings.

Other icons in various stages of completion lie on this desk, or on a large tilted drafting table behind us. There is an almost-complete icon of St. Michael the Archangel, with wings of flaming red and gold and an expression of rapt contemplation. It will go to parishioners Ina and Mark. "That one's almost finished," Carolyn says. "This is the hardest part for me, when I want to just go on fiddling with it." An icon of Carolyn's patron, St. Eudokia, has only the colors of her robes laid in; the face is an oval of white. Since she's doing this one for herself, "It tends to go to the bottom of the list," she says. An incomplete work shows the figures of Mary's parents, Joachim and Anna, standing and embracing before a bed; this is the scene of Mary's conception. This conception happened the natural way, and the figures meld gracefully, Anna appearing to reach up on tiptoe toward her husband while he bends his head down toward hers. Their arms cross in the embrace, echoing the way worshippers cross their arms when receiving Communion. But Carolyn is dissatisfied with the icon because the bed behind them came out funny. "Most of the time the bed is shown as this big blocky rectangle, and I never liked that. So I thought I'd borrow the bed from the icons of the birth of the Theotokos, which is more like an oval." The resulting tall platform bed looks like a shoebox as rendered by Dali, and isn't very inviting. "It looks like an amoeba," Carolyn concedes.

Another board has been prepared to become an icon of St. George, the warrior saint usually depicted riding on a horse and spearing a serpent. Parishioners Joe and Liz have commissioned this one. Carolyn shows me several sketches, which she based on ancient icons she found in her research. "Joe liked this one best, because of the way his robe is flying up into the air behind him," she says. "Also, he likes how the serpent is all tangled up in a coil." Carolyn opens a book of antique icons to show me the original, which is so dark and damaged it's hard to tell what's going on. The large black horse has lost all his detail and looks like the shadow of a horse. In painting this icon anew, Carolyn will carry on the ancient tradition of iconography: keeping to the forms of the past but rendering them visible again in fresh colors.

Iconography is not a kind of art, but a kind of prayer. Icon painters approach their work with prayer and fasting; in particular, prayer is directed to that saint whose image you are painting. One doesn't properly speak of "painting" an icon, but of "writing" one, since the icon is a manifestation of the Word of God. In an illiterate culture, these scenes from Scripture and the lives of saints were the only Bible many could read.

Though images of Christ, saints, and angels were painted from the early centuries of the Church, few remain from before the ninth century—not merely due to decay of materials, but because they were intentionally destroyed. The Iconoclast Controversy shook the Byzantine Empire from 726 to 843 A.D., as opponents insisted that these images were nothing more than idols. This was, of course, the view of both Judaism and Islam, Christianity's most influential spiritual neighbors. This challenge forced those who favored their use to define exactly what the theology of icons entailed, and they based their response on the fact of the Incarnation. In coming to earth in human form, God had declared his intention to be seen. In painting icons, we affirm the Incarnation and God's will to be visibly revealed to human eyes. Destroying icons indicates a desire to overspiritualize the faith and reject the body.

The eighth-century St. John of Damascus wrote in his *Defense of Holy Images* that when icons are venerated, they are not being worshipped—not the wood and paint, not even the image appearing there. St. John drew an analogy to an impression left by an imperial seal: the wax or clay doesn't change its humble nature but exhibits the presence of the one who left his mark. Worship is directed through, not to, the icon, as through a window; icons are often described as "windows into heaven."

The final victory of the iconodules is still celebrated throughout the Church on the first Sunday of Lent, in a feast we call The Triumph of Orthodoxy. It's a triumph, because the doctrine of the Incarnation is so central to Christian faith. The worshippers are instructed to recite together "in a loud voice":

As the prophets beheld, as the Apostles have taught,
as the Church has received, as the teachers have dogmatized,
as the Universe has agreed, as Grace has shown forth,
as Truth has revealed, as falsehood has been dissolved,
as Wisdom has presented, as Christ awarded,

Thus we declare, thus we assent,
thus we preach Christ our true God,
and honor his saints in words, in writings, in thoughts,
in sacrifices, in churches, in Holy Icons;
on the one hand worshipping and reverencing Christ as God
    and Lord;

and on the other honoring as true servants of the same Lord
   of all
and accordingly offering them veneration.

Louder! the instructions read.

This is the Faith of the Apostles,
this is the Faith of the Fathers,
this is the Faith of the Orthodox,
this is the Faith which has established the Universe.

It took over a hundred years to settle the controversy surrounding
the meaning of icons. When that long discussion was over, they
weren't feeling timid about their conclusions.

Another icon is resting on the drafting table, a damaged and fairly
modern one from Greece that a friend asked Carolyn to restore. It's
in a different style from the others, less stylized and Byzantine,
more painterly and European. There is a large central standing figure of St. Marcella of Chios, with a small angel reaching out of the
upper left corner to hand her a wreath of roses; at the bottom there
are two boxes showing scenes from her life—or, rather, her death.
    Poor Marcella lost her mother when she was young, and her fa-
ther, lapsing into insanity, developed a feverish lust for his daughter. (As the classic Orthodox collection of saints' lives, *The Prologue
from Ochrid,* delicately puts it, "he desired to live with his daughter
as if she were his wife.") The girl fled and her father, in a fury, pursued her to kill her. In the left-hand box we see the man building a

fire to burn his daughter to death, while she peeks out of hiding from a nearby bush. She looks tiny and her terrified expression evokes helpless pity. In the other box her father has captured her, and hauling her up by her hair raises a sword to hack off her head. Her hands are lifted in prayer. "So that's how he killed her," I say, and Carolyn says, "Yeah, and he'd already done a mastectomy." Then I notice that her red robe lies open and both breasts have been sliced off, leaving bloody disks on her chest.

I have to admit that the style of this icon appeals less to me, though I'm not sure why. Carolyn acknowledges that not everyone resonates with every icon, while reminding me that every icon is a prayer and deserves respect. She looks over the composition. "For one thing, it's not usual to dwell on the manner of death in iconography," she says. Unlike bloody western crucifixes or martyrdom scenes meant to impress the viewer with brutal reality, Orthodox iconography tries to go beyond what any onlooker would have seen. It aims to portray the spiritual reality behind the scene, the serenity or triumph that only the eyes of faith could perceive. Thus, our images of the crucified Lord are quiet and serious but not agonized. In them, the sign above his head reads, not as Pilate wrote, "The King of the Jews," but "The King of Glory."

Also, St. Marcella wears a facial expression more emotive than that typical of icons. This is hard to explain, but the more an icon reveals emotion, the less it moves me. Strange to say, an icon that looks too much like a portrait likewise seems less effective. It's earthbound in its detail. Carolyn shows me some sketches she'd made for an icon of the nineteenth-century Russian monk St. Theophan the Recluse, based on photos. "Oh, look at his eyes!" I exclaim; the eyes are full of tenderness and subtle sorrow. Though they're sketched in with only a few strokes, Carolyn has captured here a personality and an expression that draws the viewer instantly in.

"That's the problem," she says. "It looks like a portrait, not like an icon." I see what she means. Something needs to change to make this more like an icon, to draw the viewer *through* the image rather than halting in admiration at the surface.

Icons are so different in style from western religious art that I didn't like them at first. I preferred the warm, elegant, beautifully lit religious scenes from the fifteenth century on, paintings which showed humanly accessible emotion. A typical western view of the Resurrection, for example, would depict Jesus draped in white and standing in the garden near his tomb, the stone rolled away from that gaping dark entrance, and perhaps the stupefied guards in the background. There would be flowers and sunlight and the delightful, familiar freshness of spring.

The traditional Orthodox icon of this event is utterly different. We do not see the events of Sunday morning but those of Holy Saturday, the period between Jesus' Crucifixion and his first appearances to the disciples. In the icon, Jesus is standing on the broken doors of hell. The massive portals lie crossed under his feet, a reminder of the Cross which won this triumph. He stands braced and striding, like a superhero, using his mighty outstretched arms to lift a great weight. That weight is Adam and Eve themselves, our father and mother in the fallen flesh: Jesus grasps Adam's wrist with his right hand and Eve's with his left as he pulls them forcibly up, out of the carved marble boxes that are their graves. Eve is shocked and appears almost to recoil, and her long gray hair is streaming. Adam gazes at Christ with a look of stunned awe, face lined with weary age, his long tangled beard awry. Their hands lie limp in Jesus' powerful grip as he hauls them up into the light.

Behind him some are already standing. In gorgeous robes, in crowns and halos, stand King David, King Solomon, the Prophet Isaiah, the Prophet Jeremiah, clustered tightly like a standing-room-only crowd to see this marvelous sight. There is an air of joy, even conviviality, among them. St. John the Baptist is in the throng, still clothed in camel skin, now in full repossession of his head. Behind them are ranks and ranks of the righteous dead, dead no more, for Christ has set them free.

Christ has set them free from someone. Beneath his feet, beneath the broken doors, there is a black receding pit, and in the pit are floating silver shards of metal, chains, locks, ominous forms designed solely to cause pain. These are broken, shattered, and the locks are unhinged. Except for one set, still intact and in use. It binds the body of that vicious old Satan, who grimaces in his captivity, bound hand and foot and cast into his own darkness.

The Greek iconographer of the mid-twentieth century Photios Kontoglou contrasts that icon to the typical western image of the Resurrection. His comments are instructive, though not particularly tactful.

"Western painters depict 'Christ' as rising from the tomb naked and ostentatious . . . with his hair neatly combed and with a plump, pink body like a man who has just taken a bath . . . Five or six soldiers make certain pretended gestures, like actors . . . The face of 'Christ' has a milky white hue, and rosy cheeks, like a well-fed woman, and an inept beard. Behind, the sky looks like a postcard photograph, with clouds painted from an actual sunset. Thus do

Western painters strive to represent the world of immortality and truth that Christ has revealed to us—by means of well-fed bodies, angels who wear well-starched clothes, actors, and sunsets such as one sees in motion pictures."

Western religious art, Kontoglou says, has a fundamental flaw: the artist puts actors and actresses in period costumes, asks them to assume emotive expressions, and paints their portraits just as he would paint any other. This may result in a lovely evocation of earthly beauty, but it doesn't go beyond earth; it doesn't transform. It may generate tenderness and sentiment, but not awe or life-changing contrition. This is why I initially disliked icons; they seemed so remote and strange. Gradually I came to feel, however, that even the best conventional art is earthbound. Icons pull me up into another realm.

I wonder if there are rules or guidelines that iconographers can consult so they don't have to figure out how to do things like this by themselves. Carolyn shows me the *Painter's Manual* of Dionysius of Fourna, which was written about 1730 but draws on earlier manuals dating back to the ninth century. The volume opens with a prayer addressed to the Virgin Mary, in which Dionysius says that he set about to be an imitator of St. Luke the Evangelist. St. Luke is credited with being the first iconographer; it is said that he painted the Virgin from life, in an icon applied directly to her kitchen tabletop. "I wished to become his unworthy imitator, and started to practice the art of painting icons, thinking that the desire to fulfill my duty to your most high and laudable magnificence was the same as the ability to do so. However, in my arrogance I failed greatly, as nature did not assist me sufficiently, or accompany my intention and wishes." It is reassuring for budding icon-painters, I'm sure, to open this lesson-book in the company of so humble a teacher.

The first section of the book is filled with recipes and practical advice: "How to make charcoal," "On the making of brushes," "How to work on cloth with egg in such a way that it does not crack." The next covers in detail how various people and scenes should appear, ranging from simple to extremely elaborate. Here is how one would paint an icon of Judith, the heroine of the book in the Apocrypha which bears her name. "A high fortified town, with many tents below it in which soldiers are sleeping. In the midst is one tent decorated all over with gold, and in it is the headless body of Holofernes on a golden bed, wrapped in a gold quilt. The just Judith in magnificent clothes stands by him holding in one hand a sword covered in blood, and with the other she places his head in a bag which her maid holds out to her. The same town appears again further on, with men on the walls holding flags, and having the head of Holofernes impaled on a tall spear. Outside the city are the Jews, pursuing and killing their enemies."

Not all icons are so busy. Another is described this way: "Christ seated, holding a child before him with one hand; with the other hand he blesses the child and shows him to the apostles, saying, 'Whosoever shall humble himself as this little child, the same is the greatest in the kingdom of heaven.' The apostles look at each other in wonder."

Simpler still are icons merely depicting individual saints. St. Paul the Simple is "an old man with a small beard," St. Romanus the Melodist, "a young man with an incipient beard," St. Peter the Athonite, "an old man, completely naked, with a beard down to his knees. He holds a cross and says, 'A true monk is one who owns nothing in this present life, but only Christ.'" My son Stephen selected an icon like this to keep in his bedroom icon corner, a reminder of the intensity of the spiritual life.

The most familiar icons are the ones of Christ as ruler of all (Pantocrator), blessing and holding a Gospel book, or of the Virgin holding her child. When she holds him upright and gestures toward him with her hand, the image is called the Virgin Hodegetria—"one who shows the way." When she cuddles him near, pressing cheek to cheek, it is the Virgin Glykophilousa—"sweet-kissing" or "of tenderness." The famed Russian icon known as the Virgin of Vladimir, by legend painted by St. Luke, is of this latter type. The image that will be at the top of Carolyn's icon of St. Romanos, showing Mary with the unborn Christ in her womb, is the Virgin of the Sign, as in the scripture: "The Lord himself will give you a sign. Behold, a virgin shall conceive and bear a son" (Isaiah 7:14).

A couple of years ago I stood in a church just outside Chicago, looking at the icon of the Virgin on the iconostasis. It was a large image of a Virgin Hodegetria, holding her son in her left arm and gesturing toward him with her right hand. And tears were rolling out of her eyes. A clear, oily substance would bead up along her lower lids and then spill down, crossing in their path over the raised blessing hand of the child Christ.

This had started happening only a few weeks before, and I'm told continues to this day. My husband stepped behind the iconostasis to look at the wood from the back and saw only plain wood. There were numerous stories of people being healed after being anointed with the tears.

I visited again not long ago and talked with the old Romanian man who had first come to the site when the icon began to weep, in order to pray for his dying wife. After her death he simply moved into the church building and started sleeping in the basement; when the parishioners discovered this they welcomed him, gave him a bed, and fed him, and before long the bishop tonsured him a monk. On this visit I learned that there had recently been a fire in the church, which raged right up to the edge of the iconostasis and stopped. Monk Symeon showed me a photo of the charred wall and pristine edge of the oak iconostasis frame. "On the back of that last icon there was a hook where we all hung our robes," he told me. "The robes were all burnt up. The icons weren't touched."

This phenomenon of "weeping" icons is an ancient one; similar stories go back for many centuries. They seem to be proliferating lately, and every few months a new one appears in the news: another icon of the Virgin in Texas, a similar one in California, an icon of St. Nicholas in Wisconsin. In a suburban home, a tiny paper copy of the Chicago icon began weeping. The owners put it into a bowl, and by morning the icon was floating in clear oil.

What to make of all this? Some people dismiss it out of hand, believing that the supernatural is a sham and all such stories are fraudulent. But even those who do believe in God can be made uneasy by something like a weeping icon. God can do anything, but why would he do this? It strikes them as kind of tacky—showy and sentimental. God, if he's any kind of respectable deity at all, must be a paragon of exquisite taste. He wouldn't do something this offensive.

That's where I think they've missed the point. Giving offense turns out to be a pretty consistent part of the Christian story. It begins with God in a diaper, and proceeds to God on a cross, beaten and bleeding and shamed. It's a brutal story, one that isn't easy to take.

Christian Scriptures speak of the Cross as a stumbling block and a scandal. It breaks our complacency, our notions of dignity, and turns us again to be as children. God keeps doing things beyond our comprehension—sometimes things which seem designed to show us how little we comprehend.

Part of Carolyn's icon studio is workplace and part is set aside for something else. On a bureau top near the door there are candles and incense and a prayer rope, and above it on the wall are half a dozen icons of various sizes and scenes. Icons lead one to prayer, to standing before something beyond comprehension and resting in it in trust. Their meaning cannot be exhausted by analysis but only by entering in on their own terms and allowing the icon to speak to you, perhaps to change you.

This is the secret, at last, of the icon's eyes. They should not be painted dramatically cast up to heaven, or so full of human emotion that there is no room for the viewer to get past. The best icons look at you; you find yourself not contemplating them but being contemplated by them, by steady eyes that plumb the soul. After all, you can look through a window from both sides. You have to be ready for that to happen, or else looking at icons will just make you uneasy. I have been standing here visiting on this warm evening, chatting with Carolyn, making evaluations based on my personal taste, looking from icon to icon. Now I realize with almost a chill: they have been looking at me.

CHAPTER 7

Holy Texts and Holy Doubt

While we're singing the third antiphon, they're lining up behind the iconostasis. My son David peeks out of the "Deacon's Door" on the left; he's holding up the processional cross, which is painted with an icon of the Crucifixion. Behind him stand Zach and Elliot, holding candles. The candlebearers try to match up for height, and these two young teens come near enough, though they don't match for coloring or temperament. Zach is a blond with dark eyebrows and a natural inclination to take charge, even of teens much older. Elliot, with brown hair in a bowl cut that fringes over his glasses, observes the world from a reserved, amused perspective that might have been appropriate to the poet for whom he's named.

The acolytes come forward with my husband behind them; he's holding the silver-covered book of the Gospels up before his face. They process to the center of the iconostasis and stand before the Holy Doors, the candlebearers on either side and my husband in the middle, with David, the crucifer, behind him. Father Gregory prays that as they enter the sanctuary angels will enter with them and assist in worship. He sings, "Blessed is the entrance of thy saints, always, now and ever, and unto ages of ages, Amen," making the sign of the cross with the book.

Obviously this is an entrance ceremony, which seems out of place since we've already been here awhile. The preceding antiphons, however, were not originally part of the service. Worshippers would have completed those on the way to church, and at this point be gathered waiting for the entrance procession of the clergy. Father Gregory cries out, "Wisdom! Attend!"—an admonition that recurs in the Liturgy, and is sometimes translated "Pay attention!" Another admonition, "Let us stand aright!" is sometimes translated "Stand up straight!" People's minds have been wandering in church for many centuries. Father Gregory proceeds through the Holy Doors, placing the book on the altar.

After a few more hymns we come to the distinctive Trisagion, or "Thrice-Holy" hymn, one of the most significant prayers of Orthodoxy. It became part of our tradition in a dramatic way. When St. Proclus was bishop of Constantinople, in the fifth century, the city was rocked by one of its recurrent earthquakes. As grand buildings crumbled around them, the screaming citizens fled out to the fields around the city. St. Proclus and his clergy followed them in procession, attempting to console them and to lead them in singing intercessions with the familiar refrain of "Lord, have mercy." As the sound of crashing masonry resounded from the city and the ground shuddered, as the people wailed and cried for mercy, a young child was suddenly caught up into the air, ascending so high that he was finally lost to sight. Then, just as suddenly, he plunged back to earth. He reported that he had heard something up there: angels were singing the words "Holy God, Holy Mighty, Holy Immortal."

"Have mercy on us!" the people responded, and began repeating this new hymn. According to the story, the earthquake ceased immediately. The Trisagion hymn immediately swept throughout the Orthodox world, and it is still sung in nearly every service. It recalls the vision that Isaiah had of God "sitting upon a throne, high and lifted up, and his train filled the temple." Six-winged angels, seraphim, flew above him and called to each other, "Holy, holy, holy is the Lord of hosts; heaven and earth are full of his glory!" At this "the foundations of the thresholds shook at the voice of him who called, and the house was filled with smoke" (Isaiah 6:1–4).

"Holy God, Holy Mighty, Holy Immortal, have mercy on us," we sing, crossing ourselves and bowing to touch the floor. Then we sing it in Arabic: "Qudduson Allah, Qudduson ul-qawi, Qudduson ul-ladhi layamut, urhamna." Well, we try to sing it. We're an Antiochian Orthodox parish, one whose ecclesiastical authority is rooted in the Middle East, but there isn't a single Middle-Easterner in this parish. Mostly we're converts, though there are a few Greek and Russian families who have joined us. Our service is otherwise in English, but we're trying to learn this one verse in Arabic as a gesture of unity with our sister churches.

The varieties of Orthodox labeling confuse many newcomers. Though there's no exact analogy, it might be likened to the Roman Catholic Church's plantings in this country. In a big city a generation ago you could skim the yellow pages and predict with some confidence, "That's an Irish Catholic church, that's an Italian

Catholic church, that's a French Catholic church"—all the while knowing, of course, that these ethnic markers are laid over a common core, and the churches all Roman Catholic underneath.

It's a similar story in Orthodoxy. The yellow pages spell out: that's a Greek Orthodox church, that's a Russian Orthodox church, that's an Antiochian Orthodox church. As with the Roman churches above, these are all really one Church. But although (like Rome) Orthodoxy is one Church, it doesn't (like Rome) have one Bureaucracy. Constantinople isn't the central powerplant of the Orthodox Church, in the way Rome is for Catholics; likewise, the Patriarch of Constantinople is not empowered to command universally or set doctrine, like the Pope is.

This is one practical reason why Orthodox-Catholic reunion is problematic. The Patriarch of Constantinople does not have the authority to sign a document binding on all Orthodox everywhere. No one does. Orthodoxy is a communal faith, rather than one controlled and dispensed by the hierarchy; the ancient beliefs are held in common by all, and it is the responsibility of the leaders to keep them intact. Bishops and clergy do not enjoy power over the faith any more than a night watchman enjoys power over a bank's deposits.

It might seem that such a communally maintained faith would be slippery and ever-evolving, while a hierarchically developed and imposed faith would be comparatively unchanging. Surprisingly, the reverse seems to be true. A hierarchy empowered to interpret the faith is a location for change to take place, whether from internal conviction or as a result of outside pressures finding a handy focus. In Orthodoxy, there is no site for agents of change to target, since the historic faith is distributed into every heart. A startling discovery for those who begin reading Orthodox spiritual literature is how consistent it is in style and flavor, despite vast shifts of time and geography. St. Theophan the Recluse, the Russian saint of the late nineteenth century, reads like St. John Chrysostom, our liturgical saint of fourth-century Constantinople. As the joke goes, "How many Orthodox does it take to change a light bulb?" "'Change'? What is this—'change'?"

In fact, the split between the eastern and western churches occurred because (in the eastern view) the West wanted to change something. In an attempt to defend the divinity of Christ, the Pope wanted to add something to the Nicene Creed: instead of stating that we believe in the Holy Spirit "Who proceeds from the Father," we would say, "Who proceeds from the Father *and the Son*." In Latin, this addition was only one word, *filioque*.

While the controversy initially seems picayune, an important principle was at stake. The eastern bishops protested that the Creed had already been in use for six hundred years at that point, and that no such belated change was reasonable, or even possible, without the united consent of the whole Church. They protested the addition on theological grounds as well, as diluting the distinctive role of the Holy Spirit. The periodic outbursts of Pentecostal enthusiasm in the West, Orthodox would say, are an attempt to revitalize a "Holy Ghost" that this addendum rendered too subsidiary, vague, and ghostly. It also changes the nature of the Trinity: as St. Gregory Palamas said, "Those who say that the Holy Spirit proceeds from the Son divide the divine monarchy into a diarchy."

The Pope believed he possessed authority to impose this change to the Creed without other churches' consent; the other bishops disagreed. One day in the year 1054 A.D. the legate of the Pope delivered a Bull of Excommunication to the Patriarch of Constantinople, placing it on the altar during the Liturgy. Shortly thereafter the Patriarch responded in kind. Though the excommunications have been lifted, the split has not been healed, and is unlikely to be. Orthodoxy rejects key Roman Catholic doctrines, like papal infallibility; it considers the "filioque" non-negotiable; and, even if these could be resolved, it lacks a centralized power structure that could implement a reunion. A patriarch who signed such a concordat would be swiftly repudiated by those furious laity, clergy, and monastics who saw it as a betrayal.

It should be obvious by now that Orthodoxy has a long memory. One that isn't diminishing is that of April 13, 1204, when Roman Catholic Crusaders sacked Constantinople. Historian Sir Steven Runciman has called this "the greatest crime in history." Drunken soldiers burned and looted, stealing ecclesiastical treasures and carting them back to the West. (One friend of mine noted, "You can be sure that the 'Shroud of Turin' was the 'Shroud of Someplace Else' before the Crusades.") The Pope condemned these brigands, then installed a Latin patriarch and a Latin emperor in Constantinople. Byzantines did not retake control of the city for fifty-seven years. No wonder Orthodox, with their elephants' memories, are suspicious of Roman Catholics' open arms. If Orthodox soldiers had conquered Rome, stolen its treasures, and installed a Byzantine patriarch in the Vatican, Roman Catholics would no doubt feel the same.

Rather than having a single, ultimate head of the Church in Constantinople, Orthodoxy grants to the faithful of different geographic regions the right to be self-governing, or "autocephalous." Gaining autocephaly has not always been a smooth process historically—there can be disagreements about when a new regional church is ready to go solo—but time generally heals these disputes. Thus, just as there is a Greek Orthodox church in Greece and a Russian Orthodox church in Russia, there should be a single American Orthodox church in America. That there is not is the result of some historical anomalies.

Russian missionaries were the first to reach the shores of this continent, coming to Alaska over the Bering Strait in 1794. All through the nineteenth century the project of establishing the Orthodox faith in American soil was struggling forward, but with the turn of the twentieth, two events knocked the plans askew. The first was the Russian revolution, which derailed our spiritual mother's ability to continue the project; the second was the arrival of wave after wave of Orthodox immigrants from Eastern Europe and the Middle East, all of whom wanted to start worshipping immediately in their native languages.

Separate churches for each ethnic background were swiftly established, with separate bishops and bureaucracies, each tied to a hierarchy in a separate Old Country. There are now some dozen different Orthodox "jurisdictions" operating in America. We belong to the Antiochian Archdiocese, which has its headquarters in Damascus, on the "street called Straight" (Acts 9:11), where St. Paul was taken after he was struck blind. For us, turning to Antioch was a practical choice: this jurisdiction was the one most ready to assist pastors who wanted to convert from other denominations. When you're making a life-changing decision like that, you appreciate all the help you can get.

The high proportion of converts at Holy Cross is an example of a national phenomenon, one which was inaugurated by a group of former Campus Crusade for Christ clergy who became Orthodox with their congregations about a decade ago. These enthusiastic campus evangelists had gradually become dissatisfied with the results of their efforts; conversions didn't always last, and making converts that way was, as one of their members said, like having babies and abandoning them on doorsteps. They decided that what was lacking was the ongoing support of a teaching and discipling community—in short, a church. They began years of study into the tenets and practices of the earliest Christians, committing themselves to abide by whatever they found. Father Peter Gillquist, in his book about their journey, *Becoming Orthodox,* called this "the phantom search for the perfect church." After much study, the group had come to conclusions that overturned their assumptions about worship, the interpretation of Scripture, the Virgin Mary, clerical orders, and other issues. They could see a continuity in the Body of Christ from the first century till the Great Schism of 1054, when Rome had a permanent break with the Orthodox bishops of the East.

Reviewing history to that point, the group came to the conclusion that the Orthodox had taken the correct path at the split, but none of them had any acquaintance with Orthodoxy today. "Most of us did not know it existed," Father Peter writes. "For that reason, I am chagrined to report that we decided to start it over again!" The fledgling group began ordaining each other and setting up churches with postcard-sized icons. Gradually they came into contact with Orthodox clergy and scholars and began to see their way into the Church. Two thousand were chrismated at a series of services over several months in early 1987.

Converts are attracted to Orthodoxy for a variety of reasons. Evangelicals like these may stumble across it while searching for the "original" first-century Church; they may visit, get their first taste of liturgical worship, and be smitten. Converts from liturgical mainline churches may be looking instead for a stable church, one less influenced by the zeitgeist. Still others come from Buddhism or other eastern religious philosophies, and find here a comparable tradition of spiritual disciplines leading to divine union. Some don't have any prior religious background but are seeking in response to a growing spiritual hunger. Orthodox would say that in all cases, the real reason the person is drawn toward this faith is the jewel at its center, the Lord Jesus Christ.

As converts continue to stream into Orthodoxy, it is being transformed from a community of immigrants to an indigenous church. A couple of statistical snapshots show the moment the balance shifts: about half the students in the nation's two largest seminaries are converts, as are half the bishops in the jurisdiction known as the Orthodox Church in America. In our jurisdiction, the Antiochian Archdiocese, the number of American churches has tripled in recent decades, and convert clergy outnumber "cradle" clergy by two to one. Since 1993, when Holy Cross was founded, a new mission has begun on average every month and a half.

Overall, there are 3.5 million Orthodox in the United States (comparable to some Protestant denominations, for example the 2.5 million-member Episcopal church), and 250 million in all, making it the second largest Christian church in the world, after Roman Catholicism. In the United States, Greek, Russian, and Antiochian Orthodox jurisdictions report a combined total of about three thousand conversions per year. (These are conversions of already baptized Christians; conversions that include an adult baptism cannot be separated statistically from infant baptisms.) Orthodoxy is not likely to be the next Hula Hoop craze, but as it roots into the American landscape it will continue to grow.

As we sing the last notes of "Holy God," Carolyn comes forward to read the epistle. She stands near the icon of the Theotokos and, after Father Gregory calls out "Let us attend! Wisdom!" begins to chant the day's assigned reading.

We take turns reading the epistle each Sunday, with some variation in delivery: some merely read it and some chant. The liturgical preference is for chanting because, contrary to what you might expect, we believe it's better for the Bible to be read *without* expression. A talented reader's emphasis on one phrase or another would amount to a distracting personal interpretation. A clear chant lets the passage speak for itself.

Personal interpretation is the bugaboo of personal faith, of course. Every faith that has personal impact must leave some individual marks: elements that, due to the follower's particular history or experience, are particularly cherished or taken as guide. Too much of this, however, and the devotee ends up swept down the oubliette of his own head. There must be a counterbalance of objective authority, some core of Truth where all believers meet and agree, from which they all partake. The conciliar nature of Orthodoxy both creates and provides a common well that all draw from, while anticipating that this shared treasure will be personally applied in individual lives.

When Carolyn finishes reading the epistle, she kisses the cross my husband holds out for her, then heads back toward the choir. She threads her way carefully past Nicholas, who is now lying on the rug, pounding his fist idly into Andy's leg. Andy steps to the side, closer to Annette's front-row seat, but Nicholas scoots over as well, to keep in pounding range.

As we begin to sing the Alleluia, those who have been sitting stand up. Tiny Lillian is carrying a cane today but seems to stand with no difficulty. In her matching lilac cardigan and skirt, and tuft of white hair topped by a crocheted cap, she looks like an Easter decoration. We are in the season following Easter, which we call Pascha, and the church is full of flowers. Last Sunday, on Pascha, we heard the nearly unbelievable story of the Resurrection. Today we will hear a gospel story about not believing it.

My husband circles the altar, swinging the censer, as Stephen chants psalm verses, and we respond with "Alleluia, alleluia, alleluia." The smoke of rising incense wreaths the air, and symbolizes the ascent of our joined prayers. The scent is both pungent and laden with roses. Father Gregory hands the censer to David, then takes up the silver-covered gospel book and comes out through the Holy Doors.

"Peace be to all," he says, and blesses us with the sign of the cross. We respond, "And to thy spirit," and he goes on, "Let us hear the holy gospel."

Today is the first Sunday after Pascha, and the story appointed is that of Doubting Thomas, which occurs only in the gospel of John. It tells how, when Jesus appeared to his disciples on the night of Pascha, Thomas wasn't there. When they later told him the astonishing story, he wouldn't believe them. "Unless I see in his hands the print of the nails, and place my finger in the mark of the nails, and place my hand in his side, I will not believe" (John 20:25).

Goodness knows what Thomas thought; probably that his buddies had lost their minds. It was a reasonable inference, since they'd had an unbearably intense week. Thursday night at dinner everyone was vowing that they'd stick with Jesus no matter what; a few hours later they were snoring while he wept and prayed in the garden of Gethsemane. When the soldiers arrived to arrest him they fell into confusion, some attacking the soldiers, some fleeing, and all ultimately hiding for fear of their lives. When questioned, Peter famously claimed he'd never heard of Jesus. (A striking thing about this incident is that it never would have become known if the repentant Peter had not told it on himself. He even revealed that, after speaking the words of frightened denial, he "went out and wept bitterly.") On Friday, Jesus was beaten and tortured, then led out carrying his cross, as his mother and the women disciples followed; among the twelve apostles, only John showed up at the foot of the cross.

It was incomprehensible that Jesus could be crucified or that he could die; they thought he had supernatural powers, that he was "the Christ, the Son of the living God" (Matthew 16:16). This bloody, humiliating death, the one devised by Rome to make an example of criminals, was impossible for the Lord of Glory whom they had seen transfigured in radiance on the top of Mount Tabor. But there he was, dying; and then he was dead and gray in his mother's arms; and then they were walking away from the tomb into the onrushing twilight of a world that had suddenly been stripped of meaning. They felt stunned and afraid, probably. And they probably felt like fools.

Imagine Thomas, then. Nutty stories had been cropping up all week, which he found most reasonable to attribute to overstretched nerves and hysteria. The women who went on Sunday to complete burial preparations came rushing back to the apostles, reporting that the tomb was empty and an angel had told them Jesus was risen. "These words seemed to them an idle tale, and they did not believe them" (Luke 24:11). John and Peter went to verify the story and found the tomb was empty, then left perplexed; had someone stolen the body? Why? Mary Magdalene remained behind weeping, and when a man appeared and asked her why, she thought he was the gardener and begged him to show her where the body had been taken. "Mary," the man said, and she replied, "Rabboni!"; when he spoke her name, she recognized him as her Lord. After this, appearances kept popping up: to Peter alone, to the gathered apostles minus Thomas, to two men walking to Emmaus. Yet there was no proof, just incredible stories.

Thomas was frustrated and determined not to be suckered like the rest. In fact, with a name like Thomas ("Twin"), he may have known better than most the possibilities of mistaken identity. Twins can look so much alike that even good friends can't tell them apart. You have to check for distinguishing marks—like scars. He'd only believe it was really Jesus if he could touch the wounds of the nails.

Eight days had passed since the tomb was found empty, and this time Thomas was with the rest when Jesus appeared. Jesus immediately invited Thomas to touch his wounds, admonishing, "Do not be faithless, but believing" (John 20:27).

"My Lord and my God!" Thomas exclaimed, the clearest statement in the Gospels that Jesus is God, a statement that Jesus immediately affirmed. "Have you believed because you have seen me? Blessed are those who have not seen and yet believe" (John 20:29).

When Father Gregory finishes reading the Gospel, he returns the book to the altar, and the congregation settles itself to hear the sermon. Those near chairs take them, and the rest sit on the oriental rugs that cover the middle of the floor, wherever the rugs aren't already covered by babies and toddlers. Father Gregory takes up a cross, which he will hold in his right hand throughout the sermon, and comes forward to stand before the Holy Doors. He doesn't preach from a pulpit or use notes but simply tells what this most recent week's study of the passage—on top of previous decades of study—has disclosed. His sermons aren't long. While some churches treat the sermon as the service's high point, our Sunday-morning focus isn't on the pastor's thoughts but on worshipping God. More extended time to explore Scripture is provided after worship during our coffee hour, and at the several regular Bible study groups.

"Every day this week we have celebrated the Resurrection," he begins. "Every day the hymns of the Matins service have been the same Paschal Matins we used last Sunday morning, and every evening Vespers have been the same Agape Vespers we used to conclude our Paschal celebration. Every day we've stated in the strongest possible terms that Christ is risen from the dead.

"In light of this, we come to church today and hear this Gospel—a story about not believing the very things we've been saying all week. What are we to make of Thomas, anyway? The very thing for which Thomas is criticized by Christ, for doubting, is the reason he's held up to us as an example. To tell the truth, we all live with some amount of doubt."

Father Gregory goes on: "I'd say that there are two main categories of doubt. First, there's a kind that has belief as its goal. It's a good and healthy kind of doubt, because it's asking questions in order to get answers. It comes from an open heart and a mind that is receptive and seeking.

"But a second kind of doubt comes from a closed mind. Some people don't want to believe, because they fear the implications; they fear that it might change their lives. Christ might say to them, 'I have work for you to do' or 'I'm going to send you out.' Perhaps he will challenge how they're living their daily lives and call them to change their behavior. For some people, it's a lot easier to choose skepticism and doubt than to accept these implications.

"If you don't want to live according to the Gospel, you will find a way to build an anti-Gospel case. If we don't want to believe something, because it would challenge what we want to do or avoid doing, we can find a way out.

"The Church calls Thomas a saint because Christ met him at his point of doubt, and he responded. Doubts will come, but they can be transformed as long as they are the kind that sincerely seeks answers, rather than the kind that is trying to hide from uncomfortable truth.

"In Jesus' words we hear some criticism of Thomas, but because of his great love for him he wanted Thomas in the Kingdom. Then he said, 'Blessed are those who have not seen, and yet believe.' That's us. Our belief is not based on nothing, it's not blind trust, but it's based on an event two thousand years ago. Ever since, men's and women's lives have been changed by the Risen Christ and the power that flows from the empty tomb. We can see it throughout history, as brothers and sisters reach out toward one another, as they put their lives on the line.

"Would the martyrs have been willing to go to death if Jesus were not risen? Would they have found that kind of courage and meaning if the apostles had only experienced a nice warm feeling a few days after the Crucifixion? Would they have gone to the ends of the earth to bring the good news if that's all the news there was? There had to be something that overturned everything they knew, everything that had always before been dominated by the fear of death. Death was overthrown. Suddenly things could be done that seemed impossible before, both in their individual lives and in the whole world.

"Go then, in faith and in sincere, seeking doubt, in the company of the apostles, martyrs, and saints, in the company of your brothers and sisters here today. Go, because a mission has been given to us and a message has been given to us: that Christ will be all in all, that Christ will be king."

CHAPTER 8

Sad Santa

AT A THRIFT SHOP IN GLEN BURNIE

Ken Myers, host of the Mars Hill Audio Journal, once said, "To get an overview of our current culture, stand in a 7-Eleven and turn around 360 degrees." The "cultural artifacts" visible in such a sweep, he said, would tell us a lot about what we value.

It is a few days before Christmas, and my daughter Megan and I are standing in a thrift shop. I can turn 360 degrees here and see a whole different world from the one at the 7-Eleven, but one no less revealing of our culture. The difference is, everything here is something that somebody didn't want anymore. It's an index of what we *no longer* value. For this reason I find a thrift shop a sweet place to be, tender and forlorn. Still, it carries a dash of hope. Maybe someone else didn't want it, but I might; I believe in the Resurrection.

We pause just inside the door of the shop, a cavernous place that I suspect was originally a grocery store. The inventory of a thrift shop is unlimited; anything anyone might buy and then discard ends up here. Near us there are used magazines (does anyone actually buy these?), old vinyl records, children's clothes, and shelves and shelves of books. A sign nearby reads, "All bikes on sidewalk, $1.00," but there is only one bike left, a pink girl's banana seat. The windows behind us are framed with lights and plastic greenery, and clothes strung up on hangers alternating red and green. Several bent, denuded Christmas trees stand near the door, leaning like convivial drunks.

Nearby, a shelf of glassware demonstrates the jumble of decades come to rest here, united only by the melancholy comradeship of being out of date. There are green glass tumblers with big white polka dots that strike me with nostalgia. I can remember grown-ups drinking their grown-up drinks from these at my parents' parties, back when grown-up-land was a vastly different place from where I lived. It was as clearly defined as a spot on a map but, like a mirage, somehow evaporated as I grew closer. There are some tumblers with faded, dishwasher-etched rainbows—these look more like my college years. There is a beer mug stamped in gold, "Hunter High School, 1984," and a plastic tumbler showing an ocean liner and the banner "Titanic." We've leapt seventy-two years in a twelve-inch span of metal shelving.

There are plenty of Christmas shoppers to sample all this bounty. The aisles are jammed, and Megan and I decide to stroll around a bit before trying to penetrate the clothing arena. I'm still a little surprised that I buy clothes at thrift shops. I first ventured into a shop a decade ago, when a friend told me it was a great place to buy hardback books. After a few visits I noticed a set of art deco chairs with backs steepled like the Empire State Building; now painted cobalt blue, these look great in my kitchen. My prowling the store grew bolder, and one day I found a bit of embroidery sticking out of a bin of curtains. It turned out to be a giant piece of visionary folk art, an apocalyptic scene of Jesus appearing in the sky over a multicolored mansion, with the legend "Gained the Whole World, Lost Souls." It is signed, "ARTIST, Jeannie Gates." Do the all-caps indicate that some of her acquaintances doubted she was really an ARTIST? Whoever disposed of this by dumping it at the Salvation Army probably did.

But I took it home to cherish, and from then on found that shopping, or rather hunting, at thrift shops was a great way to un-wind. It's a poor-man's antique shop; you never know what you'll find in this jumble of discards, but whatever it is will be cheap enough to take home. Within a few years you can have a home full of very unusual stuff, which can be a bad thing or a good thing, and if your neighbors are tactful you might never have to know for sure. Since most of these shops operate as charities, a dollar is better spent there than at the mall, and is spent in an alternate economy based on recycling, far outside the grinding consumer machine. For the same reason, a thrift shop is also a much more *intriguing* place to shop: guileless, unpackaged, unplugged, full of surprises.

Still, making the leap from the book and furniture sections to the clothing section was not easy. It seemed to me too strange, somehow, to wear used clothes. Of course, I reasoned, I wear used clothes every day; once these were washed they'd be no different from clothes I had bought firsthand. Somewhat reluctantly I strolled over to the clothing racks, where all coy resistance was swiftly overcome. Here were labels that I'd never seen before outside ads in glossy magazines, and never imagined with a $4 price tag. I couldn't afford such clothes new, but the nice people who can eventually donate them here, and I'm not too proud to give them a second wearing.

I can now honestly say that I've walked a hundred miles in another woman's shoes. I've ironed her blouse, hemmed her skirt, and carried her handbag. It's not just one person, of course, but dozens of women, all ages and races and creeds. There is only one thing all these women have in common: they were all more or less my size.

Megan and I stroll toward the shelves of Christmas decor. She is humming "O Come All Ye Faithful," and it makes me want to rest my head on her shoulder and just listen. We pass boxes of old glass ornaments, artificial wreaths, and a string of plastic popcorn that looks prechewed. There are stockings inscribed "Katie" and "Roger," and I wonder why Katie and Roger didn't want these anymore. There are various incompetent Santas: one with pursed lips and narrow eyes glowers from a homemade ceramic cookie jar, and a walking wind-up Santa looks ghoulish with his scalp removed and brainworks revealed. There is a bag of Santa candles, but these have been warmed, stretched, and flattened to El Greco dimensions. They would look eerie alight and melting from the head down. This whole train of thought is taking a disturbing turn. There is a mug shaped like Santa's head, which causes Megan to say, "Can you imagine this? If you had hot chocolate in it, the inside of his head would be brown and steaming."

All this Santa business has nothing to do with St. Nicholas, the fourth-century bishop of Myra whose feast was a few weeks ago. Though St. Nicholas was a kindly man who loved children and rescued prisoners unjustly condemned to death, he was not always mild-tempered. At the church council which considered the theo-logical innovation of Arianism, St. Nicholas got so frustrated with Arius that he struck him. For this outburst, the leaders of the coun-cil expelled him from the assembly but later reinstated him follow-ing a series of dreams indicating that the Theotokos's sympathies lay with St. Nicholas.

Then Megan notices a snow globe that shows a cluster of Vic-torian carolers standing in a mound of fine white gravel. There is no water in the globe. She turns the globe upside down and rights it, and the gravel falls on the singers' heads, pinging like meteorites. "I really like this," she laughs. "I like this a lot!"

Meg has always been a laughing girl, casual, easygoing. I'm grateful that my only daughter has been free of vanity, sparing me the no-your-nose-*isn't*-too-big agonies some moms of teens go through. Today Meg's hair is an emblem of her insouciance: the lower six inches are black, the upper four inches are copper, and at the roots a hint of natural brown is just beginning to appear. The girl with the Neapolitan hair. It has been like this since Thanksgiv-ing, when a hair-dyeing plan went tragically awry, and somehow she has never gotten around to correcting it.

"Do you think your hair just might be hip?" I ask.

She makes a face. "Not really," she says. "A young teenager might think so. A fourteen-year-old would look at this and wish her mom would let her wear her hair this way."

Not long ago I experienced sartori—not satori, spiritual en-lightenment, but rather a sartorial revelation about how I should wear my hair. I have been associated with this hair for several decades now, and it has been a bumpy relationship. When I flipped through my old high-school yearbook not long ago I remembered when all my troubles began. Every girl in those pages had hair as shiny and straight as a pane of glass, Breck-girl glossy and parted on the side. I did too. I got mine that way by ironing it.

Allowed to run wild, my hair is exuberantly curly and propels from my head as if trying to escape. Years of fighting this natural curl were eventually resolved with a short cut that let it twine in un-restrained bliss. I was proud to go natural, an independent woman unswayed by fashion.

Then, strangely enough, fashion came after me. As it grayed, my cap of curly hair began to look disturbingly like the coiffeur popu-lar with women a few decades older: permed, sprayed, blue-rinsed hair in short curls. Frequently, older women were telling me how much they admired my hairdo and envied its natural curl. Hmmm. I don't mind looking older, but I didn't want to look *that* kind of older. I wanted to still look hip. That old serpent, vanity, hadn't been clubbed to death as thoroughly as I hoped.

The irony, of course, is that older women now wear their hair short and curly because, earlier this century, it *was* hip—it was the daring new style. Away with long tresses, braids, and Gibson-girl buns. Cutting your hair short was a mark of rebellion, of libera-tion. It was so daring it could be traumatic, as in Fitzgerald's short story "Bernice Bobs Her Hair."

A couple of generations later, long hair was back in fashion: the style for flower children of both sexes was trailing, tangled hair ac-centuated by misplaced daisy stems. There was even a shampoo marketed under the unlikely name of "I'll Never Cut My Hair!" (This was the era of conversational shampoo. Another was "Gee, Your Hair Smells Terrific.")

But I found even hippie long hair to be a bother, so I was re-lieved to discover a short, workable cut. Now I'm going to have to grow my hair out again, to get away from yesteryear's curly-bob fashion. Once it's long, I don't know what I'll do with it. Maybe I'll put it in a braid, or a Gibson-girl bun. I think it could look very hip.

All these linking issues—the concern to look hip, fashionable, 7-Eleven rather than thrift shop—could be subsumed under the heading "vanity." It's a topic about which the faith has much to say. Orthodox monks wear their hair and beards long because trimming is considered unnecessary and vain. Any attempts to improve one's natural appearance occur on a continuum that could well be endless. St. John Chrysostom noted that it is a good thing that the attainment of physical beauty is impossible, or else pursuing it would consume all our time and energy: "Because we cannot really create bodily beauty, we cunningly devise imitations by means of paints and dyes and dressing of hair, and arrangement of garments, and penciling of eyebrows, and many other contrivances. What time would we have set aside for soul and serious matters if it were in our power to transfigure the body into a really symmetrical shape?"

Of course now it is possible, with surgery, diet, and exercise to transfigure nearly any body into any desired shape. But it's a chase that's hopeless in the long run and pitiable in the short. I see so many women my age fretting about their figures and wish I could advise them: Oh, go ahead and buy larger clothes. Imagine a composite of all the women all over the world who share your age and childbearing history. Apparently that's what God has in mind.

According to the third-century African bishop St. Cyprian of Carthage, redesigning the body meant rejecting the beauty God had created in his own image. What is natural is from God, and what artificially distorts this nature comes from the one who would distort our souls: "Does anyone dare to alter and to change what God has made? They are laying hands on God when they try to re-form that which He formed, and to transfigure it, not knowing that everything which comes into being is God's work, and everything that is changed is the devil's."

St. Cyprian even imagines God failing to recognize his children if they arrive at his doorstep forcibly changed. "This is not my work, nor is this our image. You have polluted your skin with a false medicament, you have changed your hair with an adulterous color, your face is violently taken possession of by a lie, your figure is corrupted, your countenance is another's. You cannot see God, since your eyes are not those which God made."

Is there a difference between being beautiful and being attractive? Though these words are forceful, St. Cyprian was beloved by his age for his compassion and gentleness of spirit. When he was beheaded, in 258 A.D., he left twenty-five gold pieces as a gift to his executioner. There's no reason to think St. Cyprian looked like a movie star, but it's evident that those who knew him were attracted to him in love and admiration. It's a strange thing, but a really intentionally beautiful person, one whose beauty is pronounced and aggressive, can fail to be attractive. People like that can be cold and supercilious. You don't enjoy being around them, and it's a relief to get away.

A truly attractive person, on the other hand, attracts in the same way a magnet does; you want to be near them. This may have nothing to do with physical beauty. Older people, plumper people, homelier people, these can be much more attractive than the merely beautiful. The one guarantee about that kind of beauty, anyway, is that it's bound to be fleeting, and desperate attempts to hold onto it are craven and sad. Attractiveness, on the other hand, can be forever. No makeup or cosmetic surgery will make your eyes as beautiful as setting aside more time for prayer.

And I will show you a still more excellent way.

"A scholar attracts by his knowledge, a wealthy man by riches, a handsome man by beauty, an artist by his skill. Each of these attracts a limited number of individuals," wrote Bishop Nicolai Velimirovic. "Only love attracts all human beings. The attraction of love is unlimited. And educated or uneducated, rich or poor, skilled or unskilled, beautiful or ugly, healthy or sick, and young or old—all want to be loved. Christ spread his love on everyone, and lovingly drew all to himself. With his great love he encompassed even the dead, long decomposed and forgotten by men." And you can't be any more obsolete than dead.

Megan is still delighting in the Christmas thrift shop goodies. She picks up a toy brass bugle and attempts to play it without actually making contact with the mouthpiece. "I know it's totally unsanitary," she says, "but I'm just so curious!"

Mixed with the Christmas gear are other items: a framed portrait of a middle-aged bride, circa 1950; a saccharine version of the Last Supper on a pine plank (on the back it reads: "B 5, Last Supper, Dark Picture"); a homemade ceramic wedding plate inscribed "John and Ellen, July 23, 1960."

Homemade ceramics are big at thrift shops, as are homemade paintings, plaques, and needlework. One could carpet a townhouse with the granny-made afghans and baby blankets. Every time I come to a thrift shop I notice this phenomenon, but I never quite understand it: why are humans compelled to decorate things? Who glued lace around this measuring cup? Who painted hearts around this wooden picture frame? Why was Jeannie Gates so determined to pronounce herself an ARTIST? It seems like the crocus pushing through the spring snow, this insistent, almost urgent, need to beautify. And of course, much of it I don't find very beautiful. I don't know whether this makes me discerning or a snob.

I find something spectacular: a diorama staged in a small box of orange knotty pine. A border of seashells and abalone frame a central figure of the crucified Jesus. His body is entirely of gold; its voluptuous pose, with tilted hip and discreet sash, resembles Goldfinger's painted girl more than Golgotha's blood and sweat.

Towering far above the figure is a pink plastic flamingo. I don't think this is meant to be a joke, not any more than the abalone shells; the artist has merely put every beautiful thing he had into his work. The flamingo looks sincere, in fact looks like it bears an aching weight of emotion. It's size alone would make this inevitable. If someone were to stage this scene as a full-scale tableau vivant, that pink neck could reach up forty feet. His beak hovers near the golden torso, as if about to nudge it in concern.

I pick up a paint-by-number rendition of hummingbirds. "I understand these are becoming valuable," I tell Meg. We look at the blocks of hard color, which seem a little somber for the subject, as if base-tinted olive green. It is not lovely.

"Why would this be fashionable?" Meg asks, and I think she's chosen a better word than I have, because this painting could never be valuable.

"I don't think the interest could be sincere," I say. "It must be one of those irony things." I feel a little sorry for the person who tried to make something lovely with this picture, and who will now be collected by people making fun of him. Sometimes I feel like saying, Can we stop being ironic now? Because it's making my face hurt.

There is a large print of the familiar sentimental scene of an old man praying over a loaf of bread at a rough table, and a small cubist print labeled "Lyonel Feininger, 'Zirchow VII,' 1918." This is composed of blocks of dark blue and green, and because of that has an odd resonance with the scene of the hummingbirds. There's a sofa-sized textured landscape printed on cardboard, and a cartoonish original acrylic of a girl sniffing a flower, and a somewhat damaged string-art representation of a baseball player. Of all these, the only one I would want to go on looking at is the old man praying, though I know that's the wrong answer.

A thrift shop is full of what nobody wants anymore, and a 360-degree turn here reminds you of the transience of fashion. As Thomas Franks explains in his fascinating book *The Conquest of Cool,* the booming postwar economy resulted quickly in a sense of malaise; people feared they were lapsing into a cookie-cutter existence, buying mass-produced products and living in little boxes all the same. This fear was not confined to the anxious elite class but was widespread and treated even in popular magazines like *Life* and *Reader's Digest.* In a 1957 essay, Norman Mailer proposed the solution: "The White Negro." Instead of being a conformist "Square," one could be a "Hipster" by adopting the style whites attributed to blacks: jazzy, free, hedonistic. It's a solution that worked, and which endures to this day.

As Franks points out, one aspect of this hedonism was greeted enthusiastically by the supposedly square, un-hip business world:

profligate spending. Part of the hipster package was the incessant hunger for new stimulation, easily translated into hunger for new stuff. Only squares were thrifty and budget-conscious; only squares resisted buying a new car every three years. Thus, one could paradoxically demonstrate superiority to the mindless, mass-produced consumer society by buying stuff. It is an ingenious "perpetual motion machine," Franks says.

Those business figures who saw in this new economic philosophy promise of larger profits embraced it for personal reasons as well. The Establishment had been just as frightened by the soul-sickness of conformity as the general public. The original "Man in the Grey Flannel Suit" was, after all, an advertising executive. Business feared that rigidly "efficient" management practices were stifling creativity and the American genius for entrepreneurship. The truth was that there was no clear distinction between Hipsters and Squares. People were Squares by day, when making a living required discipline and foresight, but by night everyone wanted to be a high-consuming Hipster. Thus, the business establishment was as hungry as anyone else for revolution.

Though we imagine the late sixties counterculture as the force that turned things upside down, it was actually a late arrival to the scene. The Volkswagen anti-ads began in 1959; the Pepsi Generation made its debut in 1961. When the hippies showed up a few years later they were embraced like a party's latecoming guests of honor. Not only did they embody the Hipster free spirit that Big Business had been hungering for, but they also represented a wonderful new free-spending market, philosophically dedicated to pursuit of the new.

The thing that perplexes me is how old this posture of hip new-ness is. Why does it never age? How can it still seem daring, when the counterbalancing Establishment the dares were aimed at has been defunct for decades? Hipster style now controls nearly every variety of power in our culture, from advertising to academia to journalism. Opposition to hipness scarcely exists in real life, though it remains an indispensable foil; Franks describes the "central casting prudes and squares (police, Southerners, old folks, etc.)" hauled out to recite their lines as needed. Otherwise, they are invisible. Franks quotes historian Rochelle Gurstein: "By now it should be obvious that there is something fraudulent, if not perverse, in the endless rehearsal of arguments that were developed to destroy nineteenth-century Victorians in a world where Victorians have been long extinct."

Believe it or not, I used to be hip. Not long ago I got down the old box of buttons from my husband's and my college days. I had recently seen a young woman wearing an "Uppity Women Unite" button and wondered if I still had mine, though mine would have been manufactured about the time she was in diapers. I rustled through the box of hundreds of buttons. Couldn't find one of those, but there were "Women's Equality" and "Repeal All Abortion Laws," "Nixon You Liar, Sign the Treaty," and "Clean for Gene," McGovern and both Kennedys, and a couple of arm bands. "Smile America, Say Chuck E. Cheese" appeared to come from a different era of my life. There were various "March on Washington"s, even a treasured one from the 1963 event that unveiled Martin Luther King's famous speech. Though he was too young to attend, my husband knew what side he was on.

Some were predictable: "Black Power," "Viva Che," "Boycott Grapes," a golden profile of Mao framed in a sunburst of red.

Some are less predictable: "Draft Lodge," "Salinger for Senator," "George Wallace 1968," "Alert Republicans say LBJ." Some were antique: "Willkie and McNary," "I Like Ike," a tiny sunflower reading "Landon and Knox." "I am an enemy of the state" looked semi-appropriate all over again. "Burn Baby Burn," "Viet Nam Wants Peace," "Hubert Humphrey: boy, did you turn out to be a schmuck." I returned "If it moves, fondle it" to the bottom of the pile.

David and Stephen got into the act, bringing the old hippie box down from the attic and lifting the goodies out by layers. My husband's Earth Shoes, the ones he wore to our wedding—these fit David fine.

"Can I have these?" he asked.

"Why in the world would you want them?" I asked.

David looked down admiringly. "I think they're cool," he said. I think they're ugly—broad brown balloon toes and dipped-down heels, supposedly permitting a more natural walk. Earth Shoes, the footwear of the revolution, were modeled on a semi-scientific discovery so stubbornly natural that it has its chin stuck out, daring a rejoinder: when you walk in the sand, your heel makes a deeper mark than your toes. There's probably a gap of logic between how you walk on a soft surface, and how you should always walk, but such things were of little importance in those days. We lived by romantic allusion.

Stephen pulled out a white t-shirt with an image in faded red on the front. Is it possible that this ever fit me? It looks like it was made for a child. But I wore it constantly, defiantly. There's a picture of a head wrapped in mummy bandages with a large pin over the mouth, and angry eyes glaring out. Above it the words run in jazzy script: *Une jeunesse que l'avenir inquiète trop souvent.* "A young woman too often troubled by the future," but not in English of course. Boy, was I a jackass.

A long strand of red love beads. A leather cord with a metal peace symbol. A floor-length dress of Indian print that likewise looked unreasonably tiny. Their dad's student movement t-shirt, with a fist and the word "STRIKE" stenciled across it in large red letters. I don't think this would fit him now, either. Wire-rim glasses with once-again-fashionable oval frames, and never-fashionable little brass safety-pins holding the temples together. A poster detailing student grievances and demanding an end to "John Foard's witch hunt."

Stephen pondered the poster. "Who was John Foard? What was he doing you didn't like?"

"He was a local official—I don't remember exactly what. Chief of police, maybe?" I fumbled. I remembered being outraged, but not why. "I think we felt he was persecuting people, but I don't remember for what."

My memory must be slipping. Just when I should be moving by right of age into the broad pleasure of nostalgic reminiscence, I'm losing my grasp of the details. Previous generations probably had details much more noble to remember (or forget, if I'm any pattern). Does any of this past count? Can I still be a Hipster today?

There's probably some sort of subliminal Hip Grading System going on, whereby we evaluate everyone according to their acceptability or credibility. My husband and I should get some points, for example, because we were grinding our own French Roast coffee and brewing it in a drip Chemex pot decades before Starbucks began to proliferate. Long before the microbrew craze, twenty years ago, I brewed my own beer. Let's say that's good for 8 points.

It was *terrible.* Minus 5 points.

I'm still vegetarian about half the year, because fasting is part of my Church's tradition. No, let's try that again: because fasting is one of my faith disciplines. Even better: because it's part of my spiritual journey. Depending on how effectively this is phrased, it rates from minus 2 to plus 8 points.

I was briefly a volunteer on the staff of "off our backs"; I had a movie review in the same issue celebrating the Roe v. Wade decision. 20 points.

I have a copy of *Our Bodies, Ourselves* so old it's printed on newsprint stapled together. 5 points.

I used to surf. This is a questionable entry, particularly because it was quite a while ago. Pre-"Point Break." Back in the Gidget era, in fact. Let's just pretend I didn't bring this up.

My husband went to Woodstock—the original one. 10 points.

He says that all he remembers is "lying on the ground a lot." 10 more points.

We had a dark-green Volkswagen beetle, which we drove cross-country one summer. Only 1 point, because *everybody* had a Volkswagen beetle, and half of them drove it cross-country.

When we got married, I hyphenated my name. 2 points.

When we got married, my husband hyphenated *his* name. 8 points.

My husband still has longish hair, a beard, sandals, and incense, and starts each morning with ancient spiritual chants. 7 points.

This is because he's an Eastern Orthodox priest. 0 points, because nobody knows what this means. It's not a hip-perception minus, like it would be if he were a Baptist preacher or a Catholic priest (though if my husband were a Catholic priest I'd have other problems to reckon with). Eastern Orthodoxy, whether Russian,

Greek, or whatever, is a mystery to most people. Since it's "Eastern," it just may qualify as cool.

But the bottom line is—this makes me a pastor's wife. BRAWP BRAWP EMERGENCY EMERGENCY MELTDOWN

All points automatically erased. No pastor's wife gets to be cool. It's the law.

All in all, it's a profusion of strange things. "Imagine what a nightmare it would be to be with Robin Williams in here," Megan says, glancing around. "What does God think of all this?"

In this jumble of objects desired and discarded we are moving toward Christmas, that highest of consumer holidays. Today the malls are full of people buying stuff that they hope will impress or thrill, and some of it will be here in this thrift shop in six months. Fashion is a kaleidoscope of change, but the compulsion underneath it is anxiety about what others think.

We will celebrate an alternate Christmas at Holy Cross, one where things don't change, but which includes a story about fear of what people will think. These fears did not receive a reassurance that those onlookers would understand. At the service of Royal Hours on the morning of Christmas Eve we will sing Joseph's thoughts. He had found out that his fiancée was pregnant, and he knew he wasn't the dad. How could he bear the shame?

Joseph said to the virgin:
What has happened to you, O Mary?
I am troubled; what can I say to you?
Doubt clouds my mind; depart from me!

What has happened to you, O Mary?
Instead of honor, you bring me shame.
Instead of joy, you fill me with grief.
Men who praised me will blame me.
I cannot bear condemnation from every side.
I received you, a pure virgin in the sight of the Lord.
What is this that I now see?

Later in the service the answer comes:

When Joseph went up to Bethlehem,
His heart was filled with sadness.
But you cried out to him, O Virgin:
Why are you so troubled?
Why are you in misery seeing me with child?
Do you not understand at all?
I bear a fearful mystery!
Cast your fears away, and learn a strange wonder:
God in his mercy descends from heaven to earth.
Within my womb he has taken flesh!
When he is pleased to be born, you will see him.
You will rejoice, and worship him, your creator.
The angels ceaselessly praise him in song,
Glorifying him with the Father and the Holy Spirit.

This explanation is not likely to mollify Joseph's critics, but for those who receive it, it is the best news in history.

Today he who holds the whole creation in his hand is born of
a virgin.

He whose essence none can touch is bound in swaddling-
  clothes as a mortal man.
God, who in the beginning fashioned the heavens, lies in a
  manger.
He who rained manna on his people in the wilderness is fed
  on milk from his mother's breast.
The bridegroom of the church summons the wise men;
The son of the virgin accepts their gifts.
We worship thy birth, O Christ.
We worship thy birth, O Christ.
We worship thy birth, O Christ.
Show us also thy holy Theophany!

On a shelf a homemade papier-mâché Santa is perched up on
one toe as if twirling. He is ineptly painted, and his mouth is not
jolly but stretched in a long oval like a howl. His eyes plead under a
tented brow, as if he longs to stop his endless spinning but doesn't
know how. Some other hand flung him circling and then turned
away. His shoulders are dusty. No one wants him anymore.

CHAPTER 9

Not Seeker-Friendly

At the end of the homily we get to our feet again, and Father Gregory peers around the church. "Is Emelia here? Where's Emelia?" he asks.

Behind me a woman holds up a hand, then begins to walk toward the icon of Christ on the iconostasis. Emelia is a catechumen, one who is studying to join the Church. She wears her brown hair in a round Clara Bow cut, and is usually dressed in black—sweater, skirt, stockings—right down to bright orange leather thong sandals.

She stands next to my husband and together they face the icon. It is a rather severe one, showing a frowning Jesus holding a large book with a gold cover in his left arm, while his right hand is held up in blessing. We bought this icon, and the matching one of the Theotokos, when we first started the church; I remember the day the UPS man carted the huge, flat boxes up to our front door, and we took them into the dining room to unpack and lay on the table. From the first time I saw this Jesus' stern expression I felt awkward, as if facing someone who understood something about me that I didn't, someone who understood why I have a murky bag of disconnected guilt rambling about under the surface all the time. I know that I ping back and forth between this guilt, and oh-yeah? behaviors like overeating or showing off or gossiping or thinking luxuriously about how spiritual I am. I don't know this landscape fully, I've only jolted over it in a sprung-seated carriage in the dark, and it's a little scary to me. When I look into the eyes of this icon, I think he knows, and it makes him very serious.

I had looked at this icon, somewhat shrinkingly, for several years before I realized that his right hand is held up *in blessing.* That is his will for me; he wants to bless me. He loves me. It's serious, my condition; it's going to require major surgery. But it is his love for me that drives all of this forward, his uncompromising will to bless me.

A prayer of St. John of Damascus, the eighth-century champion of icons, acknowledges this vacillating self. "I know indeed, O Lord, that I am not worthy of thy love . . . But, O Lord, whether I wish it or not, do thou save me. For if thou savest the just, it is nothing great; and if thou hast mercy upon the pure, it is nothing marvelous; for they are worthy of thy mercy. But upon me, a sinner, show the wonder of thy mercy; in this manifest thy love toward all." That "whether I wish it or not" interests me. I know there are times that I cannot yet pray, "Yes, Lord, I am willing." I have to start further back: "Please help me be willing to be willing."

Father Gregory and Emelia stand facing this icon, and he chants, "Pray to the Lord, you catechumen." He speaks several prayers of intercession over her, while we all respond, "Lord, have mercy." At last he sings, "Bow your head unto the Lord, you cate- chumen," and Emelia bows her head. He prays, "O Lord, our God, who dwellest on high and regardest the humble of heart, who hast sent forth as the salvation of the race of men Thine only-begotten Son and God, our Lord Jesus Christ: Look down upon Thy servant the catechumen who has bowed her neck before Thee; make her worthy in due time of the laver of regeneration, the remission of sins, and the robe of incorruption. Unite her to Thy Holy, Catholic, and Apostolic Church, and number her with Thy chosen flock. That with us she may glorify Thine all-honorable and majes- tic name: of the Father, and of the Son, and of the Holy Spirit, now and ever and unto ages of ages."

The entry of new members into Orthodoxy is cautious, and al- ways has been. Traditionally, inquirers were introduced to a small portion of the Church's mysteries at a time. The fourth-century nun Egeria wrote back to her Spanish convent what she encoun- tered during her travels in the Holy Land, including a bishop's words to catechumens. At the end of their years of instruction, which culminated with a Lent of three hours' instruction a day, the bishop said, "During the past seven weeks you have been given in- struction in the whole of scripture. You have been taught about the Christian faith and the resurrection of the body, and you have also learned as much as catechumens are allowed to know of the mean- ing of the Creed. But the teaching on baptism itself is much deeper, and as long as you remain catechumens you have no right to hear it. However, do not think it will never be explained to you. You will be told everything after you have been baptized. But catechumens cannot be told about God's secret mysteries."

This seems strange in our era, for a couple of reasons. In the first place, American churches tend to display everything they have vigorously, rushing toward any vaguely curious inquirer with the entire boatload of services the church can provide. There's nothing that a seeker isn't yet entitled to know.

In the second place, it's generally assumed that there are no mysteries, anyway. The faith is made as open and cheerful and accessible as possible. People who want mystery don't go to church; they watch *The X-Files* or phone the Psychic Network. They know in their bones that there is mystery out there somewhere, and if the Church won't provide it they look elsewhere. A line often attributed to G. K. Chesterton goes, "When a man ceases to believe in God, he doesn't believe in nothing, he'll believe in anything."

In the early Church the burden was on seekers, to listen and learn. They knew that the gathered community, the Church, had knowledge they didn't: it knew how to draw closer to God. They committed themselves to be instructed and expected that with time they would be initiated further. Catechumens understood that they were receiving a great gift—one worth waiting for—and that only those who had made a commitment to the community could enter its mysteries.

It's my unprovable hunch that this is the better course. People newly coming to church *should* have an unfamiliar experience. It should be apparent to them that they are encountering something very different from the mundane. It should be discontinuous with their everyday experience, because God is discontinuous. God is holy, other, incomprehensible, strange, and if we go expecting an

affable market-tested nice guy, we won't be getting the whole picture. We'll be getting the short God in a straw hat, not the big one
beyond all thought.

Coming into the community of believers at worship *should* be
disconcerting. It should leave the visitor with several impressions:
whatever this is, these people take it very seriously; I don't understand it; if I join I might have to change.

The well-intentioned idea of presenting the appealing, useful
side of faith fails, I think, because it doesn't question deeply enough
the basic consumer ethos. The transaction that takes place between
a shopper-seeker and the goods acquired (groceries, furniture, the
key to the meaning of life) is one that leaves the seeker in control,
in a position of judging, evaluating, and rejecting the parts he
doesn't like. But entering faith is more like making a promise or beginning a marriage. It involves being grafted into a community and
requires a willingness to grow and change. If it didn't, if it merely
confirmed us in our comfortable places, how could it free us to be
more than we are?

Emelia kisses the cross my husband holds out toward her, and
returns to her place with a shy smile. On her chrismation day he
will anoint her forehead, eyes, nose, lips, ears, chest, hands, feet, and
between her shoulders with blessed oil, announcing each time,
"The seal of the gift of the Holy Spirit." All of us in the congregation will shout back each time, "Seal!" Over the course of many
months Emelia is being initiated into ancient mysteries, and I appreciate her patience.

Not long ago I spoke at the Sunday morning service of a large church
outside Pittsburgh. It was an evangelical mainline service: heartfelt,

friendly, but not overly casual. We marched into the century-old stone church to the tune of a century-old hymn, preceded by a pretty young crucifer and a vested choir. I took my seat all by my-self, up front, in a chair of dark carved wood next to the pulpit.

After an antiphonal reading of a psalm, the overhead projector was snapped on and lyrics were displayed for a couple of "praise choruses." These are exceedingly simple hymns, with minimal words conveying the barest ideas. The point is not the words, it's the mu-sic, which leans toward hand-clapping, high-spirited celebration. In fact, the first song began with just that idea: "Celebrate Jesus! Cel-ebrate!" we sang repeatedly. In the third row I could see the nice gray-haired lady I was talking with before the service, joining in en-thusiastically. I couldn't see much of her, but I could see the top of her hair and the tips of her fingers swaying back and forth through the air like a metronome.

Much of the congregation, like her, was smiling, clapping, and singing. It reminded me of a comment a friend made at a similar gathering: "For a minute there, we almost didn't act like white people." White people never do this sort of thing with the focus and discipline—a funny word, but I think it's the right one—of a black congregation. We look sheepish but happy, like a dog in a floppy hat.

I didn't clap. I stood on the rise behind the pulpit, on display, and clasped my hands and sang politely like Alice reciting "You are Old, Father William." I was wondering what my church was doing that morning. At home that day it was the yearly observance of the Holy Fathers of the First Ecumenical Council. This was the coun-cil which settled the matter of Arius, the council at which St. Nicholas lost his temper. It took place in Nicea in 325 A.D., and re-sulted in a statement of belief now known as the Nicene Creed. On this Sunday my church family at home was celebrating the triumph of the council of Nicea, and gloating over the downfall of Arius as if the news had just hit the headlines.

Arius, as we've noted before, taught that Jesus was created by God, and is not eternally one with the Godhead. Thus, he said, Jesus was not really "the Son of God," and his mother could not be called God-Bearer (Theotokos). These teachings enjoyed widespread popularity, and even after their rejection by the Council Arius did his best to be reinstated. On the eve of his triumphant return to the Church, he died in an outhouse in a manner, his opponent St. Athanasius says, similar to the death of Judas. Scripture describes Judas' end this way: "This man bought a field with the reward of his wickedness; and falling headlong he burst open in the middle and all his bowels gushed out" (Acts I:18).

At home my son Stephen was chanting:

"Of the Father before the morning star thou wast begotten from the belly without mother before all ages, even though Arius did believe thee to be created, not God, classing thee in ignorance and impudence with creatures . . . When thou wast asked, O Saviour, Who rent thy garment? Thou didst reply that it was Arius, who divided the headship of the Trinity, united with honor, into parts . . . He it was who taught the transgressing Nestorius not to say that the Virgin is Theotokos . . .

"Pretending blindness that he might not see the light, Arius toppled into the pit of sin, and his bowels were torn by a divine hook that he might give up his whole substance. In a repulsive manner his soul came out, and he became another Judas by his own purpose and character, but the Nicene Council proclaimed openly that thou are Son of God, equal in the throne to the Father, and to the Spirit also."

There is a lot of complicated theology packed into these lines, though phrased poetically. It's not the sort of thing western Christians sing. While Stephen was chanting that, our group in Pittsburgh had moved on to "Mighty is our God! Mighty is our King!"

Orthodoxy is strongly concerned with enunciating and preserving the elements of right belief, down to reviewing the foolishness of Arius once a year. It's called "Orthodoxy" for a reason. But this is not done merely as a study drill of dry theology. For Orthodox, theological truths convey the beauty of God.

While a theologian in the West is one who has acquired intellectual understanding of religious theory, in the East a theologian is one who has approached union with God and been flooded with light. A theologian is not one who grasps the truth but who has been grasped by the truth and transformed. This doesn't make the specifics of faith any less precise, but it makes doing theology an entirely different sort of enterprise: not cogitating but entering into illuminating union with God. While in the West an artificial division between head and heart resulted in a separation of theology from personal transformation, in Orthodoxy they remain united. The purpose of doing theology is to come into union with God.

One of the several saints named Symeon is called "the New Theologian" because he is relatively recent; he died in 1022. He is a theologian because he saw the uncreated light of God, an event more significant, and ultimately more beneficial to his readers, than the mere ability to rearrange theological principles. St. Symeon wrote in his Hymns of Divine Love:

> I partake of light; I participate also in glory,
> And my face shines, as does also His for whom I long;
> And all my members become bearers of light.
> I then become the most beautiful of beautiful things.

This is what it means to be a theologian. As Evagrius of Pontus, another of Arius's fourth-century adversaries, said, "A theologian is one whose prayer is true." Theology is, at root, prayer—specifically, adoration. This is why our worship is the center of all we do. There is not an Orthodox tradition of removed, deductive theological reasoning; one searches in vain for a *Summa Theologica,* or even a complete systematic theology. Yet there are whole libraries of books on prayer.

Further, our prayer is not merely "Celebrate Jesus! Celebrate!" It's about the glory of Christ, threatened by that weasel Arius, rescued by God-illuminated theologians after pitched battle, vindicated in the graphic judgment of God. Recounting this story is worship, because theology is prayer, adoration is being filled with the light of capital-T Truth.

A popular informal hymn in evangelical circles is based on Psalm 42: "As the deer panteth for the water, so my soul longeth after thee; you alone are my heart's desire and I long to worship thee." The melody is lovely and haunting, somewhat like "Greensleeves." It speaks of yearning, even if the lyrics can't decide if they're addressing "you" or "thee."

Once my husband commented on this song, "Back when we were Protestants, we were always singing songs like this, about how we longed to worship. The truth was that we didn't know how to worship; we just glimpsed it from time to time. As best as we could tell, it was about emotion."

I remembered that, that intense hunger for God and the frustrating sense that it would never be satisfied. Since we became Orthodox, I realized, that hunger has diminished. Not because our worship is particularly emotional; sometimes emotion appears, but when it doesn't, the dignity and authority of the ancient prayers are sufficient to bear you beyond yourself. In fact, when worship is emotion-powered, it's like a fun-park ride, and you're being carried around as a treat. It's only when those emotions fade and you get down to the business of doing the work, following the way, saying the prayers even when you don't feel like it, that your stony heart begins to budge. It's only the offerings done from deliberate will that bend the will and shape it to fit the will of God. Giddy emotions feel good, and all of us might need a bowl of ice cream from time to time, but they don't produce spiritual growth.

Orthodox worship doesn't engender that kind of emotion, I find. I'm less likely to face the twins I knew so well before: flushed sentimental weepiness, or vexed, restless yearning when that treat was absent, the yearning I believed this song was about. Instead, the spiritual emotions I find prompted by walking the path Orthodoxy teaches are complex and hard to describe: the overwhelming, deliciously terrifying riptide of God's love; the rapturous joy of weeping over my sins; the sweet, stinging desire to bring others to see the beautiful face of Jesus.

I don't have to "long to worship thee" anymore; I do worship him. The longing is satisfied, not by emotional thrills but by something that just feels right, like a key in a lock, like "food is meant for the stomach and the stomach for food" (I Corinthians 6:13). I was made for this.

Orthodoxy means "right teaching." It also means "right praise."

CHAPTER 10

Twelve-Inch Mohawk

AT A CAMPSITE IN BUSHNELL

As I come up the dusty, gravel-pocked road from the lake I pass one of the music tents, and its white canvas sides are trembling with the tumult within. Slipping through a side flap I'm engulfed in the loudest music I've heard during the entire festival. My rib cage feels like an accordion, struggling to keep pace with the thundering percussion. My feet vibrate so much on the dirt floor that they feel like they're falling asleep. I ask by gestures (speaking is impossible) which band this is, and a guy with a silver hoop in his lower lip shows me in the program: "Left Out."

I've never liked heavy metal, but this is the first time I've seen it live, and I must admit it's a terrific show. The guys on stage are having a great time. The lead singer, bare-chested in droopy black jeans, is a skinny pale guy in Buddy Holly glasses. He spins and grins and pogos, and sweat flies into the crowd. I can't understand a word, even though he's screaming. The rest of the band—it looks like a lot of them, six or seven—are banging away at maximum force. At other concerts over the last few days, I've seen moshing, stage diving, and crowd surfing, but the late afternoon heat and sheer volume has left this crowd looking bludgeoned. Near the stage a few prone bodies are circulating like offerings to the volcano god.

The song crashes into a wall and dies, and the hopping lead singer grabs up the microphone. "This next song is for the pastors out there," he says. "If you're feeling on the downside, come on back up. God is here, his Holy Spirit is here. That's what's important."

A roar of agreement goes up from the crowd, and the band slams into the next song. Again, no individual lyrics are discernible, but I hope any pastors in the audience feel cheered all the same.

I am a lone Orthodox, as far as I know, in a crowd of twenty-five thousand screaming, stomping, tattooed, metal-studded Christians. It's the fifteenth annual Cornerstone Festival, which once again has overwhelmed the little town of Bushnell, Illinois. You can tell Bushnell looks forward to this each year: every movable-letter sign in town reads "Welcome, Cornerstone!" and all along the last stretch of dusty road to the farm the ranch-house lawns are festooned with yard-sale abundance. Some town businesses, I'm told, make more this week than in the whole rest of the year.

Cornerstone is more than a rock fest; it's also a record label, a magazine, and an inner-city community. The last came first: in the early seventies, a group of Jesus freaks, calling themselves "Jesus People USA" (or "JPUSA") began living together on the rough side of Chicago. Nearly thirty years later they're still there, running a shelter for homeless and abused women, a home for the elderly

("Friendly Towers"), a transition-to-work housing program, a day-care center, boys' and girls' clubs, and a pregnancy resource center. Funding for all this is of the elbow-grease variety. "We feel that Jesus has called us to provide the majority of our community funding as Paul did—through work" reads the festival program. "We support ourselves with a roofing supply company and a custom cabinet business. This is definitely an integral part of missionary outreach. Is it for you?"

I thought it was for me. When my husband was first considering leaving his career as a mainline Protestant pastor, a half-dozen years ago, he was drawn toward the high liturgical churches and the ancient forms of Christian faith. I didn't get it. I thought we ought to move to Chicago and join Jesus People USA. I thought this, with fervor and warm romance, because I knew there was very little chance we'd actually do it. In truth, I was forty with three teenagers and a station wagon, and had never been the most flexible and cheerful person in the tent at summer camp. It just seemed to me that living in the inner city, serving the poor, sharing goods in common, and living in community was the most excellent life another Christian besides me could have.

I never even got around to visiting JPUSA in their Chicago digs, but having been invited to give a few speeches during the annual festival I now have the opportunity to observe the operation in motion—perpetual motion. It resembles what I've been reading in *Cornerstone* magazine for the last twenty years. At some point I must have sent in a subscription card, because issues have continued to arrive at the rate of two or three a year, persistent as a puppy. There is never an expiration notice or renewal request; the magazine is free, and once they have found you, they never let you go.

Unlike many free mags, it is excellent both in content and appearance. A full-color production with the heft of the *New Yorker*, it has the jazziest graphics of any Christian magazine (like *Wired*, maybe, but different). Contents include heavily footnoted reporting, including some exposés of Christian charlatans; poetry, essays, fiction, reviews, and diary-like descriptions of life among the poor of Chicago. There's even a two-page comic strip. I try to remember to send a check from time to time, but not as often as I should, so someone in Chicago is underwriting my subscription by refurbishing kitchen cabinets.

Interviews with Christian rock bands are interesting, but even more so are the interviews with secular bands. The reporter always brings the topic around to the Christian faith, with some surprising results. Cris Kirkwood of the Meat Puppets, for example, admired the sacrifice of the Cross, but concluded, "There's a certain point where I say 'Forget you.' If I have to be nailed to a cross, I'd just as soon not be."

When the interviewer began talking about Christian faith, Mick Jagger mumbled continuously, "You can't be telling me this, you can't be telling me this." Then, looking up from his drink, he blurted "in a stage whisper": "Hey . . . aren't you afraid the Lord will put a curse on you?"

Ozzy Osbourne enthused about Jesus' message, which he said was "Just believe in the spirit that is within you."

"But that's not what he said," the *C'stone* interviewer put in. "If you look in the Bible, you'll see he said we had to follow him."

"Well, so did Adolf Hitler!" Osbourne rejoined, with impressive facility.

Before coming to the festival I'd never paid much attention to Christian rock groups, about forty of which will be performing here over the course of several days. I arrived presuming this music would be like Mr. Rogers sitting by a campfire with a guitar and a fish lapel pin, singing songs from the category derisively termed "Jesus is my girlfriend." (Take any pop love song, change the pronouns so it's about Jesus.) The attendees, I thought, would be the variety of overly clean-looking young men and women who pump my hand and call me "ma'am."

I'm glad these clean-cut kids exist, and admire purity as a mysterious virtue that previous centuries knew to be a generator of spiritual power. This is a wisdom we have simply lost, and unable now to comprehend it fall back to easy ridicule. I admire these kids and can acknowledge the communal support they derive from their culture, but I thought that spending more than fifteen minutes exposed to that kind of music would have me looking for an exhaust pipe and a rubber hose.

I don't know where that music is, but it isn't here. Nor is its culture. I strolled on the campsite my first day here and saw a guy with tangled green hair and a t-shirt reading "Turn back to God, America." Another, with spiked green and yellow hair, wore a hand-lettered t-shirt with a more direct request: "Looking for a Christian chick." Nearby a group in bristling dog collars and chrome chains were admiring a friend with a brand-new giant safety pin through his cheek. "That *had* to hurt," one was saying.

Skaters were swooping up and down the skateboard pipe, concentrating hard and pretending they didn't hear the whoops and leisurely applause of the standing crowd. Graffiti was sprayed on the pipe's interior: "Can't you see this filth? Ignorance—Racism—Prison—Politics." A giant skull was painted at the base of a cross, and a balance scale showed "Rich" favored over "Poor."

A woman in full Goth gear—floor-length black, chains, lace, ripped sleeves, drooling eyeliner, and purple hair—was pushing twins in a stroller. Her gloomy expression may have been part of the costume, or due to navigating tiny wheels over the rutted ground while wearing lots of black and metal in ninety-degree heat.

It's strange to recall that there was a time when you could predict the opinions of total strangers merely from their appearance. Donning certain clothes or hairstyles expressed voluntary membership in an ideological group: hippies looked one way and straights looked another. Not cutting one's hair meant "letting my freak flag fly." There are reasons I'm glad that during my college years none of my friends owned a camera. But I'm not sure the costume of these young Christians is actually intended to mean anything.

Fashion has become a tossed salad during these intervening years. People dress in ways they enjoy, ways that seem cool or fun, without much strategizing. These festival-goers seem to say that clothes and accessories are for fun and aren't inherently good or evil or even significant; it's what's in the heart that counts. At least I *think* that's what they're saying, but it's hard to say anything clearly with a safety pin through your cheek.

I find all this bemusing, but a couple of Orthodox monks who read over this chapter told me they found it dismaying. My friend Father Andrew, previously a Protestant, is concerned that evangelicals adopt elements of contemporary culture wholesale and without discernment, in the name of being "Incarnational." Anything can be sanctified by sticking a fish symbol on it, he says. "They seem to interpret the Incarnation as meaning that God 'came down' to us and, apparently, just stayed here," Father Andrew says. "As I understand the Patristic vision, God comes down to effect an immediate rescue program. He doesn't just set his seal of approval on whatever he finds."

I'm an immature Orthodox and know that Father Andrew's dis-

cernment is keener than mine. At this conference I am mostly occupied with observing; though much of what I see strikes me as
strange, I respect both the size and the sincerity of the effort, and
I'm trying to comprehend it.

Today I stroll inside the exhibition tent and find that the album
covers and t-shirts for bands show surprisingly sophisticated
graphic design. The standard Christian-message t-shirts, however,
are hokey and disappointingly obsessed with replicating advertising
logos and slogans. How about a giant hand nailed to a board, with
the caption "This Blood's For You"? A perky chihuahua saying
"Yo Quiero Jesus"? The UPS logo rendered "JPS—Jesus, Personal
Savior"? No matter what the text says, the subtext says "Let's get
trivial."

I see faux logos for Calvin Klein, Tommy Hilfiger, Adidas, Con-
verse, M&M's, Ford ("Have you considered the Lord lately?"),
C.O.P.S., Hot Wheels, Gap, and Reese's. The only one I like is hot-
pink Mr. Bubble rendered with a sneaky expression and horns:
"Don't Mess Around with Mr. Trouble." Some may find these
clever, but to me they so far betray the dignity of the faith as to
communicate nothing true. Looking over this display I feel like I
know what Jesus meant about not throwing your pearls before
swine.

The band t-shirts are more interesting. Knowing nothing of the
music represented, I buy for David a "Pedro the Lion" shirt, which
shows three square black-and-white photos of a boy wearing a costume lion head. I'm not sure why, but it reminds me of him, that
large, kind, shaggy head and the comparative vulnerability of the
undershirted boy who carries it on his shoulders. (When Megan
sees this later, she says, "Isn't that shirt just perfect for David!") I
get Megan one that announces in purple letters "I am not your

demographic." Though I know she'll have to explain it everywhere she goes, I don't think she'll mind doing that. For Stephen, it's a baby-blue t-shirt for the faux-fifties band Thee Spivies, which shows on the back their jovial cartoon heads and "Ready or not, here we come!" This is to become one of his favorite shirts.

These t-shirts, as I've said, show more sophisticated graphics than the Christian-message ones, but on the other hand they don't convey any Christian message at all. This seems to be a prevalent dilemma. Christianity has become so overexposed that any hint of it seems hackneyed. In the secular mainstream world, the most successful efforts by Christian novelists, filmmakers, musicians, and other artists are those which reveal their faith the least. When genuine faith pops up in a work, it clangs like a cracked bell—obviously, a frustrating situation for the artists.

Some protest that it's not fair, that if a Buddhist rock group is accepted as mainstream, a group that sings about Jesus (along with other topics) should be treated the same. But things don't work that way. The Christian group must either proclaim itself so, and wind up in the ghetto singing only to fellow Christians; or subdue the faith message to such a subtle level that it becomes inaudible; or attempt to pass as normal and risk being "found out" and viewed as phonies and sneaks. Fair or not, Christianity is *different* from other faiths in our common culture, because of its overbearing historic weight. The culture is so saturated with superficial familiarity that deeper engagement is often blocked. Everybody already knows about the cross, Jesus, salvation, the whole et cetera bagful; shut up or we'll change the channel. We've been innoculated against Christian faith, and when it insists on reappearing in the secular world it is annoying but ineffective, like a flock of gnats.

What sweat-stained labors are expended on overcoming this

block. Church leaders have been worrying about making Christian faith "relevant" since the sixties; this seems to mean scrambling behind the culture by a few years' remove and copying whatever has proved itself a safe bet. (Admittedly, originality that housed a Christian message would merely baffle.) Nothing is more agonizingly dated to me now than my own hip 'n' earnest faith of the early seventies. The human potential lingo, the Fritz Perls posters, the trust-building exercises, the felt banners, the role playing, the passing an apple around a circle so everyone could, like, really *look* at it, all these now strike me as pretty cringeworthy. Some church leaders still talk that way, not realizing that the parade has passed them by. I occasionally see a "gut feelings" quote in the newspaper from a clerical *eminence grise* and think, "Boy, I know what year *he* graduated from seminary." He's *griser* than he thinks.

More up-to-date attempts to make faith relevant can make the mistake of adopting the ever-present vernacular of consumerism, and offering Jesus as a product that will solve all your problems and make you happy. This justifiably provokes a "What kind of a fool do you take me for?" response. But strangely enough, in a way it's actually true; not the fixing-all-your-problems part, but the way in which his presence takes root and spreads, producing peace and joy no matter what life's circumstances.

But there's no way to say that without sounding sappy and, frankly, like an idiot. Life hurts—how can you say Jesus makes it all O.K.? Well, it's hard to explain—you kind of have to come and see for yourself, and try it on for a while to get it. It doesn't mean that you get everything you want; rather, that gradually you get to want only Jesus. "He will give you the desires of your heart" (Psalm 37:4) turns out to mean that God gives the desires themselves; our impulsive and conflicting hungers are transformed, tuned, and ordered to receive what God intends to give.

In light of this, much Christian output of every genre seems shallow because it fails to grapple adequately with suffering. It's not that Christians don't suffer, but the expectation that there will always be a peaceful resolution to the story, even if it is just the peace of acceptance won through anger and tears, tends to make any preceding anguish inevitably seem artificial or contrived. Yet from a Christian perspective, a work that culminated in pessimism or cynicism would be the truly artificial one; we know that's not the end of the story. This is not an easy problem to resolve.

Finding ways to cross faith with culture is a persistent concern at a festival like this. A further complication is that we don't all participate in a single broadcast culture anymore but are a nation of niches, tiny virtual communities linked by hundreds of narrow-cast channels. At one booth I stop and look over a display of CDs representing the unlikely phenomenon of Christian death metal. The groups have names like Mortification, Dead Pharisees, Corpse, and Ultimatum. Regulations seem to require a black album cover with either red or poison-green lettering, in a font I'd call New Vampire Opulent (Obscure). The album cover for Forthwright shows blood dripping down from giant hands onto a naked figure in a fetal position with its head cupped in its hands. Tourniquet's cover shows a wasted hand reaching through prison bars to pick up a bug. Hey, you have a nice day, too.

The proprietor of the booth notes my lack of familiarity with the genre and produces a portable CD player and some earphones, saying, "Want to do some?" I begin listening to a song by a group called Crimson Thorn. The lead singer has a voice like James Earl

Jones in a very bad mood. I think it's meant to sound like growling, but sometimes it sounds more like belching. Curiously, the CD's back cover shows the band standing in front of a Russian Ortho- dox church, complete with onion domes and three-bar crosses. I guess this was the scariest-looking church they could find. Sample song titles: "Dissection," "Putrid Condemnation," "Suffering," "Grave of Rebirth," and "2nd Timothy." The song rumbles on and I watch the CD counter: a minute and a half and I still haven't un- derstood a single lyric.

Just then the Crimson Thorn lead singer walks up to the booth and the proprietor introduces us. Luke Renno is an immense guy with a waist-length ponytail and seven earrings. On his calf there is a large tattoo of the device called "chi rho"; it looks like intersected X and P, representing the Greek monogram of Christ. Renno is twenty-three and has been singing with the group for seven years.

I ask how he got his voice that low, and whether it's electroni- cally enhanced. No, he says in quite a normal voice, it's just from practice, and he looks embarrassed. I ask, "Why death metal mu- sic? What aspect of the Gospel does it represent?"

"The Gospel's pretty intense," Renno replies. Is it meant to ex- press anger? "Not really. We have a good time, smile and stuff," he says. "It's not that we're angry at Satan, but we're proclaiming Jesus with everything we have. We really put it out there."

I tell Renno that I listened to his song "Beaten Beyond" and couldn't understand any lyrics. Could he give me an example of the sort of thing he sings? He recites a verse from "No Exceptions," which begins, "Hanging on the cross the price was paid, blood shed for sin." The quatrain ends with the rhyme ". . . be born again."

I ask what sorts of themes Crimson Thorn sings about. "We don't get into social issues too much," Renno says. "It's all about a personal relationship with Jesus Christ. We're against drugs, but that's not our main focus. If somebody got off drugs but didn't come to know Jesus Christ, he's still going to hell."

So why use this type of music to get this message across? "Secular death metal bands seem depressed," he says. "We want to plant seeds. People come up after our concerts and talk with us, they say they had always been against Christians because they thought we were against them. We smile at 'em and talk to 'em and it gives 'em something new to think about."

Christian death metal music, then, is not aimed at Christians, but is intended to reach secular metal enthusiasts who otherwise wouldn't consider the faith. I meet another performer, Matthew Harper of One Flesh, who reiterates Renno's image of seed-planting. He goes on, "We're kind of like sheep in wolves' clothing. Death metal kids are not going to listen to CCM," he says, referring to the genre called Contemporary Christian Music, encompassing soft rock, worship music, and other non-threatening sounds, mostly played on Christian radio and bought by Christian consumers.

"CCM is—" he hesitates "—kind of cheesy. But secular kids listen to our music, and they can tell we're serious, we're for real. You know, evil is not a matter of your appearance. It's what's in your heart." Two silver thorns protrude from the septum that divides his nostrils. "People listen to the music, they like it, then they read the lyrics and get interested. My band gets letters from people who say they came to faith through our lyrics."

Harper explains that there is some debate in the Christian metal community about whether to enclose lyric sheets with the album. Some kids might take a glance at the lyrics, figure out that it's that icky Christian stuff, and throw the CD away. Bands concerned about this try to build in a delay so that the kids can form an affection for the music before confronting the content. Instead of enclosing lyrics, they might give an address where buyers can write away for a free lyric sheet, or an Internet address where the lyrics can be downloaded.

What is One Flesh like? Harper, a jazz theory major, explains, "It's technical metal, *extremely* heavy." And what is its message? "We sing about sexual purity, sex abuse, porn. We do a lot of secular events."

The combination of hard rock and sexual purity is surprising, but I suppose not inherently incompatible. On a staff golf cart outside sits an exhausted-looking Edie Goodwin, who with her husband make up the band Headnoise. Edie is not very conversational; she worked hard the night before. A friend who caught Headnoise's act was enthusiastic. Edie, she said, had hammered the crowd about sexual purity. She'd told them that anyone sleeping with a boyfriend or girlfriend at the festival had to cut that out and go to the prayer tent and repent. She offered to find any left tentless another place to stay.

Edie has a stunning mohawk, twelve inches high, black at the bottom and orange at the top. It looks a little crumpled in the back, and I realize that if you have a hairdo like this, you can never let the back of your head rest against anything. No wonder she looks tired. Are mohawks still around? I don't see any others at the festival. Is this just out of date? Or is it trendy retro? Is it ironic, or a homage? When did this get so complicated? Most troubling, is it time to be nostalgic for the eighties already?

Except for serendipitous connections like that between the *Death to the World* monks and punk street kids, Orthodoxy does not expend much effort in resonating with contemporary culture. When the faith enters a new geographic area, a few basic adaptations are made: the Liturgy is translated into the common language of the people, and, though the prayers are unchanging, they may be set to melodies that feel more comfortable to local worshippers. (Since these prayers are free-verse expressions a few sentences long, however, the Church Lady musical form of four-lines-and-a-chorus familiar to westerners is not really practicable.) Other than that, the Church just does what it always has, and expects outsiders will accommodate its timelessness. The liturgical year makes its round just as it did for centuries of previous years, paying no regard to headlines or hemlines. Once my husband was talking with a Baptist pastor who complained that his congregation had dwindled down to a handful of elderly members, because they refused to update. "They still want to worship like they did in the fifties," he complained. My husband thought, "Oh—*those* fifties."

Standing between oblivious changelessness and a twelve-inch mohawk, I wonder if there's a middle road that might be more culturally responsive. I suspect that for some seekers, the very detachment and timelessness of Orthodoxy is a primary appeal. But judging from the frequency with which members refer to the Church as a "best kept secret," I wonder if we Orthodox can find some appropriate way to be less secretive. Something that doesn't involve body piercing.

Toward the end of the day I get to hear Tourniquet, a band whose bug-picking cover artwork I admired earlier. They sell a black t-shirt with the name of the band in dripping, daggerlike red letters; on the left there is the dictionary definition of "tourniquet," and on the right the band's definition: "A spiritual process by which the living Triune God can begin to stop the senseless flow of going through life without knowing and serving our creator." Sample song titles: "A Dog's Breakfast," "Vitals Fading," "Broken Chromosomes." This band is deafening—in fact, I notice that many of them are wearing earplugs. The drums churn like machine guns, and the screaming singer gets the crowd to chant along. I can't discern the lyrics, but it sounds like they're defiantly shouting, "Bassinet!" Another performer is holding a blond two-year-old on his arm as he sings. She's wearing red airport-style earprotectors. A fan clambers onto the stage, motions the crowd to come toward him, and leaps onto their arms.

The lead singer pauses to instruct, "God is not a salad bar. It's a two-way street—you're supposed to talk *and* listen. Not just go, 'Pal, can you help me out of a jam.'" As he goes into the song "White-Knuckle It," the crowd jostles the surfer off balance, and he reaches up and nearly grabs the electric wires strung to stage. Some in the audience rock their heads violently back and forth on their necks; some cheer and bounce; some just stand and nod their heads thoughtfully, like wine connoisseurs.

Not all the music is metal variation; among the alternatives is a good number of ska bands. The group Not for the Crowd has a large and grinning audience skanking in the afternoon heat. Between the songs, the lead singer urges listeners not to let the joy of the faith grow cold in their hearts. I hear several bands give messages like this between songs, which makes me wonder if cooling emotion is a recurrent problem. It doesn't seem to be a concern that listeners will actually lose their faith, but rather that they'll fail to experience a sufficiently vivid level of emotional engagement with it, that they may gradually grow numb or take it for granted.

A liturgical Church has an advantage over one where worship is relatively spontaneous, in that people powered by religious emotion simply do run out of steam. Where there is a Liturgy, you show up each week and merge into that stream, and allow the prayers to shape you. But where the test of successful worship is how much you felt moved, there's always performance anxiety; even the audience has to perform.

I had been a Christian about ten years when I noticed to my dismay that my spiritual feelings were changing; the experience was growing quieter, less exciting. I feared that I was losing my faith, or that I might hear the Lord's words to the church at Ephesus, "I have this against you, that you have abandoned the love you had at first" (Revelation 2:4). Then I came to sense that my faith had undergone a shift of location. It had moved deep inside and was glowing there like a little oil lamp; if I was swept away with emotionally noisy worship, it might tip and sputter. Silence and attentiveness were now key.

I think this happens naturally in a believer's relationship with God, just as it does between two people who are in love. At first, being in love is all so strange, and the beloved is so other and exciting, that every moment is a thrill. But gradually over long years the couple grows together and grows alike. They no longer find each other a thrilling unknown but drink deeply of a treasured known that will always extend to mystery. At the beginning, the heart pounds just to see the beloved's handwriting on an envelope; at the end, two sit side by side before a fire and don't need to speak at all. When these rock bands urge their audience not to let the joy fade, they may be calling them to fight a fruitless battle against moving to the next stage of spiritual communion, the one where God moves deep inside. When years shape us to be like him, his presence is less electric and strange; yet as we draw nearer, deeper faith yields deeper awe.

Music like this is a huge boost to Christian teens, like Kris Wolfe of Cedar Rapids. She is a fan of the band MxPx, which she describes as "Cal punk" and says sounds like Green Day. Wolfe tells me, "I'm gonna change this country when I grow up. It's completely too liberal." What kind of changes? I ask. She's momentarily at a loss, then says, "Everything. My version of this country would probably result in a lot of anarchy." She laughs self-consciously. "I like to think that if there weren't laws and a government everything would be cool, but probably it wouldn't be." Before coming to Cornerstone I haven't heard of a conservative agenda to fight liberalism by introducing anarchy, but then again I hadn't heard of Christian death metal either.

Wolfe lost her pocketwatch while crowd-surfing the night before, which leads her to give me some advice. "If you go crowd-surfing, tuck your shirt way in, because people's hands go up your back and eventually your shirt gets pulled up. And that's cool if you're a guy but not a girl." She reflects. "And it's good to have pockets with buttons. If I'd put my pocketwatch in my pocket I wouldn't have lost it, but they took me by surprise. My friend just said, 'Let's put her up,' and they did."

Wolfe's favorite, MxPx, is one of the bands considered in the cover story of the *Abba News* tabloid being handed out at the festival. This is an endearingly breathless mag, with minimal editing that puts the "creative" back in creative writing. The resulting reading experience is sort of like *Finnegan's Wake*. "My Lord's love propounds me every day." "You always feel a little erie when you get back." "Reminds the listener where the roots of ska orientated from." The group Payable on Death's live album is described in a passage so charming I can't bear to clutter it with [sic]s: "Raw with a sense of meekness, never compromising and incredible show only to leave you in awe of the Spirit. When I listen to the CD I just image how the crowd was out of control with their heads bumpin' up and down . . . You will not forget what realism is all about."

The cover bears a big headline: "Not Christian Enough !!!" The story is a defense of major Christian rock bands which have been accused of compromising, because they don't stress the Gospel in every song. The writer recounts being at a concert and seeing a guy wearing an MxPx t-shirt, which he'd adorned with a circle-slash. "My first thought was then why are you wearing the shirt?" The guy told him that he was fed up with MxPx because "they're sellouts."

The writer admits that he once felt the same, "Then God showed me how much damage I was really doing for the strong man"—Jesus speaks of defeating Satan as binding "the strong man"—"by running my mouth against MxPx. Who am I to view anyone other than myself? . . . Do we really know what impact for God MxPx is making? Only God knows that. And it really doesn't matter because Jesus is savior and he knows what's going down." The writer cites a *Spin* magazine article about MxPx which didn't mention their faith but did say they were committed to abstinence until marriage. "They were willing to take a chance at persecution from the world for saying that in order to stand up for what they believe. Yet they are still accused of not being Christian enough."

In the late afternoon, the band Ignited Soul is singing about suicide. "Temporary problem—PERMANENT SOLUTION! Temporary problem—PERMANENT SOLUTION!"

During an instrumental bridge, the singer instructs, "Close your eyes . . . don't pay any attention to the music . . . Look at your Lord . . ." He describes the passion and death of Christ. "He paid the price with his blood, and still you push him away. And still you push him away. And still you push his love away."

At the end of the song, he speaks to the audience. "A lot of bands sing about suicide, but I know about it. About three years ago I took a razor to my wrist. And if it wasn't for our Lord, I wouldn't be here today."

He pauses. "If you're feeling that way, please come and talk to us after the show. Don't leave with this inside you. The devil will use it to attack you."

Even Christians get the blues, sometimes the black-and-blues that leave them racked and stumbling. At a lonely time like that, hope in Christ can seem pretty theoretical. This singer knows what that's like, and his voice cuts through the afternoon heat, through the dusty air hanging over the heads of this crowd. Yes, even Christians suffer, and sometimes we can't remember what the hope is without each other's help. The singer's eyes search the crowd, looking for the ones who know what he's talking about. Maybe someone will drift up to the stage when the set is over, ready for a heart-to-heart talk. Even when you know in your head that Jesus Is the Answer, it helps to have another person, someone with skin on, put his arm around your shoulder and help you see it fresh. It's like somebody said: you will not forget what realism is all about.

CHAPTER 11

Something Specific

10:15 AM: CHERUBIC HYMN,
GREAT ENTRANCE,
KISS OF PEACE, CREED

As the second half of the Divine Liturgy, the Liturgy of the Faithful, begins, Father Gregory stands at the altar and prays, "Cleanse our souls and bodies from every defilement of flesh or spirit, and grant us to stand blamelessly and without condemnation before Thy holy altar." Both spirit and flesh need cleansing, sins of the heart as well as those due to overindulgence or misuse of the body. The congregation then begins to sing the first part of a subdued and slow-moving prayer, known as the "Cherubic Hymn":

> Let us who mystically represent the cherubim
> And who sing the thrice holy hymn to the
>   life-creating Trinity
> Now lay aside all earthly cares.

We sing this several times, until the priest finishes his preparations and is ready to begin the Great Entrance, a procession bearing the bread and wine through the church and back to the sanctuary. When he places these gifts on the altar, we will sing the last lines of the hymn:

> That we may receive the King of All
> Who comes invisibly upborne by the angelic hosts.
> Alleluia, alleluia, alleluia.

The Cherubic Hymn recalls the ancient Roman practice of a newly elected emperor being borne out to the people on the uplifted shields of his legionnaires. In this procession, the priest bears the bread and wine just as Christ is being invisibly borne to us by the angels, and we take the part of cherubim to welcome him. During the Eucharistic prayer we will sing the "thrice holy hymn," as angels sang in Isaiah 6: "Holy, Holy, Holy is the Lord God of Hosts; heaven and earth are full of his glory."

In this hymn, as elsewhere, we remind ourselves to *pay attention.* Sixteen hundred years ago St. John Chrysostom was reproaching his congregation for allowing their minds to wander during the Liturgy. Much of the discipline of Orthodox prayer has to do with focusing and corralling the mind—or, in the Greek word which has a slightly different meaning, the *nous.* The *nous* is the "eye of the soul," the living, aware center of a person's being. It precedes but does not include the powers of the mind—thoughts, fantasies, reasoning. The work of prayer is to bring the full concentration of the *nous* into constant awareness of God, which is cultivated in the heart. The process is often described as bringing the mind down into the heart, or immersing or capturing it in the heart. A prime way of doing this is through capturing the *nous* in the repetition of the brief Jesus Prayer, which then reverberates through the day, creating peace and setting all things in order.

But the *nous* does not like to be corralled; it is restless and worried and distracted by many things. The fifth-century monk St. Isaac of Syria described the *nous* out of God as being like a fish out of water, bewildered and rapidly dying. The state of a person in such a condition is sometimes described as "insane"; the disordered *nous* misperceives the world and reacts spastically and irrationally. In his excellent book on the Jesus Prayer, *A Night in the Desert of the Holy Mountain*, Metropolitan Hierotheos Vlachos quotes an old monk, "The *nous* looks like the dog who wants to run all the time and is extremely agile at running away." Training this restless dog is the first step of prayer.

While we are repeating the first part of the Cherubic Hymn, Father Gregory stands facing the altar and prays an unusually intimate prayer, one of the few in the Liturgy in the first person singular. He is praying for himself. He begins, "No one who is bound with the desires and pleasures of the flesh is worthy to approach or draw nigh or to serve Thee, O King of glory, for to serve Thee is a great and fearful thing even to the heavenly powers."

What is pleasurable is not innately evil; God did not set up a world full of beguiling temptations just to taunt us. The problem is *bondage* to earthly pleasures, an inebriation with material things that dulls the mind and spirit. We've earlier seen this impulse to fly headlong into bondage termed "the passions." In much of Orthodoxy literature, as in St. Paul's writings, "the flesh" conveys this negative aspect ("For the desires of the flesh are against the Spirit,"

Galatians 5:17), while "the body" is positive ("Do you not know that your body is a temple of the Holy Spirit?," I Corinthians 6:19).

The priest's prayer goes on to say that, though his own worthiness is questionable, God established the ministry of the holy table through his "boundless love toward mankind."

"Wherefore I implore Thee, Who alone art good and art ready to listen: Look down upon me, a sinner and Thine unprofitable servant, and cleanse my soul and my heart from an evil conscience . . . For I draw near unto Thee, and bowing my neck I pray Thee: Turn not Thy face from me, neither cast me out from among Thy children, but vouchsafe that these gifts may be offered unto Thee by me, Thy sinful and unworthy servant."

Father Gregory then lifts his hands and recites the Cherubic Hymn three times, privately, as we continue to sing it slowly. He moves around the altar swinging the censer, then censes the icons in the sanctuary, and, coming out through the Holy Doors, censes the icons on the iconostasis. Turning around he censes us as well. There is a continuity of meaning in the gesture. We are the original icons, since God was the first iconographer, making us in his image. During this time he continues his prayers, concluding with the penitential Psalm 51. After delivering the censer to the altar boy he comes out to us once more, bows, and says, "Forgive, O God, those who hate us and those who love us." We return the bow.

It is in asking each other's forgiveness that we are closely bound to each other. Once a year, on the night that Great Lent begins, we line the interior of the church in a big circle. The ends of the circle then overlap, as the last person in line faces the first, the priest. "Please forgive me, my brother (or sister), for any way that I have offended you," the priest says, crossing himself and bowing to touch the ground. The parishioner responds, "I forgive you." He or she then asks and receives the same forgiveness from the priest. The two exchange the kiss of peace, then move on to the next people in line. Gradually the two ends of the line loop to meet again, until every person in the church has asked for and received forgiveness from every other. There are a lot of tears, and a lot of smiles.

My daughter Megan once said, "I feel closer to the people I go to church with than to all my friends in the dorm, even though I know them a lot better. The girls in the dorm I know backwards and forwards, know everything about them. But I feel more connected to the people in the church, because we're doing this spiritual path together. We understand each other, and we're linked together in a way that I don't have with people outside the church."

I think it must be things like Forgiveness Vespers that creates that deep bond. The other element, of course, is receiving Communion, which we are moving toward now.

Behind the iconostasis the altar party is lining up. Elliot, first in line, holds the processional cross and peeps out, and the choir knows from that signal it's time to wind up the Cherubic hymn. Father Gregory ties around his shoulders a fringed square of brocade called the aer, then picks up the chalice and diskarion which hold the wine and bread. The procession exits through the left door of the iconostasis: Elliot carrying the cross, then Luke and David with candles, then Subdeacon Gregory walking backward swinging incense. Last, Father Gregory comes chanting intercessions, those prescribed by the Church and those names added by members of this parish. The person who baked the day's Communion bread in particular submits a list of people to pray for, and they are included in this litany. We respond "Amen" to each one. The procession moves down the left side of the church to the back, then returns up the center. Standees group themselves to create aisles; Rose swoops up the now-sleeping Nicole in her arms.

As the priest passes, people lean in to touch or kiss the aer or the edge of his chasuble. Many visitors don't know what to make of this; are people worshipping fringe? No, this is just a symbolic way of attaching our private petitions to this intercessory litany of the whole Church. Doing this by kissing something looks strange in the West, but in the East it's a familiar and reverent way of making a connection. Orthodox worship emerged from a culture that simply does more kissing than westerners do; Middle Easterners kiss each other in greeting, for example, when we would shake hands. So we kiss icons, crosses, the Gospel book, the aer, and each other. Our worship is physical, not solely mental. As a result, Orthodox worship engages all the senses: we touch and kiss these things we venerate, smell incense and beeswax candles, taste bread and wine, and hear chanting and hymns. The sense of vision has the most to savor: we see the priest moving through the congregation carrying the brocade-draped gifts, preceded by a cross and candles, surrounded by icons, and our friends and fellow worshippers bowing, praying, and touching his vestments as the smoke of incense swirls around us. The body is good, and we worship with our whole bodies.

Father Gregory returns to lay the gifts on the altar, and the congregation sings the second half of the Cherubic Hymn. Then we begin a new round of intercessions, during which Basil starts taking up the collection. He moves through the crowd with a small basket in his hand, and those who have donations toss them in. Basil has recently dyed his hair, and it's a helmet of black, courtesy of Miss Clairol. Megan has coincidentally used the same product, in the same shade, on her hair, but she regrets it more than Basil does.

"Peace be to all," Father Gregory says, and we respond, "And to thy spirit." He continues, "Let us love one another, that with one accord we may confess . . ." and we sing, "Father, Son and Holy Spirit, the Trinity one in essence, and undivided."

At this point we exchange the kiss of peace with those standing nearest us. This is a practice of the ancient church which is being recovered by modern Orthodoxy, but is not yet in use everywhere. I turn to Rose and we give pecks on each cheek, and I give a fingertip kiss to the top of Nicole's drowsy head. As I turn, Hardworking Jeannie is there with her arms spread wide. She's bigger, stronger, and generally more competent than me, so in her arms I feel once again like a safe child. Then there's just enough time for me to reach over to Lillian and duck my head into that lavender embrace.

As the Trinity is undivided, so this community must be, and this exchange makes visible our love for each other. It is not just a chummy time to say hello to each other, but a part of the Liturgy, an act with mystical significance. The peace must be genuine. Those who are so out of sorts with each other that they cannot exchange the peace should not receive Communion. Jesus said, "If you bring your gift to the altar, and there recall that your brother has something against you, leave your gift there at the altar, go first and be reconciled with your brother, and then come and offer your gift" (Matthew 5:23–24). This community has witnessed people who were deeply at odds with each other making genuine, teary reconciliation at the peace. I know, because it's happened to me.

Ina, the mother of altar boys Luke and Zach, tells a story from when she was attending a previous church and shared the responsibility for bringing to worship a very old, very direct lady from the Old Country. One Sunday there was a mix-up as to who was to transport Victoria, and as a result the old woman was late to church.

She stood in the aisle and shouted in stentorian tones, over the chanters' voices, "Why you not pick me up?" As she moved in next to Ina, she remained visibly annoyed, and Ina felt compelled to make amends before Communion.

After a pause, Ina turned to the small lady and whispered, "Victoria, please forgive me, I . . ."

"No!" Victoria snapped.

Ina pondered this. Some minutes later she tried again. "I'm sorry about this morning. I hope you'll . . ."

Victoria darted a glance at her. "NO!" she repeated, more sharply.

The Liturgy proceeded to the point of the Kiss of Peace. Ina realized that she couldn't receive Communion unless Victoria forgave her. She took Victoria's hands and looked her in the eye. "Victoria, I really hope that you'll be able to forgive me *sometime.*"

"No!" said Victoria. "I love you! You my daughter!" and threw her arms around her. In Victoria's eyes, it was obvious: they were united in the Body of Christ, there was nothing to forgive, and all Ina's pestering was just making her more irritated.

Why are we humans stuck here on earth with all these other people, anyway? If God's sole purpose in creating us is to forge a relationship of love with us, why doesn't he just go ahead and take us home?

Maybe God has a subtle purpose in leaving us here to rub up against each other, getting our pride bent, learning to forgive, learning to ask for forgiveness. St. Theophan the Recluse, who should know, said that it takes longer to grow in humility in the peaceful seclusion of a hermitage than it takes in the knockabout world where people step on your toes every day.

In the story of the great flood, Noah builds his ark, fills it with animals, and the day comes when "all the fountains of the great deep burst forth" (Genesis 7:11). Noah and his wife, and their three sons and their wives, all climb into the ship, a dark and humid jumble of every kind of living creature on earth. Among the eight humans, all in-laws to each other, there must have been the usual stresses and irritation. "They went in as God had commanded him, and the LORD shut them in." I picture the giant hand of God firmly closing the little toy door of the ark, and a couple of hundred pairs of eyes staring at each other in the dark as the rain came thundering down.

We are shut up together in this church, here for the long haul, and we have to learn to get along. This is why we need to kiss each other in peace every week, and ask face-to-face for every other person's forgiveness once a year. The spiritual life is not just me-and-Jesus; we find him in the midst of a community, and we have to learn to love all of them too. It's a package deal.

Jesus said, "By this all men will know that you are my disciples, that you have love for one another" (John 13:35). Our love for each other is a sign of our allegiance to him. Historically, the Church has not always done such a good job of exemplifying our discipleship by love for each other. Here in this little stone church we try again fresh every week.

Father Gregory calls us back from our paired exchanging of the peace with the words, "The doors! The doors! In wisdom, let us attend." In the earliest days of the Church, the doors would then be shut and guarded against intrusion by non-believers. The second-century African Christian Tertullian mocks with his usual tartness the heretics' open-door policy: "Alike they approach, alike they hear, alike they pray, even the heathen if they come upon the scene; they will cast that which is holy to the dogs, and pearls, though they be only false ones, before swine." St. John Chrysostom, more kindly, says that the closing of doors is to shield those who "are still imperfectly prepared" from the sacramental mysteries. It is dangerous to be exposed to spiritual power without sufficient preparation and the right sort of receptivity, like that of a grounded electric plug. "Anyone who eats and drinks without discerning the body eats and drinks judgement upon himself. That is why many of you are weak and ill, and some have died" (I Corinthians 11:29–30).

It's significant that the recital of the Creed comes now, *after* the closing of the doors, rather than before. The Creed was not meant as a witness to the world of what Christians boldly believe. It was a recital of mysteries that could not be comprehended except by initiates. There were creeds from the earliest days of the Church, mostly associated with the entrance rite of baptism, since new Church members were expected to affirm the faith they were joining. Because this faith was held in secret, early creeds were not written down but taught orally and preserved only in memory. These early creeds were probably very simple, but as various disputes arose more precise definitions became necessary. The Creed we recite now, called the Nicene Creed, was initially composed at the Council of Nicea in 325 A.D., then expanded at the Council of Constantinople in 381 A.D.

> I believe in one God, the Father Almighty, Maker of heaven
> and earth, and of all things visible and invisible;
> And in one Lord, Jesus Christ, the Son of God, the Only-
> begotten, begotten of the Father before all worlds, Light of

Light, Very God of Very God, Begotten, not made; of one
essence with the Father, by Whom all things were made;

Who for us men and for our salvation came down from
heaven, and was incarnate of the Holy Spirit and the Virgin
Mary, and was made man;

And was crucified also for us under Pontius Pilate, and suffered and was buried;

And the third day He rose again, according to the Scriptures;

And ascended into heaven, and sitteth at the right hand of the
Father;

And He shall come again with glory to judge the living and the
dead, Whose kingdom shall have no end.

And I believe in the Holy Spirit, the Lord and Giver of Life,
Who proceedeth from the Father, Who with the Father
and the Son together is worshipped and glorified, Who
spake by the Prophets;

And I believe in One Holy Catholic and Apostolic Church.

I acknowledge one Baptism for the remission of sins.

I look for the Resurrection of the dead,

And the Life of the world to come. Amen.

We chant the Creed loudly, especially Basil, who leans into the
wind as he declaims it, as if picturing a scoffer saying, "Oh, come
now, you don't *really* believe that, do you?" This is about the loudest
hymn in the Liturgy, and we thunder it out in four-part harmony.
It is bracing, and very enjoyable. On the heels of considering the
story of Doubting Thomas, we are glad to proclaim what we believe.

There is a story about a group of Orthodox who wanted to advertise a church event on Christian radio and were confronted with a sales manager skeptical as to whether they were really Christians. She asked, "Do you have a statement of faith?" This stumped them; the evangelical Protestant practice of drafting organizational "faith statements" is not common among Orthodox. Eventually they decided just to fax her the Nicene Creed. After reading it over she phoned to say, "Well, this looks very orthodox."

There's another reason why we might want to say this with the doors closed; it sounds kind of rude in our society to say that you believe specific things. The preferred stance is to believe, in a general way, in almost everything, as if strolling happily through a garden of boundless blooms. The very diversity is delightful; we would not want to limit it in any way. We want to sample and celebrate it all.

Well, not *all* of it, of course. Some ancient faiths sacrificed children, for example, or commanded slaughter of unbelievers. Some forbade sex and marriage. We can't affirm that. Some faiths taught a view of women that by today's standards would be called sexist. Can't have that, either.

Watch closely, now. What is the principle by which we accept some elements and reject others? How can we feel confident accepting a faith's view of the ecology, for example, while dismissing its view of women? What's our authority? From inside that faith, the teachings about men and women might appear just as necessary, profound and sacred truths unfolding the sacramental mystery of gender. How do we know they're wrong? What's our principle for making these judgments?

Well, um, it's us. Our principle for accepting or rejecting elements is simply what we like or dislike: what fits our prior world-view, our sense of true and untrue. How do we know our worldview is more accurate than that of the original believers who accepted all elements of this faith, both what's currently appealing and what isn't? How do we know we're smarter than they were? Where does our authority come from?

Do we respond, "I look deep inside and find it"? As with the bottom kitchen drawer, people can look deep inside and find a number of things, some useful and some downright harmful, and the latter occasionally masquerading as the former. We can look inside and find noble truths and selfishness, an urge to rescue children and an urge to seduce one's neighbor, and an urge to just get a can of beer and flip around the channels for a while. All of this can be influenced by elements as discouragingly ordinary as how much sleep you got last night, and whether those deep-fried peppers are settling the way they should. There's lots of stuff deep inside, and not all of it can be taken at face value.

Where does this rattling drawerful of deep-inside come from? The humbling truth is that we're not nearly as original or intellectually liberated as we fancy. We are heavily formed by our surrounding culture and subliminally adopt attitudes and values that we can't even see are there, so automatically are they acquired. What's more, we're the targets of an entire consumer economy aggressively trying to stuff us with fashionable ideas like a pâté goose, in hopes that we'll want to buy the emblematic products to show our participation in the ideas. We take Communion in the sacrament of Nike. It is foolish to think we're immune to this. Eighth-graders know that peer pressure is the most powerful force in forming their worldview and shaping their decisions. Grown-ups don't know it.

The principles that guide us in choosing or discarding elements of a faith—or make us blind to them altogether—are those of our surrounding culture. We are fish in a fishbowl, squinting out into the living room, trying to make out what's there, and unable to measure just how much the water and the curve of glass distort our view. We should at a minimum acknowledge that the view *is* distorted. We look at reality as the fish looks at the sofa—a dark green bulge with stubby feet curving together. We look at the garden of spirituality as citizens of our class, culture, and century.

One of the best pieces of spiritual advice I ever received was one I fortunately gained early, while still in college. It was that I should give up the project of assembling my own private faith out of the greatest hits of the ages. I encountered this idea while reading Ramakrishna, the nineteenth-century Hindu mystic. He taught that it was important to respect the integrity of each great path, and said that, for example, when he wanted to explore Christianity he would take down his images of the Great Mother and substitute images of Jesus and Mary.

I grasped that we are so indoctrinated by our culture that we can't trust our standards of evaluation. We can only gain wisdom that transcends time by exiting our time and entering an ancient path, and accepting it on its own terms; we only learn by submitting to something bigger than we are. The faith I was building out of my prejudices and preconceptions could never be bigger than I was. I was constructing a safe, tidy, unsurprising God who could never transform me but would only confirm my residence in that familiar bog I called home. I had to have more than that.

It is not too scandalous to urge people to choose one of the ancient paths and stick to it. What is more awkward is the next thing that happens: people begin to perceive that different paths teach different things about reality, and some of these teachings are mutually exclusive. If Christianity teaches that Jesus is the only Son of God, and Islam teaches that he is a prophet among other prophets, both cannot be true. This is akin to having one group of historians teach that George Washington was our first president, and another teach that he was the third. Both groups may be sincere, both are perceiving that George was president sometime, but one has come to a mistaken conclusion. (At *least* one has, that is. A third faith—Judaism, to name one—might say that Jesus was neither of these things, and that the historians are arguing over whether George was third president or sixth.)

This is a discovery that makes citizens of our time and culture feel distressed, because it violates one of our cherished presumptions, namely that all religions are the same underneath. There's a kernel of accuracy here: Truth is indeed One, and all sincere spiritual paths are questing toward that one truth, and all grasp some aspects of the light.

Our culture is inclined to extend this insight to a fallacious conclusion: that where religions agree with us, with our current ideas, is truth, and where they disagree is falsehood. This belief is a modern invention, a quirk of our culture, and though innocently well-meaning is finally imperialistic. We are likely to perceive and approve those "points of agreement" that accord with our popular idea of what religion ought to be, and dismiss, or simply miss, those that confuse us or violate our imagined universal faith.

Worse, in the process of pursuing this notion we fail to get at the heart of what committed spiritual faith is like: it is commitment to something specific. It is not vague good-neighborly sentiments that prompt a pleasant smile. There is currently popular reluctance to forming any particular ideas about spiritual reality;

the journey is deemed more important than the destination. Yet the journey must be going somewhere, it must be aiming to arrive sometime, or it's mere idle wandering. If we prefer uncertainty to conclusions, our questing is insincere. We're playing a game rather than truly seeking. A person may seek long years for a spouse, but on the wedding day we rejoice with them that the search is at an end. We don't deplore their decision to stop seeking.

Making a faith commitment is similarly specific, not vague. This makes it offensive to those outside; the Christian faith in a crucified Messiah was described by St. Paul as "a stumbling block to Jews and folly to Gentiles" (I Corinthians I:23). The experience of living a specific faith is often challenging and humbling; it confronts the follower with a grid for reality that can shake up his previous assumptions. It may require profound life changes, perhaps even willingness to sacrifice one's life. People don't undertake such obligations for the sake of general good feelings. Only the demands of a specific faith can elicit such fervor.

Our current culture mistrusts fervor; we think it means danger to those following other paths. It is true that some faiths teach war against unbelievers, while others teach love of enemies. No matter what the teaching, followers of nearly every faith have been persecutors of those on other paths, and followers of nearly every faith have been victims. But this is not inevitable; in many lands people hold different beliefs about a number of issues without killing each other. In fact, most "religious wars" through history are actually wars over property or power, with religion as an excuse. Even where strong faith is present, if the tension of conquest is absent, violence doesn't arise. In my neighborhood, people of all faiths live side by side, and no one invokes the Deity to forcibly seize his neighbor's shrubbery.

It is possible to believe strongly that smoking tobacco is wrong, without rounding up and executing smokers. It is possible to believe that one's faith is the most right one, and that others must logically fall short in comparison, while intending no ill to those who follow other faiths. In fact, intending them good, you might wish that they would look into your faith and perhaps be persuaded to join you. A committed follower of any faith could believe that the spiritual food he has found is the most nutritious of all, and wish to share it. Open-minded followers of other faiths can sample it and draw their own conclusions. Nobody has to kill anybody. Killing has been historically demonstrated as an ineffective tactic for gaining conversions.

When I was a spiritual seeker, I wasn't persuaded to become a Christian by the Nicene Creed. It took a spiritual encounter with Christ to accomplish that, over my stubborn resistance. But once I became a follower of Jesus, helplessly in love with him, I recognized that this was an explanatory summary that other addicts before me had arrived at. The Creed was the consensus of a group of previous pilgrims on this same journey, about sixteen hundred years ago. They had written it down and passed it along, and each succeeding generation in every nation had been able to agree, "I believe."

I had to trust this vast community of other believers, so I gradually began to be able to say the Creed. Not all at once; at first I had to just be silent at some phrases. But I was willing to listen, willing to believe that I didn't know everything already. Gradually the fullness of the Creed became my prayer too. This morning I can stand in the community and sing it loud, awed at the beauty entrusted to me, the ringing truths that I Believe.

CHAPTER 12

My Father

IN A PLACE UNKNOWN

In my dream my father looks stricken. His eyes are wide and alarmed, and his face is pale. I see him for just a moment and our eyes meet. "Please help me," he pleads. Then he is gone.

I understand that he is trapped somewhere and cannot escape. He has no more strength. I understand that he is begging me to pray for him.

My father died in a car accident seventeen years ago. In life, he was not a stricken kind of guy. He was a good guy, a good-natured guy, popular at parties, a favorite with friends. Though he made his career in his father's business (the old man was an entrepreneur of the old scale, a high-school graduate who taught himself naval architecture and eventually built his own shipyard), my father was an admirer of the arts, widely read in French and English, with an educated eye for antiques and painting. Midlife testing showed him to have a vocabulary several times larger than the average person's, comparable to Shakespeare's. He enjoyed showing this off by dropping odd newly discovered words into conversation in a manner he believed to be nonchalant, and then watching eagerly for someone to take the bait.

My dad was generous, warm-hearted, and had a roaring laugh. When his mind was made up, he was utterly tenacious, extending a disagreement long after everyone else was weary, for the sheer fun of debate. Even when he was exasperating, he was delightful, and his death was widely mourned.

Where has he been for seventeen years? Has he been trying to get through to me all this time? Was this his one chance to communicate with someone on earth, and he chose me?

Once he attended an auction at a house in Charleston; an estate was being sold off. The auctioneer put forward a large, badly aged mountain landscape; probably eighteenth century, probably European. No one was interested. The auctioneer added to the lot a smaller painting which caught my dad's attention. It was a winter scene, a frozen lake with hunters, one kneeling with a gun at his shoulder. Something about it looked promising, looked of finer quality. My dad bid one dollar for the two paintings and took them home.

Years later a visitor peered at the hunters on the ice. "I feel sure that's a Hendrick Avercamp," he said. "You should have it appraised." It was indeed a painting by that venerable Dutch Master, whose anniversary was conveniently just coming up. The painting was auctioned at Sotheby's in London, bringing a very handsome return on a fifty-cent investment.

In a painful spurt of imagination I picture my father flying up into blackness and paintings are falling away from him, large paintings in gold frames, brilliant colors, Matisses and Cézannes, they are no use now, they are falling, and he is soaring up into black, with a look of terror on his face.

I came home from college one weekend to find by his chair a stack of eight paperback Japanese novels. He said he'd gotten curious about current developments in Japanese fiction.

Oddly, he never showed any curiosity about spiritual things. It was like a blind spot, like being tone deaf; it couldn't catch his ear. My conversion to Christian faith soon after college graduation seemed to be faintly embarrassing to him. His only frame of reference, I suspect, was, "She got religion"—like the neighbors down the street who "got religion" when I was young, making them the butt of many a joke over at my house. To "get religion" was to become stupid. It was to abandon intelligence in favor of emotion; not even noble emotion, but sentimental, gullible emotion. Anyone who "got religion" was a "Holy Roller" in this economy. The grown-ups in the library were snickering over their scotch as my father described the probable scenes down the block; he had a gift for hyperbole, and the presence of an audience egged him on. I sat hunched on the stairs, holding onto my toes, trying to picture these nice neighbors actually rolling on the floor.

In the old joke, an enthusiastic visitor to an elite mainline church persists in hollering, "Praise the Lord" all through the service, even after repeated shushing by the usher. "Why will you not be quiet!" the latter eventually demands. "I can't help it," the visitor shrugs, "I got the Holy Ghost." "Well," the usher returns haughtily, "you certainly did not get him here."

My father was not opposed to religion, he just believed in

everything-in-its-place. He was taught to make his Sunday obligation, and all my childhood we did: scooting into St. Mary's
Catholic Church right before the Gospel reading, scooting out
again just after Communion. My dad had been taught that to intentionally avoid Sunday obligation was a mortal sin, and if you
died without confessing it, you would go straight to hell, no second
chance. He obeyed that teaching; he had faith to that extent, at
least, which could arguably equal that of a mustard seed. Making
that twenty-minute-a-week visit was the token he paid to stay on
God's good side, and as he once told me, he was afraid that if he
did more he might attract God's attention, with results that might
not be comfortable. "'There's Buddy Green!'" he said, and pan-
tomimed throwing a thunderbolt.

I think about his stricken face and I feel helpless.

I also feel on guard. My faith is not big on getting messages
from dead people. We believe in the communion of the saints, that
great "cloud of witnesses" (Hebrews 12:1) who join us in worship;
we surround ourselves with their images in icons to remind us of
their invisible presence. We frequently ask them to pray for us, but
we don't expect to get messages in return. Spiritualism, summoning
up the dead, consulting them about the future, is forbidden in both
Hebrew and Christian Scriptures. But I didn't seek or summon
this—it came to me out of the blue. I say "in my dream," but it
didn't seem very dreamlike. It seemed like one sharp clear moment
breaking into the fog of dreams. I wonder where my father is. I
wonder if he is suffering.

"Fire and brimstone" preachers are known for conjuring worlds
of horror after death, but they can't claim originality for the concept; it was Jesus who likened the afterworld of the damned to

Gehenna, the burning trashpit outside Jerusalem. It was "the place of outer darkness where men will weep and gnash their teeth" (Matthew 8:12).

I can imagine people saying, "Surely you don't believe in that!" and I feel bashful responding, Well, why not? A lot of people smarter than me have believed in that. A lot of people have believed in that, period, in a wide array of times and places. There's a multicultural consensus of a larger community here, and I don't feel confident proclaiming that all of them are wrong.

Maybe such images are meant to be taken symbolically; I imagine that, when you're beyond space and time and no longer inhabit a body, to insist on a specific trashpit outside Jerusalem as your destination is probably being overly literal. But there's no doubt that what's meant to be conveyed here is suffering. Suffering which I imagine as being more psychic than physical, pain of loneliness and alienation from all that is safe and good and beautiful; pain of being lost in the cold universe with no boundaries, falling forever in emptiness, out of touch with light. And God is the opposite of that—not cozy warmth, but brilliant light that burns through everything to clarity, and orders all reality in its course. Calling him "sovereign" or "ruler" is a weak earthly analogy for this kind of vast authority. And the energy of it is love. To be outside it is to be outside love, a fate worse than burning in garbage and offal. A fate that would make anyone weep.

It's this in-between I don't understand, where my father seems to be frightened but not irrevocably exiled, seems to be on a journey, and implores my prayers to help him. But how can anything I do accomplish that? Christians have always believed that we have this life only to choose to follow Christ; due to the overwhelming radiance of his beauty, no free choice could be possible afterward. Today is the time to decide: "'Today, when you hear his voice, do not harden your hearts' . . . While the promise of entering his rest remains, let us fear lest any of you be judged to have failed to reach it" (Hebrews 3:15; 4:1). A life spent turning away from this invitation, choosing sin and self-will, "hardens the heart." The heart calcifies, cramped and turned inward, at last satisfied by nothing on this earth or beyond it. The will, daily bent in this way, cannot in the end love light.

How can a loving God permit this? It's the inevitable price of freedom; he won't force us to accept his love against our will. Yet being outside that love, though it's what we chose, will hurt. His love is not a Hallmark card, it's the motive and energy of the entire universe. If you recollect that you can't fight city hall, you can imagine how much more damaging it would be to oppose this, disorienting and fragmenting. This searing love will ultimately singe those who try to wall themselves against it, who repeatedly choose flimsy self over reconciliation with their source and Creator. God is only love, but those who hate him won't feel it that way. As they say, the same sun that melts ice hardens mud. People send themselves to hell by their ordinary daily decisions, one little choice at a time.

But the reverse is not true; we don't escape this suffering by choosing to do *good* things. That's what "New Testament" means: under this new covenant, we unite ourselves to Jesus, who is the means of reconciliation between us and God. Filled with this love, we will show good deeds, as a well-rooted tree puts out good fruit. Good works don't save us but are evidence of a healed and overflowing heart. How good these works are is, of course, a relative thing. You can expect to wind up a better person than you were when you started but not necessarily better than your neighbor, who might be trying harder, or just have a shorter way to go. It's the allegiance to Jesus that matters, not the measurable value of our deeds. Without that allegiance, no good deeds would be enough to save us.

My father certainly didn't take God very seriously in this life. He may be suffering now. My throat tightens. I don't know how to formulate a prayer about this; I don't think I can ask God to change his mind, or bend the rules. This is all too big for me.

I go to our icon corner, that place above the living room radiator where the icons fill the wall and vigil candles are clustered. After lighting a candle, I open the Orthodox prayer book to the funeral service. "We pray for the repose of the soul of the servant of God departed this life; and that Thou wilt pardon his every transgression, both voluntary and involuntary," I read aloud. Though he wasn't Orthodox, I am, and these are now my prayers. "That the Lord will establish his soul where the just repose; the mercies of God, the kingdom of heaven, and remission of his sins, let us ask of Christ, our Immortal King and our God."

"Lord, please forgive my father," I pray. "Please do whatever is necessary to bring him to heaven and unite him with you." I read the words of the funeral service and pray along with them, along with all the grieving people through time who have read these words. I wonder how this works.

It's that old devil time, confusing things again. I can't reach back from my present time and change the details and decisions of my father's life. And I can't twist God's arm, change his mind, change his inscrutable justice. That's the puzzler about any sort of intercessory prayer—are you trying to change God's mind? If he's omnipotent, won't he go ahead and do whatever he was going to do, anyway? But Jesus commanded us to pray, in fact said that we should be insistent in prayer, like an old widow badgering a corrupt judge for justice.

Sometimes the point of prayer is to change the person doing the praying, to bring her into line with God's will so that she can do her part in accomplishing it. Sometimes it seems that God just wants partners in his work, wants us involved in his plan and power. He *likes* us; he wants us around, like a mom likes having her kids help her bake cookies. Also, our vocal prayers prepare others to recognize a good outcome as God's handiwork, rather than writing it off as mere luck.

Intercession has its own mysteries, but when we're praying for someone who is dead, there's the added element that we're praying for someone who is no longer in time. The truth is, they're not really dead. They're alive in another dimension of reality, one no longer bound by sequential time. All times are open to God, who views our lives as a man on a mountaintop watches the progress of a train across the prairie. When I unite my will to God's, I enter timelessness. Where my father is. Where he is in misery, perhaps, but I pray will be brought to light.

The vigil candle flickers. A dozen pairs of eyes look down from the icons, the faces of the dead who live in everlasting light.

The words of the prayer are soothing and confident: "Give rest to the soul of Thy departed servant in a place of brightness, a place of verdure, a place of repose, whence all sickness, sorrow, and sighing have fled away. Pardon every sin which he hath committed, whether by word, or deed, or thought; for Thou art good, and lovest mankind: for there is no man who liveth and sinneth not, and Thou only art without sin, and Thy righteousness is to all eternity, and thy law is truth."

CHAPTER 13

Not Like Judas

10:42 AM: THE EUCHARISTIC PRAYER

 At the conclusion of the Creed, Father Gregory proclaims, "Let us stand aright. Let us stand with fear. Let us attend, that we may offer the holy oblation in peace." In the earliest centuries, this was probably something of a stage direction; the fourth-century Apostolic Canons record that the deacon says this to the congregation, along with more specific injunctions like, "Let mothers take their children in hand."

The next exhortation begins a refrain familiar to Christians of many denominations:

"The grace of our Lord Jesus Christ, and the love of God the Father, and the communion of the Holy Spirit be with you all," chants the priest.

"And with thy spirit," we respond.

"Let us lift up our hearts," he goes on.

"We lift them up unto the Lord," we sing.

"Let us give thanks unto the Lord," he continues.

We sing, "It is meet and right to worship the Father and the Son and the Holy Spirit, the Trinity one in essence and undivided."

These three invitations and responses are both ancient and universal; they are recorded in similar form in the earliest unrevised description of the Eucharist, Hippolytus's Apostolic Tradition of 215 A.D. "This same division [of invitations and responses] is preserved in all of the Liturgies in both the Eastern and Western Churches," writes liturgical historian Casimir Kucharek.

Just before we receive Communion, about twenty minutes from now, the congregation will pray, "Of thy mystical supper, of Son of God, accept me today as a communicant, for I will not speak of Thy Mystery to Thine enemies, neither will I give Thee a kiss as did Judas, but like the thief will I confess Thee: Remember me, O Lord, in Thy Kingdom."

What transpires during this interim time is the Lord's mystery. The doors have been closed and only believers are present, only those who have committed themselves to the faith. As a result, I cannot describe it here in detail.

Though prayers which follow are written, the earliest centuries expected priests to convey the essence of the prayer in their own words. Thus there was variation in phrasing throughout the Church but consistency of intent. The prayer addresses first the Father, then the Son, then the Holy Spirit. The first section thanks the Father for creating us and loving us, for "all things of which we know and of which we know not." When we fell into sin, "You did not cease to do all things" to reconcile us, the priest says. Why was this what he had to do—allow Jesus to die on the cross? Weren't there other, less gruesome ways we could be reconciled? How does the atonement work, exactly?

It's a good question, and one that doesn't have a single answer. It

seems that after the Resurrection the first disciples were overwhelmed with a sense that this spiritual reunion was accomplished.
The specific mechanism, though, was not obvious, and it's been defined in various ways through the centuries. In a similar way, people
have always seen a clear connection between abundant crops and
abundant sunshine, even long before they understood photosynthe-
sis. The first Christians knew that the Cross and Resurrection had
opened the doors of Paradise, and though Scripture makes several
suggestions as to how this works, none takes clear precedence.

A familiar explanation, though not the one most widely embraced by the early Church, is that Jesus' death pays the debt we owe
to God for our sin. This theory gained strength in the Middle Ages
with the rise of the merchant class, as transactional analogies became familiar to western culture. The idea is that the general human
failure to keep the Law rolls up into a vast unpayable debt. "The
wages of sin is death" (Romans 6:23), and even one small sin is
enough to sunder the relationship between a person and God: "For
whoever keeps the whole Law but fails in one point has become
guilty of all of it" (James 2:10). Thus, the cost for each individual
is inevitably so high that even his own death would not be sufficient
to pay it. It would take the death of someone much better than the
average human; in fact, only the death of the Son of God himself
would be sufficient.

A closely related variation on this theory is judicial, not financial: our sinful deeds are tried in the heavenly courtroom and found
to merit the death penalty, and Jesus steps in to take the punishment in our place. This theory finds evidence in the Hebrew Scriptures' description of temple sacrifice, the slaughtering of animals to
pay for human sin: "It is the blood that makes atonement" (Leviti-
cus 17:11). The Christian writer of the book of Hebrews notes

this precedent as well: "Indeed, under the Law almost everything is purified with blood, and without the shedding of blood there is no forgiveness of sins" (Hebrews 9:22). Jesus is pictured as dying to fulfill the Law: "Think not that I have come to abolish the Law and the prophets; I have come not to abolish them but to fulfill them" (Matthew 5:17). Because he fulfilled the Law, we are no longer bound by it but are under grace, and must respond by showing mercy in turn and inviting all to this freedom in salvation. Because this explanation, whether financial or judicial, pictures Jesus substituting himself for us as a sacrifice for sin, it is termed the Substitutionary theory of the atonement.

Others have thought that Jesus' death was mainly intended to be inspirational. The Exemplary theory proposes that, after meditating on Jesus' example, we would be more loving toward each other. This strikes me as pretty feeble. The bloody death of the Son of God on a cross seems a bit over the top if the only purpose is to, you know, make folks stop and *think.*

The Orthodox view is different, and does not emphasize the fulfilling of the Law. I once heard my Bishop Basil give a talk on this. He began with the proposition that the worst enemy of humankind is death. The devil wants to enslave us in death, and God wants to rescue us. To accomplish this, Jesus humbled himself to take human form, and then further bowed to death on the cross, as it says in the earliest recorded Christian hymn: "Who, though he was in the form of God, did not count equality with God a thing to be grasped, but emptied himself, taking the form of a servant, being born in the likeness of men. And being found in human form he humbled himself and became obedient unto death, even death on a cross" (Philippians 2:6–8).

Jesus willingly went through these steps, living and dying in the same way we do, until he was brought into the domain of Satan as a captive, conquered by death. And then he revealed himself as God and Lord, blasting open the realm of death and filling it with light, freeing the righteous dead from their chains and casting Satan into his own pit. This explanation of how the Cross frees us is called "Christus Victor," Christ the Conqueror.

This theory is not developed from ideas of financial or legal debt but on overwhelming love, the kind of self-sacrificial love a Father would feel toward his lost, endangered children. This is the kind of daring, costly rescue such a Father would attempt, and do it for the sake of anguished love, not that of good accounting.

When Bishop Basil had finished, I stood to ask a question. How can we explain this view of salvation to Protestant friends? I asked. It's foreign to them, because they don't figure the devil into the equation at all. They believe that the Cross was the price Jesus paid to God, in order to cover our sins.

Bishop Basil said, "You mean, they think *God* demanded that his own son be killed? To satisfy *himself?*" It took several members of the audience to persuade him that, indeed, this was a widespread theory of the action of the Cross. The bishop clearly found this formulation strange and unpleasant. "What kind of a Father would do such a thing? That's not a God of love. If the Incarnation was merely about paying for sins rather than saving us from death, why couldn't God just remit the debt and declare it paid?"

We explained that, under this theory, God can't do that. He's bound by his own rules of justice, bound by his own Law. "That doesn't make any sense," Bishop Basil pointed out. "If he can break the rules of nature to do miracles and healings, he can decide to forgive our sins."

In fairness, the Substitutionary view can be found in Scripture.

It's there among a number of explanations for how this works, not all of them fully worked out. Jesus himself says he will "give his life as a ransom for many" (Matthew 20:28), raising questions of who the ransom is paid to and why. (The question of "Many? Why not all?" is just a problem of translation; "many" is *hoi polloi*, and though it literally means "the many," the idiom signifies everybody.) Several Orthodox prayers speak of nailing our sins to the Cross, so salvation is not solely due to the descent into Hades and resulting defeat of Satan. There is a relationship between Jesus' suffering and our sinfulness; if this were not so, if the plan of salvation was solely to get Jesus into Hades, he could have died in his sleep at seventy-five. Christus Victor was the theory that emerged in the lead in the early years of the Church, but other theories harmonize around it.

The priest continues, thanking the Father for enabling us to worship him, "even though there stand before Thee thousands of archangels and ten thousands of angels, the cherubim and the seraphim, six-winged, many-eyed, soaring aloft, borne on their pinions, singing the triumphal hymn, shouting, proclaiming, and saying":

And we sing, "Holy, Holy, Holy Lord of Sabaoth, heaven and earth are full of Thy glory. Hosanna in the highest. Blessed is He Who cometh in the name of the Lord. Hosanna in the highest."

The next section of the prayer recalls the events of the Last Supper, and Jesus' words over the bread and wine, "This is My Body," "This is My Blood." Western Eucharistic theology attaches to these "Words of Institution" the moment of transformation when the bread and wine become the Body and Blood of Christ. Orthodoxy does not; we see that change occurring as the Holy

Spirit is invoked over the elements, in a prayer called the "epiclesis." This third section of the prayer is the point at which, at other times of the year, worshippers drop to their knees and put their hands and foreheads on the floor in a prostration. During the joyous season after Pascha, however, no kneeling is allowed.

After the epiclesis there are more intercessions, and a hymn to the Virgin Mary:

> It is truly meet to bless thee, O Theotokos,
> Ever blessed and most pure and the Mother of our God.
> More honorable than the cherubim,
> And more glorious beyond compare than the seraphim,
> Without defilement thou gavest birth to God the Word;
> True Theotokos, we magnify thee.

After these intercessions we pray the Lord's Prayer, some lifting their hands as they do so. The icon in the apse above shows the Theotokos with her hands similarly raised in prayer, in the "orans" stance shown in the earliest Christian catacomb paintings. She is a Queen of War with open hands and no weapons.

At the conclusion of the Lord's Prayer, Father Gregory instructs us to bow our heads to the Lord. We do so, turning toward the icon of Christ on the iconostasis.

"Look down from heaven upon those who have bowed their heads unto thee," he prays, "for they have not bowed down unto flesh and blood, but to thee, the awesome God." We don't bow to any earthly power, nor to the wood and paint of the icon, but to God.

The priest prepares the bread and wine for Communion, adding to the wine a little warm water to represent the fervor of faith.

When I sent my Protestant friend Rich an account of the Liturgy including this detail, he said, "When I read that it had to be *hot* water, boy, that was when you lost me." This rite of the "zeon," as it is called, goes back to the sixth century and probably earlier, but strikes Protestants as one more of those oddball details that makes them wary of the whole Orthodox package. As with other elements of the Faith, this can't be resolved by searching for scriptural or theological justifications for the practice. The question is, what is the Church? Orthodox claim that what the early Church did, and the Church of subsequent centuries preserved, is what the Holy Spirit guided Christians to do and what God intends. For those who think of Orthodoxy as merely another denomination, however, and not the continuation of the ancient Church, this argument is maddeningly circular: "It's right because it's what we do."

We now come to the prayer promising not to reveal the Mystery of the Eucharist. Immediately before it we pray, "I believe, O Lord, and I confess that thou art truly the Christ, the Son of the living God, who didst come into the world to save sinners, of whom I am chief."

One of the odd things I noticed after becoming Orthodox was the distinctive practice of making explicit statements of humility, of calling oneself the chief of sinners. Soon after my conversion I noticed that some of the letters and e-mail I was receiving from new friends would close with the line, "Please pray for me, a sinner." Or people might sign themselves, "the unworthy Andrew," or "the sinner, Catherine." One that stuck in my mind was, "the most sinful nun, Macaria."

In robust, confident America, such expressions of self-abasement sound dangerously self-revelatory; we imagine that next the person will be sobbing on our shoulder and recounting details of childhood trauma. But in Orthodoxy, I learned, it's a routine announcement, matter-of-fact, not necessarily intending emotional freight. Like members of AA who announce, "I'm Sam, and I'm an alcoholic," these Orthodox are merely acknowledging something about themselves they think everybody knows anyway. It's an acknowledgment that, for them, keeps things in perspective.

Is the perspective correct, though? How sinful can a nun be, anyway? Perspective is all a matter of the angle of vision. Compared to me, the typical nun probably shines like a star. Compared to God, though, both of us look pretty shabby. That's the exhilarating tension of the Christian faith: the vast radiance, energy, and majesty of God, and our own unworthiness—our weakness and selfishness. God's got our number, all right, and the astounding good news is that he loved us so much he came and died for us, in order to corral us back into the circle of his love. So expressions, like these, of our sinfulness are reminders of how vast God's love is. We see his love best in that contrast, just as we see the love of our friends and family best those times when we test it, and not when we're on our lovable best behavior.

Can this get out of balance? Yes, when the God-popularizers bring him down to our level, make him so affable that we can't imagine he even notices our sin. What isn't recognized can't be healed and taken away. Or, conversely, when humility veers into self-loathing, and we forget that God saves us because he *loves* us.

Thus, I thought it went a little off-track when I got an e-mail signed, "worthless Alexis." It may have been merely a translation flub, but to my mind there's a difference between acknowledging that you're undeserving of a great gift, "unworthy," and labeling yourself worthless. The object of such overwhelming love must be of infinite value in the eyes of the lover.

But I did enjoy imagining such a verbal habit catching on in America. Imagine hearing, "Hello, I'm worthless Antoine, and I'll be your waiter tonight." Or, "This is *60 Minutes,* and I'm worthless Mike Wallace." "And I'm worthless Morley Safer." It might be the kind of competition this stressed-out culture needs: the fight to be *lowlier* than thou.

As we sing "Praise the Lord from the heavens," Father Gregory bows to us and says, "Forgive me my sins, brothers and sisters." He turns to receive Communion.

There was a time when I wanted to be the one up there. I went to Episcopal seminary in the seventies hoping to be ordained a priest; I pictured my husband and me serving side by side in a parish. But I was ahead of the curve. The vote in favor of women's ordination had just passed, and the bishops we wrote to, asking for ordination, either were still opposed to the practice, or were so swamped with female applicants that they could take in no more. The clock was ticking, graduation was looming, I was pregnant, and we had to make a decision so that at least *one* of us could be ordained and begin supporting the family. That one, obviously, had to be my husband.

To my surprise, I felt relieved. Though I'd been fantasizing about ordination for a couple of years, deep inside I always doubted whether I actually had a calling. I found other outlets for ministry and felt satisfied in roles that didn't require ordination. We had no objections to women's ordination: over the years we sent several female parishioners to seminary and hired women on the church staff. When we became Orthodox, the all-male priesthood was a tradition we accepted along with the rest of the package, without really understanding its significance.

Once inside the Orthodox house, however, I found that the different element had not to do with my husband's role but my own. Before, as a "pastor's wife," my role was chiefly social. In Orthodoxy, I discovered, it was spiritual. I was the mother of the parish, honored with the title "khouria." (The Greeks use the word "presbytera," and Russians use "matushka," which mean respectively "priest's wife" and "little mother.") This Church prefers parish priests be married, and the husband and wife together present a leadership pair analogous to a father and mother in a home.

It had always seemed to me that the argument that the priesthood should be all-male because Jesus was male was a weak one. If the office of priest is meant to replicate the Incarnation, wouldn't it have to do so in every respect? A man would only qualify to be a priest if he shared Jesus' height, weight, and eye color. Now I gained a different perspective on this role. The priest represented not just Jesus but the Father. "Every good endowment and every perfect gift is from above, coming down from the Father of lights" (James 1:17). The distinctive thing done by a priest, not permitted to laity, is the handling of the holy gifts, the sacraments. The one who offers the sacred mysteries of bread and wine stands in the place of the Father from whom all gifts come. A woman who stood there would inevitably be a Mother, bringing a subtle shift to the meaning of the priesthood. A parish can benefit from having both mother and father, which is why the married priesthood is a good thing.

There was a point in my feminist journey when I insisted that men and women were the same. As time passed, as I lived with the same man for decades and gave birth to sons, I realized that this isn't true. I began to see that the difference between men and women is something wonderful, something fascinating and delightful, something that quite literally creates new life. There's no sense delineating roles down to minute levels—my husband cooks, I handle the budget—but in some broad, overarching areas an engagement with the realities of gender difference can be fruitful and positive, even enjoyable. I enjoy being in a Church with an all-male priesthood.

This would not be so if I felt in any way diminished, or if there were an overall disparagement of women. In fact, since becoming Orthodox I have been more welcomed to speak, write, and exercise my gifts throughout the Church than I ever was in my Protestant denomination. In Orthodoxy, laymen and laywomen stand on equal spiritual footing. At Holy Cross (though not in every Orthodox church) women do everything men do, aside from altar service: lead the choir, serve on the parish council, read the epistle, chant, paint icons, and teach both children and adults.

This equality is an intrinsic part of the Christian faith. Some writings of the early Church warn against women as temptations to sexual sin, but these messages were most often written to monks who were being reminded to resist every sort of sin from gluttony to lying to spiritual pride. They found women tempting, whether women intended to be or not, and so self-control was essential; when the tempting quality was attributed to the woman herself, it was in the same sense a weak-willed dieter calls a chocolate cake "sinful."

A better example of the early Church's treatment of women could be seen in the balance with which they handled the sin of adultery. The law of the Roman empire allowed men to divorce their wives for adultery, but women were not permitted to divorce their husbands for the same reason. St. Gregory the Theologian criticized that inequality: "I do not accept that legislation; I do not praise the custom. It was men who made that law, and on this account they legislated only as against the women." St. Basil the Great agreed in rejecting sexist Roman law, and St. John Chrysostom insisted that a married man was guilty of adultery even if his mistress was unmarried—the sin, after all, was not merely against that woman's husband but against his own wife.

St. Gregory Nazianzen wrote similarly. "The Creator of man and woman is one and the same Being. Both of them are of one and the same clay. One and the same law governs them both. There is but one resurrection. We have been born quite as much by a woman as by a man; children owe their parents a single debt . . . Christ saved them both with his passion. He became flesh for man, but also for woman. He died for man, but woman too is saved through his death. Perhaps you think that he honored man because he was born of David's seed. But by being born of the Virgin he honored woman. 'They shall be one flesh,' it says [Genesis 2:24]: that one flesh accordingly must deserve equal honor."

In classic Christianity women are honored as saints, churches are named after women, icons of women are venerated, and the woman who was Jesus' mother is honored as the Captain Leader of all believers. Though the faith is often presumed to be hostile to women, its track record is actually pretty good. John Updike compared the status of women in Christianity with their status in other faiths: "[O]n the question of women . . . Judeo-Christianity, as it has evolved in history, compares well with other cultural constructs. It was not Christianity that condoned, as late as 1910, foot-binding, a fashionable torture inflicted on female children, or the habit of female infanticide, which skews China's gender balance even now. It is not Christianity that in parts of Africa promotes clitoridectomy as a means to properly shaped femininity. It is not Christianity that inflicts upon women, as in Iran and Afghanistan, hysterical restrictions that inhibit their access to employment, education, social life, and even medical care." In the West, as we have seen, women fill Christian pews so enthusiastically that they far outnumber men, and we can presume they are there because they like it.

There are only males behind the iconostasis, my husband and altar boys. There is a last reason why I think this is a good thing, though it isn't a spiritual one. It's that nature doesn't give a very clear role for men in life. Women's part in reproduction is extensive and obvious and impossible to ignore. Men are comparatively negligible, disposable after the first fifteen minutes of fatherhood. The job of any culture is to find a role for men that directs all that strength and energy in ways that do not hurt women or each other.

Nature aids us in this. Men seem to be born with an instinctive sense that they *are* comparatively disposable, that their lives are not as valuable as women's, and they should voluntarily risk those lives when women and children are in danger. This is a good thing for women, and we maintain it by treating it as a gift we appreciate. Men likewise have an impulse to provide for women and children; only a tiny percentage have jobs that are prestigious or fulfilling, and most labor just in order to put food on the table. They don't have much choice about this, though in many circumstances women are free to choose whether or not to work outside the home. Men are expected to labor and provide no matter what their preferences. (My son David asked me when he was four, "How come girls can be a mommy or a daddy, but boys can only be a daddy?") This construct benefits women, too, and we do well to appreciate men's lifelong submission to more restricted choices than we enjoy.

When, on the other hand, men are not appreciated, when they are routinely demeaned or trivialized, their hunger to attribute meaning to their lives breaks out in less functional, more violent ways. When men cannot visualize for themselves a role of dignity and value, women get hurt. The all-male priesthood has a spiritual meaning, but I would broaden from that to affirm other merely social reasons for giving men a distinctive visible role. In the dance between the sexes, these small recognitions accorded men, often mere formalities, contribute to a sense of dignified responsibility that enables them to behave honorably toward women. Everybody wins.

C. S. Lewis wrote about the transitory dominance of the male in the sex act in "pagan" nature, and of the headship of the husband in Christian marriage, which is predicated on self-emptying love (". . . as Christ loved the Church and gave himself up for her," Ephesians 5:25). "The sternest feminist need not begrudge my sex the crowns offered it either in the Pagan or in the Christian mystery. For the one is of paper and the other of thorns."

As we wind up the "Praise the Lord from the heavens," Father Gregory turns around to face us. He chants, "With fear of God, and faith and love, draw near." It is time to go forward to receive Communion.

CHAPTER 14

Rachel Weeping

AT A PRISON IN COLDWATER

Under the blaring sun, over the cracked asphalt veined with grass, between the brick-cube buildings, I am following a large Econoline van full of ladies. I'm lost on the prison grounds, looking for our orientation session, but I think they must be headed where I'm trying to go, due to their bumperstickers. There's a Jesus fish and some Christian radio stations, and this: "Hurting from abortion? Someone still cares," followed by an 800 number.

Nearly fifty volunteers are coming to this southern Michigan women's prison today to put on a program of music and talks, the kickoff to a series of small group sessions aimed at helping inmates work through post-abortion grief. I'm here in my capacity as a free-lance writer, covering the event for a Christian magazine. Many of the women volunteers, including the event organizer and all the speakers, have had abortions themselves. They are associated with a chain of pregnancy care centers based in Grand Rapids, and are graduates of that organization's post-abortion series, called "Mourning Joy."

I am not sure why they want to do this. When I ask them, they respond with an isn't-it-obvious look and a stream of nurturing terms: post-abortion women are hurting, are in pain, are isolated, have no opportunity to talk about their feelings; they need hope, need help, need healing. It's motherly, the terms they use.

When I ask, "But why prison?" only Sydna has a personal hook. She once befriended a timid neighbor with a strangely hostile husband. One day the woman was murdered by her husband and his girlfriend, and both were convicted and sent to prison. Sydna felt great fury toward the pair, but one day realized she had to somehow forgive them for the sake of her own soul. (She didn't have the authority to forgive the murder itself, of course, but she needed to forgive the murderers for the way their deed had hurt her.) She wrote a letter to the murderous mistress, and an unlikely friendship sprang up.

During one visit, the woman impressed on Sydna the need for counseling behind prison bars. Many women inside prisons, just like those outside, have unresolved grief surrounding abortion. Too often, the abortion was coerced by the male partner, a parent, or simply by unbearable circumstances, and remains in memory as a moment of helplessness and abandonment. To these women, inside or outside prison walls, abortion does not make them feel empowered, but small, defeated, and guilty. The women at this pregnancy care center have experienced these feelings and worked through them, and want to help others come to peace as well.

The brochure each prisoner received asks if they have any symptoms of depression after abortion—nightmares, tears, anger, suici-

dal thoughts. "Do you wonder why you still think about your abortion?" The brochure goes on, "The good news is you can find happiness and healing from the hurt of a past abortion. You're not
alone with this pain. We hope you will join the thousands of
women who have found help. Come and join us for some good music, inspiring stories, and information about abortion recovery
groups that are available to you."

Like most of us, I'd never been to a prison before. We are herded
into a depressing brick educational building on the far side of the
campus from the prisoners for an orientation session. The volunteers are mostly in their twenties and thirties; trim, conservatively
fashionable, wearing Gap-flavored shirts, khakis, and sandals. Jewelry is subdued and hair is not overinflated. (Michigan Christian
women are not Texas Christian women, where, I was told, the coif-
fure rule is: "Bleach it clear, jack it up, and you're set for the day.")
These women are carrying sizable floppy-leather Bibles with titles
like *The Inspiration Bible* and *The Spirit-Filled Life Bible*. Each volume has
been personalized by wear such that it resembles a beloved teddy
bear with the fur rubbed off, and each is stuffed with a personalized
assortment of notes, clippings, photos, and prayer reminders,
which I once heard called "Biblidew."

The ladies gather in friend-clusters among the rows of seats and
begin filling out their identification forms. The room's trim is
painted the Silly Putty color that was inexplicably popular in the
fifties. There is no air conditioning. Immense floor fans push the air
violently from one end of the room to the other, and onstage the
paper on a newsprint easel flaps gaily like a flag.

Chaplain Burgess is a quiet, earnest man, kind but with a
learned wariness, and appealingly bald. As the ladies complete their
forms, he hands out a sheet of "Criteria for Volunteers." Volunteers

"will be working with convicted felons" so they should "Guard Against Manipulation." They should resist "Over-Identification with the Prisoner." They must "Safeguard their Possessions," which means that pocketbooks must be locked in car trunks and car keys turned in at the entry desk. All the volunteers may bring into the prison is their Bible and a pen.

"Some women can come across as being very truthful, and they may not be so," warns Chaplain Burgess. "Ask the Holy Spirit for wisdom." He assures the volunteers that there haven't been any assaults on volunteers, though it's not uncommon for inmates to fight among themselves. "They live in close quarters," he says, somewhat sympathetically. "They could tell you some stories about what it's like, living in such close quarters."

There are some questions about rule number 11, "Touching prisoners is not permitted, other than a handshake." Hugging is popular in Christian events that have a focus on healing. What if the woman starts weeping, thinking about her abortion? What if she prays the Sinner's Prayer and commits her life to the Lord for the first time? Can't you put your arm around her shoulder?

Chaplain Burgess allows that there can be some flexibility with this rule. He explains that he frequently had prisoners rushing toward him, open-armed for a hug. He came up with the tactic of quickly reaching up to grab both hands, then holding them for prayer. But he was reported for holding inmates' hands, and had to stop. At any rate, he says, volunteers may touch prisoners briefly, but should not let contact linger. He doesn't explain why, but I suspect it has to do with preventing visitors from passing prisoners drugs or other contraband. No exceptions, not even for chaplains or us.

It's unknown how the prisoners will respond to tonight's event.

Every inmate was sent an invitation, but only those who decided to accept the invitation and signed up would be allowed to attend. Due to a computer glitch, roughly half of those signing up were accidentally refused permission, and they won't be able to attend tonight. Along with the invitation and brochure, organizers sent each prisoner a four-page survey in tiny print seeking information about their needs, in order to guide planning. Only a handful of prisoners filled out the survey, so organizers are mostly in the dark.

At the appointed hour we shuffle into the entry building of the prison facility. Extending from either side of the building's facade are double rows of ten-foot-high chain-link fencing, each with festoons of razor wire along the top, looping another three feet high. The staff inside the prison has seen our kind before, and affect a weary smirk. Each woman is relieved of everything except her Bible and pen. One staffer flips disgustedly through a volunteer's Bible, which has been stuffed with scraps and mementos till it overflows like a teenager's diary. The book is taken aside to be raked clean of Biblidew. My desire to bring in some paper kicks up controversy, and at last an officer agrees to carry the pad until we're on-site. An escort is assigned to me and the radio reporter to ensure that we do not talk with prisoners; the escort is also under orders not to answer our questions.

I have been thinking lately about imprisonment. As the dust settles around the ruins of the Iron Curtain, books and memoirs are beginning to appear from Orthodox who were persecuted under that regime. Each night I sit in bed before turning out the light, safe and cozy, and read stories that make my hair stand on end.

White-bearded Father George Calciu appears in a photo on the

cover of the book *Christ Is Calling You!* looking spry, almost elfin. His
eyes crinkle above an endearing smile. He endured merciless physical and mental torture in Romanian prisons for sixteen years. From
1948 to 1952, he was held in the dread Pitesti prison, which prac-
ticed the experimental Russian method of "re-education." Prisoners were all young men between the ages of eighteen and
twenty-five—the target group that was to be made over into the
"new man."

In the book, Father George explains to an interviewer that the
Pitesti experiment had four distinct steps. First, a team of guards
and experienced prisoners would beat incoming prisoners and kill
one or two, whoever appeared to be a leader. Next, they would begin to "unmask," which meant requiring prisoners, under torture,
to verbally renounce everything they believed: "I lied when I said, 'I
believe in God,' I lied when I said, 'I love my mother and my father.'"
Third, prisoners were forced to denounce everyone they knew, including family. Because a diabolical element of this plan was to em-
ploy fellow prisoners as torturers, the targeted prisoners knew no
rest. The abuse never ceased, not even in the cell, and every torture
imaginable was employed.

Last, in order to show they had truly become "the communist
man," these prisoners were required to join the ranks of torturers
and assist in the "re-education" of new prisoners. This last step was
the most unbearable. "It was during this fourth part that the majority of us tried to kill ourselves," says Father George.

The experience created a spiritual crisis in Father George, who
until his imprisonment had led an ordinary, reasonably devout life.
"When you were tortured, after one or two hours of suffering, the
pain would not be so strong. But after denying God and knowing
yourself to be a blasphemer—that was the pain that *lasted* . . . We

forgive the torturers. But it is very difficult to forgive ourselves." Though often angry at God, sometimes at night a wash of tears would come, and the prisoner could pray again. "You knew very well that the next day you would again say something against God. But a few moments in the night, when you started to cry and to pray to God to forgive you and help you, was very good."

Years later, Father George attempted to write out his memories of Pitesti but found the endeavor futile. "Sometimes I was hammering at one word, timidly, then persistently, then intensely, to madness. The word became nothing other than a sequence of letters or sounds. It had no meaning. It didn't tell me anything. I would say: 'beating' or 'pain' or 'prayer' or 'curse' . . . and I would substitute one for another without any change; none told me anything! I would say 'cell' and the word would not speak. I could say instead 'lelc' or 'clel' or 'ellc' with the same result. Everything was mute and absurd. And suddenly a curse from that time would resound in my mind, or a song somebody sang during the unmaskings, and the whole atmosphere would install itself with a painfully striking character and with a reality more real than it was then. Affective memory! Proust was a genius in his intuitions, a part of the literature he wrote."

It's time to be rotated into the camp. Volunteers' hands are painted with a liquid that will show up under black light, then we're led by groups into "the bubble," a glass enclosure containing a walk-through metal detector. There we are frisked for contraband; two facial tissues stuffed in a pocket are discovered and removed. Processed volunteers wait for their colleagues in a room with an amateur Disney mural girdling the walls, and a curious framed oil reproduction of a mother and child. Ball-point pen has given the mother one black eye and one monocle, a moustache and goatee. The baby has acquired a v-shaped devil moustache, and matching v-shaped devil brows.

The reassembled pack of volunteers are led past cabinets holding gas masks, down the fenced walkway to the prison auditorium. About fifty prisoners are already there, milling about. Kathy Troccoli, the singer who will begin the program, settles into a seat in one of the back rows and puts up her boots. She's a throaty-voiced Italian from New York with a down-to-earth manner and a big laugh. The prisoners' brochure says she "sings with soulful style" and "has opened for artists such as Michael Bolton, Kenny Loggins, Color Me Badd and comedian Jay Leno."

A plump, graying prisoner comes up to Kathy and confides that she, too, is a singer; she calls herself "The Rebel With the Right Cause."

Troccoli puts her head back and laughs. "That's a new one on me! Well, hi there, 'Rebel With a Cause.' I'm 'Kathy With Jesus.'" The Rebel is invited to sing out a line or two to show off her voice, and she improvises a Gospel refrain. Troccoli immediately jumps in behind her, echoing the lines with a harmony way below. "We're gonna sing together tonight," she tells the surprised inmate. "Now, don't tell anybody!"

The audience shuffles into place, and Chaplain Burgess appears on stage to announce the first event of the evening, a song from the prison choir. Twenty women file on stage in a semicircle, wearing chevron-collared brown robes. A large young woman the color of bittersweet chocolate steps forward to begin the hymn; she bellows a line, and the clapping, swaying women behind her respond: "Spirit of the Lord, fall down!" Most of the choir is black, but along the curve on the right there is a thin, pale girl with a bandanna knotted tight over her apparently bald head. She doesn't clap; she looks weak. Overhead a banner reads "Journey to Hope & Healing."

The first speaker, Sydna, hits the right note: "Wow, how do you follow an act like that? I hope you are ready for the Spirit to come down!" The audience responds with immediate whoops and "Amen"s. The self-selected audience is enthusiastically ready to receive what the volunteers have come to bring—a huge relief to the volunteers, I'm sure. Sydna then reads a scripture that is a favorite with post-abortion counselors:

> "Thus says the LORD:
> 'A voice is heard in Ramah,
>   lamentation and bitter weeping.
>   Rachel is weeping for her children;
>   she refuses to be comforted for her children,
>   because they are not.'

> "Thus says the LORD:
> 'Keep your voice from weeping,
>   and your eyes from tears;
>   for your work shall be rewarded, says the LORD,
>   and they shall come back from the land of the enemy.
>   There is hope for your future, says the LORD,
>   and your children shall come back to their own country.'"
>   (Jeremiah 31:15–17)

"We're here for life," Sydna tells the prisoners. "Some of us have not chosen life for our unborn children. We are post-abortion women. But we know that there is no sin that God can't forgive."

Next Kathy climbs onto the stage, looks around, and says, "This is too far away." She hops down to the floor in front of the audience. "I'm Italian, so I have to come down here," she says. She knocks into a song that repeats the line "I call him Love," and by the second chorus the crowd is eagerly engaged. Some are standing and swaying, some sit with arms in the air and eyes blissfully closed, and many do their best to sing along. Near me a young woman suddenly takes a deep breath and rocks backward, as if hit by an insight that startles her. She starts to cry. She could be another Kathy—attractive, youthful, with brunette hair pinned up in tousled curls. Her friend, an elderly black woman, puts a consoling arm around her shoulders.

By halfway through the second song the party is in full swing. "We're going to do some 'Oh's together," Troccoli announces. "Here we go!" On cue, the crowd sings back, "O-oh, o-oh, o-o-o-oh!" It's hard to gauge what percentage of emotion in the room is joy and what is sorrow; tears are everywhere, and may be expressing both simultaneously. Rolls of toilet tissue are passed back and forth down the rows; inmates aren't allowed boxed tissue. Hands slap a hearty beat, and the pale girl in the bandanna taps her hands together softly. She is wearing a "WWJD" bracelet: "What Would Jesus Do?" As Kathy sings "Go Light the World," women hold up fingers as if they were candles. A large prisoner with short-cropped gray hair, in a green tank top that reveals the Betty Boop tattoo on her back, holds her candle high.

I'm odd-woman-out, in a way. Compared to what I've grown used to in recent years, this worship experience seems truncated, bereft of awe, cartoonish. It is so drunk with emotion that it rocks and disorients, disrupting any attempt to render prayerful attention to ultimate things. But this is not an evening designed to reach me.

The prisoners obviously love it; they're having a whale of a good time, rocking out on Friday night, exuberant.

The custody officers take the opposite approach and stand against the wall, arms folded, smacking gum. Every one, refrigerator-sized men and fireplug-sized women, has gum; perhaps it is part of the Michigan prison guard uniform. Both the men and the women maintain expressions of disdain. There are three groups here: the volunteers offering a tender, hopeful gift, the prisoners hollering out their good time, and the officers leaning against the wall, mauling gum in their jaws. I don't seem to fit exactly anywhere. Though I'd love to go out and have a beer with Kathy.

Father Roman Braga also spent several years in Pitesti. The charge against him and his colleagues was inventive: they were suspected of trying to overthrow the government by discussing the writings of St. Basil the Great, St. John Climacus, and St. Gregory of Nyssa. Like Father George, he found the torments at Pitesti to be beyond description. "I cannot speak about this prison because it would take volumes to describe the horrors," Father Roman said in an interview published as *Exploring the Inner Universe.* "They used not only physical torture, but especially psychological pressure. They were experts in keeping people on the border between sanity and insanity. There are former inmates of this prison who even now are still out of their minds."

Father Roman spent his first year in Pitesti in solitary confinement, and there he learned to pray. "We will never reach the same spiritual level of life as in communist imprisonment," he says. In solitary confinement there was nothing to see but four walls. "You had to go somewhere; you had to find an inner perspective, because otherwise you would truly go crazy. I'm ashamed to say that I was forced to find myself in prison . . . Only then was I able to discover how beautiful the interior life of man is. I liked it very much."

Under the strictures of solitude, Father Roman found his memory functioning with great clarity, and he could recall long passages from spiritual books. "I experienced such joys in prison, I could not detach myself from them. I was never interested when they brought me food or water. I took the ideas out of my memory to transform them into spiritual food, especially since I did not know if I would ever be liberated. When you are not sure that you will escape alive, then everything refers to yourself and eternity."

In 1978, Father George Calciu defied the communist government again, and was once again imprisoned. He had preached a bold series of sermons to students, though fellow priests, Church hierarchs, and the seminary administration all warned him to stop. They locked the church; he preached in the courtyard. They locked the gates; students climbed over the walls. Father George went to prison knowing that Ceausescu wanted to kill him, but his cellmates assigned to that task refused. Eventually he was freed, thanks to protests by Romanians in exile like Eugene Ionescu and Mircea Eliade, and pressure from the U.S. government. Both he and Father Roman are now living in America.

Father George's first seven months of this more recent imprisonment were in solitary confinement. During this time he feared that he was forgetting how to speak; his grasp of language seemed to be evaporating. He tried to befriend a fly in his cell by putting out some bread, but "her commotion exhausted me." Next, he tried talking to a spider, but "he paid no attention to me. Absolutely none! Not to my words, not to my presence—he was not impressed by me," Father George laughs. Finally, recalling the relationship between the Fox and the Prince in *The Little Prince*, Father George began with great patience and diligence to befriend a cockroach. Gradually the roach grew brave enough to venture near and eat the priest's offered breadcrumbs. "He was amazing, like a monster. If you look at him from up close, he is like a monster. Little by little I began to talk to him, and he actually came to visit me for weeks, until my isolation came to an end. I was saved in my ability to remember my language by this cockroach."

Between songs, Kathy talks about faith in Jesus. "Whether you're in here or out there, if you don't have Jesus, you don't have anything." A solid roar of agreement comes back to her. Then she calls out, "Hey, Rebel With a Cause! You come up here!" The beaming woman, in a denim prison uniform and a red bandanna tied about her round head, bounds onto the stage. When Kathy invites her to lead off in song, she first rolls her eyes to the ceiling and prays loudly, "Help me, Holy Ghost!" Then she sings a line in a clear voice: "The Spirit of the Lord is liberty!" Kathy rolls it back at a bass level. "In Jesus Christ I've been set free!" Again the response.

After the duet, Kathy asks the crowd to give a hand to the pregnancy center volunteers, which brings on an immediate standing ovation with loud cheers. She follows this by introducing a more serious song, one she says took her ten years to write: "A Baby's Prayer." The lyrics are spoken in the voice of an unborn child.

This I usually hate. I understand, at least intellectually, the desire to give the unborn child a chance to speak for herself. But in realization these songs and poems are nearly always cloying. Kathy talks, more than sings, the lyrics, in an unusually deep voice for a baby: "I can hear her talking to a friend, I think it's all about me;

how she can't have a baby now . . ." The song concludes with the aborted child asking the Lord to remind her mother that she is now in a place far from earthly pain: "On the days when she may think of me, please comfort her with the truth: That the angels hold me safe and sound, 'cause I'm in heaven with you." This song is followed by grave applause and teary eyes. A couple of prisoners are holding rolls of toilet paper and scanning the crowd, looking for someone in need. Their attitude is attentive and benign, eager to be helpful, and when they spot someone ready to wipe her eyes or blow her nose, they rush toward her with satisfaction. It's that same motherly streak I saw in the volunteers earlier. Women want to do this for each other; they want to do it for *somebody*. It's literally in their genes.

Kathy is wiry and athletic, but after one last rousing song she's sweating heavily. She winds up with an invitation to faith. "Without Jesus, I would want to be dead," she says bluntly. "Give your life to Jesus. I don't mean that the same way you've always heard it. He's a real God, he rose from the dead, and no matter where you are on this planet, he has life abundant for you."

Three speakers then recount the stories of their abortion experiences. Janina, a young Latina, says, "I did a lot of drugs and alcohol, and my boyfriend Peter and I were just not ready for a baby. I was afraid to tell my mom, because it would be just one more disappointment." When she finally did tell, her mom ticked off all the reasons she couldn't have the baby, then made an appointment for an abortion. "Everything inside was telling me to keep the baby, but everyone I knew was telling me not to."

The abortion did not make everything all right. "Since that day I've never been the same," Janina says. "I went back to partying, trying to numb my feelings. My favorite was LSD, because it kept me high the longest." Eventually she married Peter, but their early years of marriage were "terrible," she says. "Then Peter's cousin began writing to us from prison, telling us about the Lord. 'I'm in prison, but so are you,' he'd say. 'You're in prison to your guilt and shame.'"

Janina and Peter came to Christian faith, but Janina could never quite believe that her abortion was forgivable. A year ago she heard a radio advertisement for the "Mourning Joy" abortion grief group and signed up for the course. Peter has gone through the classes now, too. "On May seventeenth, the anniversary of my abortion, Peter and I went to the cemetery where they have a monument to the unborn. For the first time, we mourned our son."

A professional-looking black woman, Renee, next takes the stage, saying that she is nervous because she's never told her story before. "Do you know that song 'Amazing Grace, how sweet the sound that saved a wretch like me'?" she begins, patting her chest at the word "wretch." The hymn was written by a former slave trader, she explains, "who brutalized, maimed, and murdered. I know about that, because I brutalized, maimed, and murdered my children. Five of them," she says, holding up her hand with fingers spread.

"When I was eighteen I met a man," Renee goes on, who taught her how to use and sell drugs, and how to pass bad checks. She had two abortions with him. "Then I met a man who shot heroin, and who asked me to prostitute myself to make money"—a request she refused, though she did give him the money she earned at her job. She had two more abortions with him. "You know how we give up control to a man, and let him lead us to a place?" The women listening know this very well, and say so.

"But my mother was praying for me," Renee begins—and can't go on, because a wave of joyful, grateful shouts has propelled her listeners, applauding, to their feet. As it dies down, she reminds them that sometimes it takes years for the effects of prayer to get through. "I met another man—a married man—and had another abortion." Though devastated inside, she kept her appearance up, striving to look good on the outside.

"Do you know the woman in the Bible, the prostitute who had an alabaster jar of fragrant ointment? She would use that on herself to cover up her sins. And then one day, she met a man . . ."

The crowd sees what's coming and begins to cheer. "And I met that same man—and his name is Jesus—" Renee has to wait for order to return. "And she poured that fragrance out for him. That's a man that'll love you, just the way you are."

Renee says she was numb to the effects of her abortions, until she happened to see a film that showed a sonogram of an abortion. "When I saw that little baby's mouth open in a scream, I wailed for that baby," Renee says, and begins to weep. From the side a prisoner comes up, gratified to be helpful, and hands her a roll of toilet paper. At this Renee gives a rueful smile. "I thought it was just tissue. Well, *this*,"—holding up a wad—"is tissue." If she'd had cancer, she says, she would have researched it at the library. But with the abortion, she preferred not to know too much.

"The devil hates women," Renee concludes. "Genesis tells us there is enmity between the woman and the serpent. That's why there have been thirty-seven million abortions in this country, because the devil is working. It's our job, the hurting women, to reach out to other women and tell them, 'You don't have to do this.'"

Finally, Terri addresses the crowd. Her neat appearance and cheerful demeanor make her testimony all the more astonishing. "I did drugs—shooting speed was my drug of choice—used alcohol, joined a motorcycle gang, got into Buddhism, had a brush with Satanism, and had two pregnancies. I had an abusive stepfather who was already calling me a slut, and if he knew I was pregnant it would just confirm that. So, twice, I chose abortion." She gradually grew so dejected she decided on suicide. "I looked in the mirror and saw a loser, a failure of no use to anybody." One night she lined up her pills and vodka, planning to combine them and end it all. But at that moment she remembered some women who had witnessed to her, and instead made a decision to turn to the Lord.

Yet, like Janina, Terri kept one part of her life hidden away—her abortions. Deep inside, she said, worries assailed her: "When I get to heaven, how am I going to face my kids? How am I going to explain to them why I let them be killed in such a horrible way?" A friend counseled her to trust Jesus to convey the truth of her love to her children so that she could begin to accept forgiveness.

After this, Terri began to feel more freedom. She was working as a volunteer with prisoners, and one day found herself addressing a group of men condemned to Death Row. She tells her audience that she said to those men, "'My first baby was so far along in development that when it was aborted it had to be dismembered. Whatever you're in here for, whatever you did, it was not as bad as that—that a mother would allow that to be done to her own innocent baby. And you're in here, and I'm not, because society doesn't see my crime the way it sees yours.

"'But there is a holy God'," Terri quotes herself as telling the death-row inmates. She points one finger up, and the audience interrupts her with cheers. "'I know I deserve the same punishment you do. Now let me tell you about a Savior.'"

Terri leads the group through three steps on the "Journey to Hope & Healing." First, she says, each woman should turn to Jesus Christ as her personal savior. Some already know this step; as Terri recites supporting Scriptures, several voices in the audience chime in. "Second, admit it wasn't a 'procedure,' it was wrong! I killed two unborn children, and it was wrong! You've got to have the courage to admit it." Abortion grief counselors have discovered the importance of this step; women who spend their energy blaming the abortion on others delay their own resolution. Often, others were complicit, or may have even coerced the decision. But it is in owning her personal responsibility that a woman breaks through. Third, Terri says, forgive yourself, the last link in the chain. Even though there is forgiveness, there may still be some consequences that will never change. "I'm going to turn fifty this year," Terri says. "I've never been married. I'll never give birth to a child."

During the communist years, unauthorized religious writings circulated in carbon-copy form, the so-called "samizdat" or "self-published" books. One such book bears the name *Father Arseny: Priest, Prisoner, Spiritual Father* and is a collection of reminiscences of a priest of extraordinary holiness, written by those who knew him both in and out of prison. These stories were compiled by "the servant of God, Alexander," and circulated privately for years. With the fall of communism, four hundred thousand copies have been printed in Russia, and it has recently been published in English.

Father Arseny, before his ordination, was an art historian, author, and professor. What turned him to accept the risky life of a Christian and a priest is unknown. He was imprisoned for most of the Stalin era, in one of the "special" camps for the worst criminals and "incorrigible" political prisoners, a prison from which inmates were not intended to emerge alive. Vera Bouteneff, the translator of *Father Arseny,* writes: "Since the fall of the Soviet regime, it has been revealed that six hundred bishops, forty thousand priests, and one hundred twenty thousand monks and nuns were killed during this period . . . By the end of Stalin's dictatorship, only some two hundred priests remained active in the Soviet Union."

Father Arseny's appeal lies in his compelling character—humble, prayerful, and loving, even when treated with violence and abuse. Many of the anecdotes collected here are recounted by criminals, communist officials, and guards who were converted by the priest's luminous witness and unresting kindness. To read these stories, told by so many different voices, is to see Christ walking in our day, a non-sappy illustration of "What Would Jesus Do?" The book conveys the amazing good news that it is possible for an ordinary human being to embody the spirit of Jesus.

Many of these recollections are of incidents showing near-superhuman love, but some of them cross the line into the frankly supernatural. Once Father Arseny was thrown with a young man, Alexei, into a punishment cell—a three-by-six cabin lined with metal. The temperature was -22 degrees F, and the only way to survive was to jump up and down for the entire period they were confined—in this case, forty-eight hours. The young man collapsed, wailing that they were going to die. Father Arseny began to pray.

Alexei told the story later. He was at the point of death when suddenly he felt all his pain and fear disappear. The blackened cell which had been lit only by a shaft of moonlight was filled with brilliant light. Father Arseny stood praying, no longer clothed in his patched gray cotton vest but in white garments like the ones Alexei had once seen on a priest, the one time he went to church as a child. Two other figures in white stood beside the priest and served with him in prayer.

"Go, Alyosha! Lie down, you are tired. I will keep praying, you will hear me," Father Arseny told him. Alexei lay on the metal floor and listened to the priest pray. He found somehow he knew the words of the prayers and could follow Father Arseny in saying them. He felt flooded with warmth and happiness. Two days and nights passed. Only when someone knocked against the door, trying to turn the frozen lock, did the figures in white bless Father Arseny and Alexei and depart. The guards had come to drag out the frozen cadavers, and instead found the prisoners rested and radiant, with a thick coating of frost on their clothing.

Stories like this stream through this little book, passed hand to hand for decades. Alexander Avsenkov was a deposed communist official; he had, in fact, signed Father Arseny's sentence. Reduced to terrible circumstances in the camp, he found Father Arseny to be a friend. One night a young prisoner was late to roll call and scurried about trying to find his place in line. Guards knocked him down, and one began beating him and kicking him with his boot.

At this, Avsenkov says, Father Arseny stepped out of line, made the sign of the cross over the guard beating the young man, and announced, "In the name of the Lord, I am ordering you to stop!" The guard stopped the beating immediately. Father Arseny then turned and blessed everyone present with a wide sign of the cross and stepped back in line. The guard went back to counting prisoners.

"Did you see what Father Arseny did?" Avsenkov asked a fellow prisoner.

"Did what? He was standing as still as a statue," came the reply.

Some of the stories touch particularly on women's concerns. One spiritual daughter of Father Arseny recounts how a man dragged her into a forest to rape her. Terrified, she continuously whispered the prayer to the Theotokos, "To thee our Captain,

Queen of War." The man repeatedly halted in his attack, looked up as if he saw someone, then dragged the girl to a different part of the forest. Eventually he gave up and, to her amazement, escorted her safely back to the door of her apartment.

One year later the man returned and humbly asked her to forgive him. Then, seeing an icon of the Theotokos on the wall, he exclaimed, "She's the one!" While in the forest, he explained, he had been frightened by a woman who kept appearing standing near the girl, ordering him with a commanding gesture to stop.

Another woman tells of delivering letters from Father Arseny to his spiritual children. She realized she was being followed by a KGB agent and could not risk leading the woman to the homes of these believers, nor ditch the letters and have the addresses be confiscated, nor return home and be arrested holding the letters. In a quandary, she walked on and on at random, praying. Suddenly, when she turned a corner, another young woman stepped out beside her—wearing the same coat and kerchief, carrying the same pocketbook, as identical as a twin, except that her face was full of "an extraordinary light." The agent, catching up behind them, was startled but continued to follow from a distance. As they turned a corner, the twin whispered a command: "Stop here and stand. I will keep walking." Moments later the agent rushed up, looked the letter-carrier over, then scurried after the identical figure ahead.

A year later, the letter-carrier was brought before the police for questioning. The interrogator kept demanding to be told how she had pulled off this stunt. The woman agent angrily insisted that after following the twin for ten minutes "she suddenly simply disappeared into thin air . . . it was just like a disappearing act in the circus."

"'Well, I do not know!'" the letter-carrier replied. "'The Mother of God saved me. I had been walking and praying to her all the time.' The interrogator started laughing but didn't hit me any more."

As Laurie, the project director, wraps up the evening, she says, "We're woman-to-woman here, that's what we're about. Our prayer counselors want to talk with you tonight one-on-one and tell you there's help, there's hope, there's healing. But it's not just so you'll feel good tonight; we want to stay with you, we want to know you. We're going to be coming here for ten weeks, because we want to go through the issues of your life with you." The prisoners react with loud applause, as if this is unprecedented good news. "This lady over here did it for me," says Laurie, pointing to a friend, "and we want to do it for you!"

She now points to the front row on her left. "Look at these ladies over here," she says, and the five volunteers there sit up straighter, while the rest of the room cranes their necks in that direction.

"They've all had abortions. So have I," Laurie went on. "That's why we're here. We want to talk and pray with you. God is your Father and he loves you, and he has sent his Son for you. We want to get to know you and to help you get to know him."

How distinctively feminine this entire event has been—the motherly concern for each other, the emphasis on sharing burdens, the confident belief that just talking things over with a loving friend can be healing. There has not been particular rigor in the theology espoused tonight—just a blanket "Jesus loves you." There has been a lot of talk about resolving guilt feelings toward one's aborted babies by giving them names, sending them messages through Jesus, telling them you're sorry. Some of this sounds speculative to me, but I'm sure it must be comforting.

Perhaps comfort is the necessary first thing before any other change can be made. The sky is a brilliant cobalt blue as the volunteers troop out again, around 10:00 P.M. The air is clear and cool. The beams from a hundred floodlights set the razor wire shimmering like silver.

"This Is a Hard Saying"

10:54 AM: RECEIVING COMMUNION

Father Gregory is standing on the platform just in front of the iconostasis, holding the large golden chalice with its enamel medallions. Subdeacon Gregory stands on the left and my son David on the right, holding a red cloth up under the chin of each person. Communicants step in to close that circle, crossing their arms over their chests. Father Gregory says, "The servant of God, John, . . ." or "The handmaiden of God, Mary, partakes of the precious and all-holy Body and Blood of our Lord and God and Savior Jesus Christ, unto the remission of sins and unto life everlasting." At the same time he uses the long golden spoon to place in the communicant's mouth a morsel of wine-soaked bread, now become the Body and Blood of Christ.

Lillian goes first, leaning on Vince's arm. She is eighty-nine years old, and they were hard years, running a restaurant, raising kids, and putting up with a temperamental husband. She was sustained not only by her faith but by a vision. Lillian once told me the story, in her Baltimore accent:

"When this happened I was sixteen years old and had been out of the hospital about a week. I had got lung and kidney trouble, and I caught pneumonia with it, and was in the hospital almost a year. They still thought I wasn't going to live, even though I come out of the hospital; they still thought I could go anytime. While I was still in the hospital one doctor left and went to Europe, and when he come back, he come in the room and he says, 'Are you still living?'

"So I was home, on the second floor of our house, out on the porch. I had gotten out of bed and walked out there, and I was looking up, and all of a sudden I saw this ladder coming down from the sky, and people coming up and down like angels dressed all in white.

"And I screamed! My mother come outside, she says, 'What's the matter? What's the matter?'

"I says, 'Look at that ladder with all those angels coming up and down!'

"She says, 'I don't see anything.'

"I says, 'Well, I do!' I could still see it.

"I didn't know what it was. It was wide open in the sky, no trees or clouds around it or nothing. I looked around other places, I didn't see anything else, but straight ahead, on the east, a ladder. I looked at it until it just faded away. At first I was afraid of it, then afterwhile I says, 'Well, I guess I am gonna live now.'

"I didn't know what it was. Later I saw an icon of Jacob's ladder and it looked very familiar to me. I felt seeing this ladder was a gift to me and that I should try to do what is right the rest of my life. I had peace, oh yes."

We all expect Lillian to go first to Communion and Annette second, and so she comes up next, leaning on Andy's arm. Behind Annette, families are getting in line, and the choir will be last of all. I watch and pray for each person as they receive, all of us members of a spiritual family sharing this journey in the ark called Holy Cross. Just to the left of the altar, as people leave the chalice, stands Luke holding a large basket full of bread cut into large cubes. People take pieces for themselves, or to give to visitors. This is the remainder of the round loaves that my husband prayed over earlier today, when he removed the square center portion to be the "Lamb" for Communion. This remaining bread is blessed, though not consecrated, and though only Orthodox may receive Communion, through this bread others can share with us in the ommon loaf.

Behind the iconostasis, Zach refreshes the incense. As the long line of people filter up we sing a couple of hymns, then the simple refrain, "Receive the Body of Christ, taste the fountain of immortality." After each refrain, Stephen chants a verse from the sixth chapter of John. Babies know about receiving from a spoon, and I see little Mary Elizabeth open wide.

Everyone seems pretty serene considering the strange thing we're doing. We believe we are literally eating the flesh and blood of Jesus—of God himself. At our last Protestant church, a member family once had a French exchange student stay with them. One Sunday they brought her to church with them and explained to her about the Communion service. Her reaction was one of horror: "It sounds like vampires!"

To be honest, this is the most reasonable first reaction. In the sixth chapter of John's gospel, Jesus insists, "Unless you eat the flesh of the Son of Man and drink his blood, you have no life in you . . . he who eats my flesh and drinks my blood has eternal life, and I will raise him up at the last day." Some disciples were so offended at this they would no longer follow Jesus. To make it worse, John records that Jesus didn't use the usual term for eating, "phago," but "trogo," to munch and grind in the teeth like a cow chews a cud. It's a graphic term, putting the listener on more intimate terms with the process than might be comfortable.

Christianity is not just a mental or spiritual endeavor, not just about acquiring the right ideas or right level of spiritual enlightenment. It involves the body too. Christians believe that at the end of time there will be a resurrection of the body, and we will be reunited with bodies that have been transformed, in much the way a seed is transformed by germination, sprouting, and growth. There is continuity between earthly body and heavenly body, as between seed and plant; but the plant is a completion and culmination that could never have been imagined by one who was familiar only with seeds.

Even in a body-positive culture, the idea of disciples munching and chewing the body of their leader would naturally be disturbing. Rumors grew and mutated. Early Christians were accused of cannibalism; it was thought they hid a baby in a bag of flour and beat it to death, then ate it. This appears to be a jumble composed of several details of the faith: the baby born in a manger, the bread of the Eucharist, the belief that we partake of the Body of Christ himself. But because the actual practice of Christians was kept secret from those outside the faith (before Communion, we pray, "I will not speak of thy mystery to thine enemies"), these misunderstandings could not be decisively cleared up.

As rumors spread, disgust and horror at Christians followed, and persecution naturally came next. A typical group of Christians was arrested in Lyons, France, in 177 A.D. One of their number wrote regarding the charges against them, "They accused us of feeding on human flesh like Thyestes and of committing incest like Oedipus, as well as other abominations which it is unlawful for us to even think of, and which we can scarcely believe ever to have been perpetrated by men."

This account of the martyrdom at Lyons was written by survivors shortly after the events occurred and has been called "the pearl of Christian literature of the second century." It tells how the persecution gradually came about; first Christians were the object of a whisper campaign, then they were rejected socially and in the marketplace, then they were subjected to public insults and taunting. Next believers' goods were plundered, and they themselves were beaten and stoned, in an expanding range of hate crimes.

At that point the government took up the cause. Christians were questioned, imprisoned, and subjected to torture in an attempt to erase their convictions. When the accusations of cannibalism were made public, it was a final blow. Many who had stood up for the besieged community till then changed their minds, and would no longer visit them in prison or support them. Some of the prisoners panicked under this pressure, renounced their faith, and went free.

So there clustered in the Lyons prison a reduced, beleaguered group of men and women, deprived of all earthly encouragement. The company was particularly worried about one of their number, a slave named Blandina; she seemed weak, and they feared she might give way under torture and renounce her faith. "But she was endued with so much power that even those who in relays tortured her from morning till evening grew faint and weary." During these torments,

Blandina kept repeating, "I am a Christian, and nothing vile is done amongst us."

These martyrs weren't killed merely because their persecutors were bad guys. If what was rumored about them was true, torture and execution would have seemed justifiable to citizens of the time. Authorities truly believed that Christians were practicing loathsome atrocities, and that society had to be cleansed of their noxious presence. Christians, for their part, were left with the frustrating task of proving a negative.

In Lyons, this circle of Christians was unable to prove it. One by one the men and women were killed by cruelly amusing devices, as a jeering crowd looked on. Attalus was strapped to an iron chair and roasted alive. He cried out, "This is in truth a consuming of human flesh—and it is you who do it! We neither eat men nor commit any other enormity!" As the days passed, the martyrs' example of humility, of praying for their persecutors, began to strengthen wavering minds. Gradually, most of those who had renounced their faith returned to prison voluntarily and rejoined the martyrs. A physician named Alexander, who had apostatized to gain his freedom, was so moved by the combats that he sat in the stands each day calling out encouragement to the martyrs. This behavior had to be noticed eventually, and when the governor challenged him, Alexander announced himself a Christian. He was tortured to death the next day.

At last only two of the company remained. "On the last day of the single combats, Blandina was again brought into the amphitheater with Ponticus, a boy of about fifteen. They had been compelled day after day to watch the torture of the rest, and were now urged to swear by the idols. Because they refused and set them at naught, the multitude pitied neither the age of the boy nor the sex of the woman. They exposed them to all the torments, endeavoring unsuccessfully from time to time to induce them to swear [and renounce their faith]. Ponticus, encouraged, as the heathen could see, by the exhortations of his sister, nobly endured every torment and then gave up the ghost.

"The blessed Blandina last of all, like a mother of high degree, after encouraging her children and sending them on before as victors to the King, hastened to join them—rejoicing and triumphing over her departure as if she had been summoned to a marriage-feast instead of being cast to the beasts. After the scourges, after the wild animals, after the frying-pan, she was thrown at last into a net and exposed to a bull. When she had been tossed for a time by the beast, and was completely upheld by her faith and her communing with Christ as to have become insensible to what was being done to her, she too was immolated, the heathen themselves confessing that they had never known a woman to show such endurance."

What creates such devotion? No one would do this for a mere great teacher or inspiring example. There is a spiritual power here, a spiritual reality, that only those who have experienced it know, and to outsiders it is foolishness.

To those in the crowd on the day described in John 6, it was revolting. When Jesus spoke of the necessity of eating his flesh and blood, his followers were distressed. "Many of his disciples, when they heard it, said, 'This is a hard saying; who can listen to it?' . . . After this many of his disciples drew back and no longer went about with him" (John 6:60, 66).

Jesus then asked the circle of the twelve, "Do you also wish to go away?" Peter replied, "Lord, to whom shall we go? You have the words of eternal life."

There is a mystery about this, why some people get it, really get it, and others remain on the outside all their lives. It is a mystery Christians have pondered over the millennia. One Protestant explanation seeks to guard first God's sovereignty: that if people don't come to faith in Christ, it's because God doesn't want them to. Whatever the omnipotent God wants, he gets, and he must not want *them*. When this doctrine of predestination is followed to its end, it proposes that God doesn't love everyone but only the saved. The rest are "vessels of wrath made for destruction" (Romans 9:22), lives created solely to be destroyed. One pictures a little boy fashioning soldiers of clay and smashing them with his fist.

This is incomprehensible to me. "God is love" (I John 4:8) is the most durable and fundamental of all Scriptures, a precondition for anything else we attempt to understand. The ancient Church understood a subtle interchange whereby God the Father, hymned repeatedly in our Liturgy as "the lover of mankind," sends his Son to reconcile us to him. We, in turn, either respond or turn away. His grace precedes, follows, and surrounds us, and enables our acceptance of his love—but it never coerces. Everyone is free to refuse this invitation.

What, then, of God's omnipotence? The third-century theologian Origen proposed that somehow God's desire for reunion with all his creation will eventually be satisfied; that even the devil will be reconciled one day and all creation would join in the joys of heaven. This teaching was rejected by the Church as presumptuous, a claim to know what we cannot know, and as turning creatures into mere robots with no freedom to choose, if need be, their own tragedy. (This is why he's not "St. Origen.") We may, however, *hope* that all will come to Christ; we believe that that is Jesus' intent, and that his saving death is effective to reconcile everyone who will agree to come. He came "to seek and save the lost" (Luke 19:10), and the searching is tinged with urgency. Jesus likens it to a shepherd seeking a lost sheep, a woman turning her house upside down to recover a lost coin, and, most poignantly, a father watching day and night for his dissolute son to come home.

This story of the Prodigal Son is perhaps the most beloved of Jesus' parables. In it, a son asked his father to give him his share of the inheritance, and then took off for "a far country" where he soon squandered the entire fortune partying. When the money ran out, the boy was in trouble. He offered himself as a servant to a landowner, and got a job tending swine—one of the ugliest jobs imaginable to a people who held the animal to be unclean. The boy was so hungry he looked enviously on the swill the pigs were given, "and no one gave him anything."

Eventually the son came to his senses. He thought of how even the servants of his father ate better than he did, and resolved to return home. He rehearsed a speech in his mind: "Father, I have sinned against heaven and before you; I am no longer worthy to be called your son; treat me as one of your hired servants."

But while he was still a long way off, his father saw him coming; perhaps the father had been watching every day for his return. The father ran toward his son, embraced him and kissed him. The boy began to deliver his speech, but his father interrupted him: "Bring quickly the best robe and put it on him, and put a ring on his hand, and shoes on his feet, and bring the fatted calf and kill it, and let us eat and make merry; for this my son was dead, and is alive again; he was lost, and is found." And the music and dancing and feasting began.

An icon of this parable shows the son clad in a tunic with a rope belt, and rags wrapped around his feet. He rests his cheek in one hand sorrowfully and tentatively extends the other toward Jesus. And Jesus is running toward him; Jesus' head bends over that of the son, and his arm encircles the young man's shoulder. A scroll tumbles from Jesus' hand: "For this my son was dead and is alive again; he was lost and is found." This is a good icon to keep in mind while preparing to make a confession.

The mystery remains that there are those who don't come home, and those who do. To some, this salvation makes complete sense; either suddenly or gradually it catches fire within them and becomes the compass of their lives. No matter how difficult the way, they never want to cease following, because he has the words of eternal life. It's far from being solely an autonomous human decision. Somehow faith is planted in us by the Holy Spirit, a gift worth asking for: "Ask and it will be given you; seek, and you will find; knock, and it will be opened to you" (Matthew 7:7). Somehow our willingness to receive was preceded by the grace to be willing, and the faith which results is brought to fruition by means beyond our own powers—sometimes, as in my case, mostly against our will.

Once inside the faith, many have a dawning realization that they were being sought all along, an experience poet Francis Thompson described as being pursued by the "Hound of Heaven." It's been said that on the outside of the house of faith the sign over the door reads "Choose this day whom you will serve" (Joshua 24:15) and on the inside the sign reads "You did not choose me, but I chose you" (John 15:16). All I know is, I came home, and I don't ever want to be anywhere else.

The line trickles forward, person by person, old, young, and babies in arms. As I draw up near the front, I pass the large icon of the crucifixion on the side wall, one of Carolyn's first icons. When we were first chrismated, a friend of the parish gave us a tiny round box containing a splinter which the accompanying certificate identified as a fragment of the True Cross. A recess was set into the icon to hold this reliquary. Earlier today a stream of parishioners stood in this spot, praying and setting candles in the copper-lined box of sand, pressing a fingertip kiss to the glass lid of the reliquary. Each candle represents a prayer, and throughout our communal prayer this morning these emblems of individual intercession have been flickering.

As I draw up alongside the icon I see splayed on the floor one of Nicole's stuffed toys, a red crab named Sebastian, a character from Disney's *The Little Mermaid*. Chin down, he is crawling—not toward the altar but toward this icon and its forest of candles. His futile little comma-legs are awry, and one large claw stretches desperately forward while the other dangles useless by his side. Sebastian is, horribly, the color of a crab *that has already been boiled*. The mystery of suffering and adoration unfolds again. Sebastian's large eyes are embarrassed and apologetic, and his huge piano-white teeth cram his improbable jaw with a terrible grin.

At last it's my turn. I step up close, and with my husband and the two holding the red cloth under my chin we make an intimate circle. Father Gregory prays for me, for the remission of my sins and for eternal life. I receive the sacramental bread and wine from the spoon, and it is pungent and sweet. As the prayer ends I lean forward to kiss the medallion of Christ on the chalice. This moment seems suspended, out of time, and full of a rush of sensations and meaning beyond words.

This is Communion: a flowing union with each other, with God, that does not erase individuality but somehow brightens it. In this moment, we each know how beloved we are. The light shines through us, as through stained-glass windows, making each of us more distinct and unique. There is so much to see in this moment, and so much that we cannot see. I recall the prayer earlier, which thanked God for his many gifts to us, "all that we know and do not know." In this suspended moment of tranquillity I can relinquish all I do not know and simply gaze at his beauty.

Where Will You Spend Eternity?

AT A BUFFET IN SELMA

Stephen and I are driving north, weaving back and forth from interstate to country roads, returning from a visit with family on the South Carolina coast. This is my home, the land where I grew up, flat and hot and thickly green. On the back roads trees, bushes, vines, weeds, crowd against windowless shacks, pull down aging billboards, swamp abandoned motels. A large arrow, inscribed "Enter" in defunct neon, points into a wall of thick forest. Green eats everything, even its own: young pines, overwhelmed by kudzu, lean and shamble together like the Burghers of Calais.

Back on the interstate, the South is scrubbed away, pushed behind the outlet malls and enormous plastic motel signs. "Shop and Drop" a North Carolina billboard advises. And eat, of course; reassuringly familiar food is dispensed in bags directly into your car, nearly untouched by human interaction. We were with our Anglican friend from Uganda, Bishop William, the first time his wife joined him on a visit to America. As we turned into a Kentucky Fried Chicken, he explained, "Now watch, Harriet, this is how you get food in America. You scream into a box and then someone hands you food through a window."

Stephen is sporting an emblem of southern food culture, a Krispy Kreme donuts t-shirt, and is mostly full of Krispy Kremes right now. That doesn't mean that he can't make room for an all-you-can-eat buffet, and I'm scanning highway signs for a likely place to stop. Stephen frowns at the manual for the car stereo, still trying to figure out how to get maximum Billy Joel out of this machine. The stereo is new because the car is new (to us, anyway), and the car is new because Stephen wrecked the old one. It was his fault. He'd want you to know that.

He'd only had his license a week when he picked up his girlfriend for a picnic. A light drizzle began to fall as they headed out. When he went to change a tape and accidently drifted into the next lane, he returned both hands to the wheel and then, with a teasing glance at Sarah, jiggled the steering wheel. Immediately the car began to swerve wildly, and when Stephen hit the brakes it spun out of control, sliding across both lanes, down an embankment, spinning back to face traffic. Thank God for Swedish safety-first construction: the car was totaled, but neither kid sustained a scratch. If Stephen and Sarah were all right, I wasn't going to worry overmuch about the car: with 209,000 miles on the odometer, the old station wagon was due for retirement anyway.

But when Stephen got home from the ordeal he was concerned that I didn't realize he had *caused* the accident. I listened to his story, and then said that, though jiggling the steering wheel wasn't an act of genius, the car had always had a tendency to skid if you didn't brake just right; he shouldn't take all the blame. No, he told me, "I am a reckless driver." He stood up, pulled out his wallet, and handed me his shiny-new driver's license. Then, "I'd like you to take me over to Sarah's house so I can tell her parents the accident was my fault."

I looked down at the tiny photo, at the narrow face that I've loved all these years, wondering where this sixteen-year-old got this soldierly fortitude and sense of responsibility. As a little kid, he caused more random destruction and induced more parental hysteria than the older two combined. It was Stephen who clambered atop the highboy bureau at two, who rolled a toy wheelbarrow full of dirt and milk through the living room at four, who came home from fifth grade with a lunch detention notice every day for weeks. (It was Stephen who regularly heard from harried teachers, "Why can't you be more like your older brother?"—David the quiet, serene, attentive, industrious, who left that same fifth-grade classroom having been given the "Christian Character" award by his classmates.)

Yet for all Stephen's wild-man rambunctiousness, he never could bear to get away with anything. An hour after lights-out, he'd be at our bedside, faltering out the whole truth, compelled by a sense of fairness so exacting that he couldn't bear even for himself to escape. Not that this had any curbing effect on his mischief, at least not for many weary, exasperated years. But we could always know that if he'd done something bad, we'd find out before long; he was compelled to complete honesty. (If his older brother or sister had done anything wrong, he'd feel compelled to tell us that, too, the little angel.) His friends know that if there's a disagreement, tension, or misunderstanding in a relationship, Stephen will insist on talking things through to the point of transparency.

In the photo, he looks more intense, more serious, than he is, with dark gray-blue eyes under a prominent brow. Stephen will never be a tall guy, but he's sinewy and well proportioned, with a noble profile contradicted by a dimple in his cheek. This is a souvenir of his running into a wooden swing when he was four. Once my husband was going to anoint the kids with some blessed oil he'd received, and Stephen objected: "I'm afraid it might heal my dimple." God wouldn't take away your dimple, we assured him, your dimple is a good thing. He submitted reluctantly, muttering, "Well, I sure hope Jesus knows that."

As the youngest, he missed the Generation X bandwagon and fell over the line into the following, mystery generation we have yet to get to know. Some elements were distinctive right away. When Megan and David were doing the recycled hippie thing, Stephen was dressing like it's Casual Friday at a hip Manhattan office. The rest of us tend to have a somewhat crumpled and haphazard sartorial style, but even in an outfit completely assembled at a thrift shop, Stephen looks crisp. His short haircut is probably something more fashionable than a crewcut, but it sure looks like a crewcut to me. The wispy moustache and goatee would contribute a beatnik touch if they were visible.

It's a whole new generation. Megan painted daisies on her old brown car and kept the tape deck full of Janis Joplin, Jimi Hendrix, and Jim Morrison: "Everyone I like is dead," she said. David looped his hair in a long ponytail and worked out guitar chords for Dylan songs, just as I had attempted to do thirty years earlier—a somewhat disturbing realization. Why were my kids reliving my life? When I was in high school, I wasn't listening to my mom's old Sinatra records or copying her shiny postwar hairstyle. I felt vaguely guilty. It was that old hound dog, middle-aged nostalgia, showing up to grin and wag its tail at the Boomers as it does at every generation. But in this case, the older generation was unprecedentedly big and willful, and the younger relatively weak and aimless. We resurrected our stars and styles and told the Xers, "Isn't this cool?" And they fell for it. As Megan once complained, "We're always celebrating some Boomer anniversary. Our whole present is just Boomer past." The older two are gradually extricating themselves from tie-dye retrouvé, but Stephen has always set his own distinctive course.

I spot a sign for Oliver's, which promises an all-you-can-eat lunch. We pull in to find that it's instinctively southern cooking, so unself-conscious about this that it doesn't advertise as such. There are no cornpone elements to the decor, no humorous plaques with pigs on them, no piped-in country music; an old Nirvana song is playing softly as we walk in. The buffet offers ribs and fried chicken, turnips, collard greens, yams, and fried okra. I like okra, which probably discloses a character flaw. Okra is unique among vegetables in that it combines both slimy and hairy in one great taste sensation. Frying mitigates these qualities somewhat, which I regret.

There is a bucket of something I can't identify, rigid off-white shards with a brown edge. They turn out to be bacon rinds, so amazingly salty that after a couple of bites I can do a good impression of Lot's wife. Over on the dessert table there is a round home-made chocolate cake looking saggy in the heat (if there's air conditioning in here it's set on "swelter," though ceiling fans push the humidity around) and a big tray of that luxurious concoction assembled from sliced bananas, pudding, and vanilla wafers. Why haven't I seen this ultimate comfort food in so long? Oh yeah—I moved up north.

Near the checkout counter there is a rack filled with religious fliers. The tall, narrow ones are doubled over, defeated, victims of the heat. Printed in red, white, and blue, they are headed "Freedom in Jesus" and begin, "Attention: The following is written especially for the poor, the brokenhearted, the captive, the blind, and the bruised. Please read carefully." The tract describes trouble and despair in unflinching terms, such as people everywhere might secretly know, even here in this sticky restaurant with a bellyful of collards and Kurt Cobain drifting down between the sluggish ceiling fans. "Are you bound in some prison of your own or someone else's making, distant from God and Jesus? . . . Is your body racked with pain or disease from the very pits of hell? . . . Has Satan stolen your very reasons for living?" People anywhere might answer yes to these questions, but I don't think these questions are asked publicly very far outside the South.

"Then, praise God! Your redemption draweth nigh." Over several more paragraphs, the writer interweaves Scripture with exhortation and encouragement, highlighting Bible promises to set us (all capitals) "FREE." It concludes with this suggested prayer: "Heavenly Father, I believe Jesus to be Your Son and the One Who shed His blood for the remission of my sins. I accept His sacrifice for me. I am sorry for my sins and ask You to forgive me. I thank You, Father, for the freedom I now have in Jesus Christ, freedom from all the curse of the Law. By faith in Jesus I am now saved, healed, and made whole. I thank You, Lord, and I love You, and pray for your will to be done in my life. Amen." The tracts were provided by

"Jesus Is Coming Again Ministries," right here in Selma, North Carolina.

The smaller, green tract takes a less consoling approach. "Where Will You Spend Eternity?" it asks, over a giant question mark. "Do you know that if you died today, you would go to heaven? If you could know for sure, would you do what the Bible said?"

Inside, a spare layout follows boldface headings with answering Scriptures. "Who is good? Romans 3:10. 'As it is written, there is none righteous, no, not one.' Who has sinned? Romans 3:23. 'For all have sinned, and come short of the glory of God.'" The tract leads the reader through "Where sin came from," "God's price on sin," and "Our way out," each followed with a quote from the Book of Romans. "Now pray," it concludes. "Confess that you are a sinner, ask God to save you and receive Christ as your Savior." These are the classic elements of the "Sinner's Prayer," as shown in the example from the tract above.

The conclusion of these tracts is the same, but the intellectual foundation is different. The green tract presumes the problem is rational, informational; it presumes that people need to know facts and act on them. The "Freedom in Jesus" tract presumes instead that the problem is that people feel bewildered and in pain, and need God's healing. There is a cultural sea change at work here, from a theology based on objectivity to one based on subjectivity, and the green tract's worldview is rapidly going out of style. Of course, having religious tracts in a restaurant at all went out of style most places a long time ago.

The green tract offers on its back cover lines for the reader to write in his own name and address. "If you believe that Christ died for you, and are willing to confess Him before God and man, then sign your name and send this tract to us for further help." Below this is the address and phone number for Honda Used Parts in North Myrtle Beach, South Carolina.

I phone Charlie Walls, "Honda Charlie," to ask whether anyone ever mails these in. I was raised a city southerner in sophisticated Charleston and can hear the country road in his voice. Distinctions like these are, frustratingly, lost on Hollywood, but then again they only need one all-purpose southern accent to cue the viewer that a character is either stupid or cruel or Fred Thompson.

"People ask me, 'Do they work?' and I tell 'em, they sure do," Charlie says. "Most times I sit down and write a letter back, maybe send a Bible. I have some fun with those tracts. I wish all would come back, but enough do that the Lord lets me know I'm doing the right thing."

He uses the tract as his business card. "I met this black guy up in Wilmington. he said, 'I need some parts,' so I gave him a tract. I told him, 'On the back of that tract is me, but the person you need to know is on the front.' He looked at it and put it in his pocket, and later he called about parts and I sent 'em.

"About a month went by and it was just a few days before Christmas, and I was closing up the shop for the holiday. That phone started ringing and I said, 'I ain't answering that phone no more,' trying to close things up. But it just kept on ringing! Like they say, when the Lord wants to get your attention, he finds a way. That phone musta rung about twenty-five times.

"Finally I answered it and it was a lady saying, 'Is this Honda Used Parts? Could you tell me your zip code?' See, I had forgot to put the zip code on the tract at first. She said, 'I've gotta share something with you. You gave my husband a tract a while ago. Well, I found that tract in his pocket, on the dresser, on the kitchen table,

I even found it in the laundry and put it back in his pocket. Two days ago he came up to me and said, "Honey, I can't stand it no longer. I read this tract, and read it and read it, and I gotta give my heart to the Lord. Make sure you get the address so I can sign this and mail it back in." '

"A while after that I saw him again, and I gave him a big hug and said, 'Welcome to the family of the Lord.' People ask me, Does that tract work? It works, honey."

Charlie converted after reluctantly attending a Christmas service with his wife and kids. When they passed the Communion trays he found himself looking at the bread and wine, unable to partake. "I just held that tray, and I looked up, and I thought about a Savior who loved me so much he died on a Cross and shed his blood for me." After that he threw himself vigorously into service at the church. He made a list of his activities: "I've swept floors, I've mopped floors, I've cut grass, I've been an usher, I've been a greeter, I've driven the church bus, and I've cooked. Now I didn't show my wife this list, so don't y'all tell her." But his life changed when he felt the Lord call him to begin speaking in churches.

"I said, 'Lord, I'm not going up in front of the church, you can forget that one. Why would you want to pick someone like me? I had to quit school when I was in sixth grade and go to work. I lived in an orphanage home all my life. I can't hardly read and write. My speech is terrible, Lord.' I looked for every excuse I could find.

"Then one morning about three the Lord woke me up, and he broke my heart." Charlie had a dream, or a waking vision, of a sixteen-year-old girl abused by her drunken parents, deciding on suicide. She took her father's car, intending to smash it into a tree, but at a stop light noticed people going into a church. She joined them and sat through the service listening in wonder to the talk of knowing Jesus, crying out in her heart, "Jesus, I sure need to talk to you."

The closing hymn was "What a Friend We Have in Jesus." "This li'l girl stood up with tears rolling down her face thinking, 'Won't somebody please tell me what to do?'" But there was no altar call—no explicit invitation describing how to take Jesus as her savior. As she fled the service and pulled her car out into the street, she was hit by a truck. At the hospital the weeping doctor told the pastor, "They died." "What do you mean 'they'?" "That li'l girl was three months pregnant."

When this drama finished playing inside him, Charlie goes on, "I fell down alongside my bed saying, 'Why would you tell me something like this, Lord? You done broke my heart.'" Months passed as Charlie sought in prayer to understand. Then in the wee hours of another morning he heard the Lord speak. "What I showed you hasn't happened yet. You can stop it. Do you love me enough to leave the back of the church and go up front, and tell the people that I love them?"

"Do you love me enough to tell them?" Christianity is rare among the world religions in containing an explicit command to tell unbelievers the Good News and to urge them to convert. It is an uncomfortable calling, even for someone like Charlie Walls. This obligation to evangelize is perhaps the aspect most resented by those outside the faith, and most neglected by those inside. It is an awkward calling. But it is a command of Jesus, as blunt as the calls to love our enemies and to care for the poor: "Go therefore and

make disciples of all nations, baptizing them in the name of the Father and of the Son and of the Holy Spirit" (Matthew 28:19).

Obedience to that command brought Orthodoxy to America. In the Russian Orthodox Cathedral of St. Nicholas, in Washington, D.C., there is a large icon fresco that shows, front and center, a walrus. The walrus is emerging from the water looking serious, as appropriate to its appearing in an icon, listing slightly to the left and wearing an expression befitting oatmeal tout Wilfred Brimley.

The body of water is the chilly depths of the Bering Strait, and on either side there is land. On the Russian shore stand three black-robed figures: St. Innocent of Moscow, St. Juvenaly of Alaska, and St. Herman of Alaska. On the North American shore are a group of Alaskan Natives, accompanied by an elk and a malamute. They stretch out their hands to the Russians, who are bearing a model of a church and a Bible.

Most American religion—indeed, most American history—begins on the east coast and gradually spreads west. But the Eastern Orthodox faith came into this continent at its uppermost western point, when Russian missionaries crossed the Strait in 1794. From there, it spread down the west coast and gradually made its way east, reversing the usual pattern. Because of this our first saints on this continent have names like "St. John the Wonderworker of San Francisco" and "St. Peter the Aleut."

The call to spread the Gospel can be done well—sensitively, carefully—or badly. Russian missionaries to Alaska were strictly bound never to use coercion but only to invite Native Alaskans to the faith. Once baptized, Natives were encouraged to participate at all levels in the life of the Church, including ordained ministry. Russians felt that the burden was on them to understand and appreciate the culture of their hosts. Even distressing local practices like slavery and suicide were dealt with by rational argument and persuasion, rather than outrage or command. Interracial marriage was viewed positively, and Creole children were adopted by immigrant Russian families.

A particular element of the missionaries' work was education and language. St. Innocent developed an alphabet for the Aleut language, and with the help of an Aleut Toien (Chief) published a catechism, the first book published in any Alaskan Native language. The Sitka seminary required priests-in-training to take six years of Native languages. When the first church was built, in 1784 on Kodiak Island, a school was opened as well. Bilingual and multilingual schools were maintained by Russians until the American purchase of Alaska in 1867 brought in a less friendly administration. Though Russians maintained their presence in Alaska until the Bolshevik Revolution, their influence diminished as European-Americans came in with their own missionary and educational agendas. The care with which the Russian effort was conducted, however, has left a lasting presence of Orthodoxy in Alaska to this day.

Megan phoned us at the beach house a few nights ago, after she'd gone home early to resume work. She mentioned that she'd dropped by the local copy shop to order business cards. "Not really for me," she said. "On one side they'll have the icon of the Christ of Sinai. And on the other it has the address of the church." She paused. "And above that it says, 'You should be Orthodox.'"

"Megan! You're turning into a kook!" I exclaimed, laughing.

"Well, I thought it would be handy to have them. I could leave one with a tip at a restaurant, for instance. Or I could give one with a quarter to somebody asking for spare change."

"I can't get over it," I said. "'You should be Orthodox.' Megan, you are turning into a crazy person."

When I mentioned this to the boys later, though, they rolled their eyes. "You should talk, Mom," David said. "Yeah, she gets it from you, you know," Stephen agreed.

Me? I'm a kook? On second thought, I guess I am. I'm the person who thought we should paint flames around the cat door, so when Felix came leaping in he'd look like a lion at the circus. I'm the one who thought we could build an igloo by inflating a garbage bag with vacuum cleaner exhaust, tying it off, and packing snow around it. And I am the one who, to my memorable shame, announced one night, "Look at all those shooting stars! So many in just one night. Just think how different the constellations must have looked to the ancient Greeks, before all those stars fell."

My reputation as a kook is so well established that when Gary told the kids a few weeks ago that I wanted to go to the tow-truck lot and sit in the station wagon Stephen had just wrecked, and talk about our old memories of the car, and take pictures, and drink champagne, they believed it right up to the point when he said, "She's had me searching through the prayer books, and I finally found an ancient prayer for the burial of a mule."

But I am not this kind of a kook—not the kind to grab folks by the collar and tell them, "You should be Orthodox." Megan has always been more of a debater than I am. The only non-Catholic at her college, she gets lots of practice. She's been known to spend late-night hours on the Internet, seeking out atheists in order to spar with them about the classic proofs for the existence of God. "I was getting a little insistent," she might say the next day in describing such an exchange. Having experienced what it's like to be on the receiving end of that insistence for the entire span of her teen years, the atheists have my sympathy.

The icon known as the Christ of Sinai is one of Orthodoxy's most beloved and most ancient. It was probably made in Constantinople in the sixth century and sent as a gift to the Monastery of St. Catherine on Mt. Sinai, where it remains to this day. It shows a nearly life-size Christ holding in his left arm a jeweled Bible, and his right hand is raised in blessing.

The startling thing about this icon is the eyes. The right eye is relaxed and benign, the brow gently curved; the left eye is narrowed and dark, with a pointed twitch in the brow. One eye of judgment and one of compassion.

"Look at it, Mom," Megan said. "You can see how it goes all the way down the icon. His left cheek has more shadows. The left side of his moustache droops down more sharply. The iconographer made every single detail consistent on the right, and on the left."

I study the small copy of the icon I brought on vacation. She's right; I'd never noticed that before.

"And then you get down to the hands, and that's what completes the message. On the left, he carries the book of Law and judgment. On the right, he's blessing."

I realize that this is a very accomplished piece of painting. It's not what I assumed early painting and especially iconography to be like—perspectiveless, flat, stylized. This is a realistic portrait, full of life. It recalls the Egyptian funerary portraiture of a few centuries earlier.

Not long ago my husband received a call out of the blue from a man who said he'd been given a copy of this Christ of Sinai icon by a friend. He described himself as a lifelong humanist, a retired college professor, with no knowledge of organized religion. ("Forgive me if this is a stupid question, but does your church practice circumcision?") He said he'd never before had any interest in spirituality or faith, but somehow this icon had seized him. "When I look at it, I have the sensation that he's looking into my soul," he said. "Before this, I didn't even think there was such a thing as a soul."

I'd rather let icons do my evangelizing for me. I'm not like Charlie Walls or like Megan, boldly going where a polite Charleston girl would blush to go. I like the idea of the icon on business cards, but I'd put the Jesus Prayer on the back, not a command to convert. David recounts a story that is more my style: while taking the all-night Greyhound bus from a friend's house to meet us at the beach, he sat next to a man who asked him what he was reading. It was a biography of the nineteenth-century Russian monk St. Theophan the Recluse, and David was able to go from that topic to a general explanation of Orthodoxy. "He kept asking me questions, like he was really interested," David said. He is quieter than the other two, and somewhat shy. His luminous eyes are large and pale blue. "I wonder if God sent me that person on purpose, so the first time I tried to explain to someone what I believe it would be easy."

I prefer that, too, answering questions rather than broaching the topic of faith. It seems there's little sense in answering questions people aren't asking. But Megan disagrees; she has a sense of urgency about telling people bluntly what they need to know. I wonder how effective this tactic is. I suspect that rare is the person who reads "You should be Orthodox" and concludes "I should be Orthodox." A more likely conclusion is "What kind of a kook is this?" Rather than taking the message at face value, people tend to judge the messenger. This is simple self-protection; there are shady and duplicitous folks out there. But Megan feels that if you offend twelve and reach two, at least you've done something; you've done more than if you never raised the topic at all. Perhaps she's right.

Stephen and I are flying north up the road, back to a land where raising the topic of faith is even more uncomfortable. Down here spiritual things lie closer to the surface, are embraced in all their messy glory, devoured and celebrated like a plateful of ribs. We shoot down the back roads, past the Rapture Time Church, past the Holy Ghost Hair Salon, past a barbecue shack with a sign reading "We pray that every church will have revival." This is not what America looks like anymore; this is a life that is passing away, and with it simple, guileless, outspoken faith, and Honda Charlie's tracts wilting by the cash register. Behind the Star of Deliverance Tabernacle a housetrailer is weeping and bleeding rust in the grip of green vines.

CHAPTER 17

Lasagna

After all the other communicants, Subdeacon Gregory and David
are the last to receive. They then fold up the red

cloth and return to their places behind the iconostasis. The congregation fans back out into the
body of the church, now that the lines of people
going up and back have dispersed. As the incense
diminishes, another scent is creeping up the
stairs—lasagna. We've been fasting since last night
and are pretty hungry, so a sizable feast is just
about ready downstairs.

Father Gregory sings out: "O God, save thy
people and bless thine inheritance."

On most Sundays, the Liturgy calls for this response: "We have seen the true light! We have received the heavenly spirit! We have found the true
faith! Worshipping the undivided Trinity, for he
hath saved us."

As shocking as it sounds, we do believe that we

have found the true faith. This is not to say that Christian believers of other churches can't possibly know Jesus, or even that God is prevented from saving people in other religions. That's God's business, not ours. But we are confident that everything needed for salvation can be found here: all the fullness of faith, the sacraments and disciplines, the saints and angels. We frankly believe it is the best place for anyone to be. How God handles the eternal destiny of those who never hear the invitation to join us, or who hear it and reject it, is beyond what we're allowed to know. We only know our marching orders: we're supposed to "make disciples of all nations" and do as much as we can to bring as many as we can to faith in Jesus Christ.

This makes some of my non-Christian friends understandably edgy. Nevertheless, it *is* what we believe, and it's what they don't believe, and that's the way things stand; two ideas can't occupy the same space at the same time any more than two Volkswagens can. I think it's a misnomer, though, to call this "exclusive"—it seems to me that it's the opposite, that if we went around saying, "Nyah nyah, you can't join our church," *that* would be exclusive. This isn't a club we won't let non-Christians into; we're eager for anyone to join.

The perceived insult, I think, has to do with the idea that someone is presuming their wisdom as wiser than anyone else's. Yet that's not really what's at issue with Christianity. Our faith isn't about a philosophy or mystical insight; it's about events that happened in history, in this same communal planet-earth history that we all share. If these things happened, they affect us all, just as other historical events do. We believe that God became man, died on a Cross, rose again, and opened a whole new way for humans to be reconciled with God and each other. If that happened, it's our job to tell everyone on earth about it. If it didn't happen, "we are of all men most to be pitied" (I Corinthians 15:19).

Someday each of us will find out conclusively whether this happened or not, some of us sooner than others, and some of us sooner than we expect. In the meantime, those of us who have seen the true light and found the true faith, who have seen the face of Jesus and been transformed, are propelled to spread the news.

Father Gregory chants, "Let us depart in peace," and we respond, "In the Name of the Lord." Then he sings, "Let us pray to the Lord," and we sing back, "Lord have mercy," the prelude to more intercessory prayers. In Orthodox worship, even once you say that it's all over and you're going home now, you tend to come back and do a little more praying first. We behave here like lingering dinner guests, which I guess we are.

But at last the end does come, and since it's soon after Pascha we conclude by repeating several times the acclamation: "Christ is risen from the dead, trampling down death by death, and upon those in the tombs bestowing life!"

I love this and sing it out loudly. Basil steps out into the narthex to ring the bell again during the whole time we're singing. The scent of incense and honeycandles swirl around us here, but as the doors swing behind Basil the fragrance of homey lasagna wafts in, calling us downstairs and into the next part of our story. We are always caught like this, between two times, between the incense and the lasagna, until that time when all time ends. But whether now in the between-times or then in timelessness, we are and will be ourselves, the same: redeemed, exulting, and charged with light, fulfilling the task we were created for, "destined and appointed to live for the praise of his glory" (Ephesians 1:12).

First Visit to an Orthodox Church—

12 THINGS I WISH I'D KNOWN

Orthodox worship is different! Some of these differences are apparent, if perplexing, from the first moment you walk in a church. Others become noticeable only over time. Here is some information that may help you feel more at home in Orthodox worship— twelve things I wish I'd known before my first visit to an Orthodox church.

1. What's all this commotion?

During the early part of the service the church may seem to be in a hubbub, with people walking up to the front of the church, praying in front of the iconostasis (the standing icons in front of the altar), kissing things and lighting candles, even though the service is already going on. In fact, when you came in, the service was already going on, although the sign outside clearly said "Divine Liturgy, 9:30." You felt embarrassed to apparently be late, but these people are even later, and they're walking all around inside the church. What's going on here?

In an Orthodox church there is only one Eucharistic service (Divine Liturgy) per Sunday, and it is preceded by an hour-long service of Matins (or Orthros) and several short preparatory services before that. There is no break between these services—one begins as soon as the previous ends, and posted starting times are just educated guesses. Altogether, the priest will be at the altar on Sunday morning for over three hours, "standing in the flame," as one Orthodox priest put it.

As a result of this state of continuous flow, there is no point at which everyone is sitting quietly in a pew waiting for the entrance hymn to start, glancing at their watches approaching 9:30. Orthodox worshippers arrive at any point from the beginning of Matins through the early part of the Liturgy, a span of well over an hour. No matter when they arrive, something is sure to be already going on, so Orthodox don't let this hamper them from going through the private prayers appropriate to just entering a church. This is distracting to newcomers, and may even seem disrespectful, but soon you begin to recognize it as an expression of a faith that is not merely formal but very personal. Of course, there is still no good excuse for showing up *after* 9:30, but punctuality is unfortunately one of the few virtues many Orthodox lack.

2. Stand up, stand up for Jesus.

In the Orthodox tradition, the faithful stand up for nearly the entire service. Really. In some Orthodox churches, there won't even be any chairs, except a few scattered at the edges of the room for those who need them. Expect variation in practice: some churches, especially those that bought already-existing church buildings, will have well-used pews. In any case, if you find the amount of standing too challenging, you're welcome to take a seat. No one minds or probably even notices. Long-term standing gets easier with practice.

3. In this sign.

To say that we make the sign of the cross frequently would be an understatement. We sign ourselves whenever the Trinity is invoked, whenever we venerate the Cross or an icon, and on many other occasions in the course of the Liturgy. But people aren't expected to do everything the same way. Some people cross themselves three times in a row, and some finish by sweeping their right hand to the floor. On first entering a church people may come up to an icon, and twice make a "metania"—crossing themselves and bowing with the right hand to the floor—then kiss the icon and make one more metania. This becomes familiar with time, but at first it can seem like secret-handshake stuff that you are sure to get wrong. Don't worry, you don't have to follow suit.

We cross with our right hands from right to left (push, not pull), the opposite of Roman Catholics and high-church Protestants. We hold our hands in a prescribed way: thumb and first two fingertips pressed together, last two fingers pressed down to the palm. Here as elsewhere, the Orthodox impulse is to make everything we do reinforce the Faith. Can you figure out the symbolism? (Three fingers together for the Trinity; two fingers brought down to the palm for the two natures of Christ, and his coming down to earth.) This, too, takes practice. A beginner's imprecise arrangement of fingers won't get you denounced as a heretic.

4. What, no kneelers?

Generally, we don't kneel. We do sometimes prostrate. This is not like prostration in the Roman Catholic tradition, lying out flat on the floor. To make a prostration we kneel, place our hands on the floor, and touch our foreheads down between our hands. It's just like those photos of Middle Eastern worship, which look to westerners like a sea of behinds. At first, prostration feels embarrassing, but no one else is embarrassed, so after a while it feels O.K. Ladies will learn that full skirts are best for prostrations, as flat shoes are best for standing.

Sometimes we do this and get right back up again, as during the prayer of St. Ephraim the Syrian, which is used frequently during Lent. Other times we get down and stay there awhile, as some congregations do during part of the Eucharistic prayer.

Not everyone prostrates. Some kneel, some stand with head bowed; in a pew they might slide forward and sit crouched over. Standing there feeling awkward is all right too. No one will notice if you don't prostrate. In Orthodoxy, there is a wider acceptance of individualized expressions of piety, rather than a sense that people are watching you and getting offended if you do it wrong.

One former Episcopal priest said that seeing people prostrate themselves was one of the things that made him most eager to become Orthodox. He thought, "That's how we should be before God."

5. With love and kisses.

We kiss stuff. When we first come into the church, we kiss the icons (Jesus on the feet and other saints on the hands, ideally). You'll also notice that some kiss the chalice, some kiss the edge of the priest's vestment as he passes by, the acolytes kiss his hand when they give him the censer, and we all line up to kiss the Cross at the end of the service. When we talk about "venerating" something we usually mean crossing ourselves and kissing it.

We kiss each other before we take Communion ("Greet one another with a kiss of love," I Peter 5:14). When Roman Catholics or high-church Protestants "pass the peace," they give a hug, handshake, or peck on the cheek; that's how westerners greet each other. In Orthodoxy, different cultures are at play: Greeks and Arabs kiss on two cheeks, and Slavs come back again for a third. Follow the lead of those around you and try not to bump your nose.

The usual greeting is "Christ is in our midst" and the response, "He is and shall be." Don't worry if you forget what to say. The greeting is not the one familiar to Episcopalians, "The peace of the Lord be with you." Nor is it "Hi, nice church you have here." Exchanging the kiss of peace is a liturgical act, a sign of mystical unity. Chatting and fellowship is for later.

6. Blessed bread and consecrated bread.

Only Orthodox may take Communion, but anyone may have some of the blessed bread. Here's how it works: the round Communion loaf, baked by a parishioner, is imprinted with a seal. In the preparation service before the Liturgy, the priest cuts out a section of the seal and sets it aside; it is called the "Lamb." The rest of the bread is cut up and placed in a large basket, and blessed by the priest.

During the Eucharistic prayer, the Lamb is consecrated to be the Body of Christ, and the chalice of wine is consecrated as his Blood. Here's the surprising part: the priest places the Lamb in the chalice with the wine. When we receive Communion, we file up to the priest, standing and opening our mouths wide while he gives us a fragment of the wine-soaked bread from a golden spoon. He also prays over us, calling us by our first name or the saint-name which we chose when we were baptized or chrismated (received into the Church by anointing with blessed oil).

As we file past the priest, we come to an altar boy holding the basket of blessed bread. People will take portions for themselves and for visitors and non-Orthodox friends around them. If someone hands you a piece of blessed bread, do not panic; it is not the Eucharistic Body. It is a sign of fellowship.

Visitors are sometimes offended that they are not allowed to receive Communion, but few Christian bodies treat the Eucharist with the degree of gravity that we do. The sacrament is not just a me-and-Jesus matter but incorporates the believer into a Body. Thus any communicant at the Orthodox chalice must be a member in good standing of the Body: he or she must believe Orthodox doctrine, be under the authority of an Orthodox bishop, be making regular confession to an Orthodox priest, and be at peace with fellow worshippers. The communicant must also have fasted from all food and drink since the previous midnight—yes, not even a cup of coffee. The Church guards the sacrament closely because it is our treasure. But the intention is not to be exclusive; quite the reverse, everyone is invited to join the Church by preparing for the sacraments of baptism or chrismation. Those who are not yet ready to make that commitment may still share with us in the common loaf, by partaking of the blessed bread.

7. Where's the General Confession?

In our experience, we don't have any general sins; they're all quite specific. There is no complete confession-prayer in the Liturgy. Orthodox are expected to be making regular, private confession to their priest.

The role of the pastor is much more that of a spiritual father than it is in other denominations. He is not called by his first name alone, but referred to as "Father Firstname." His wife also holds a special role as parish mother, and she gets a title, too, though it varies from one culture to another: either "Khouria" (Arabic), or "Presbytera" (Greek), both of which mean "priest's wife"; or "Matushka" (Russian), which means "Mama."

Another difference you may notice is in the Nicene Creed, which may be said or sung, depending on the parish. If we are saying that the Holy Spirit proceeds from the Father, and you from force of habit add "and the Son," you will be alone. The "filioque" was added to the Creed some six hundred years after it was written, and we adhere to the original. High-church visitors will also notice that we don't bow or genuflect during the "and was incarnate." Nor do we restrict our use of "Alleluia" during Lent (when the sisters at one Episcopal convent are referring to it as "the 'A' word"); in fact, during Matins in Lent, the Alleluias are more plentiful than ever.

8. Music, music, music.

About 75 percent of the service is congregational singing. Traditionally, Orthodox use no instruments, although some churches will have organs. Usually a small choir leads the people in a cappella harmony, with the level of congregational response varying from parish to parish. The style of music varies as well, from very Oriental-sounding solo chant in an Arabic church to more western-sounding four-part harmony in a Russian church, with lots of variation in between.

This constant singing is a little overwhelming at first; it feels like getting on the first step of an escalator and being carried along in a rush until you step off ninety minutes later. It has been fairly said that the Liturgy is one continuous song.

What keeps this from being exhausting is that it's pretty much the *same* song every week. Relatively little changes from Sunday to Sunday; the same prayers and hymns appear in the same places, and before long you know it by heart. Then you fall into the presence of God in a way you never can when flipping from prayer book to bulletin to hymnal.

9. Making editors squirm.

Is there a concise way to say something? Can extra adjectives be deleted? Can the briskest, most pointed prose be boiled down one more time to a more refined level? Then it's not Orthodox worship. If there's a longer way to say something, the Orthodox will find it. In Orthodox worship, more is always more, in every area including prayer. When the priest or deacon intones, "Let us complete our prayer to the Lord," expect to still be standing there fifteen minutes later.

The original Liturgy lasted something over five hours; those people must have been on fire for God. The Liturgy of St. Basil edited this down to about two and a half, and later (around 400 A.D.) the Liturgy of St. John Chrysostom further reduced it to about one and a half. Most Sundays we use the St. John Chrysostom Liturgy, although for some services (e.g., Sundays in Lent, Christmas Eve) we use the longer Liturgy of St. Basil.

10. Our Champion Leader.

A constant feature of Orthodox worship is veneration of the Virgin Mary, the "champion leader" of all Christians. We often address her as "Theotokos," which means "God-bearer." In providing the physical means for God to become man, she made possible our salvation.

But though we honor her, as Scripture foretold ("All generations will call me blessed," Luke 1:48), this doesn't mean that we think she or any of the other saints have magical powers or are demi-gods. When we sing "Holy Theotokos, save us," we don't mean that she grants us eternal salvation, but that we seek her prayers for our protection and growth in faith. Just as we ask for each other's prayers, we ask for the prayers of Mary and other saints as well. They're not dead, after all, just departed to the other side. Icons surround us to remind us of all the saints who are joining us invisibly in worship.

11. The three doors.

Every Orthodox church will have an iconostasis before its altar. "Iconostasis" means "icon-stand," and it can be as simple as a large image of Christ on the right and a corresponding image of the Virgin and Child on the left. In a more established church, the iconostasis may be a literal wall, adorned with icons. Some versions shield the altar from view, except when the central doors stand open.

The basic setup of two large icons creates, if you use your imagination, three doors. The central one, in front of the altar itself, is called the "Holy Doors" or "Royal Doors," because there the King of Glory comes out to the congregation in the Eucharist. Only the priest and deacons, who bear the Eucharist, use the Holy Doors.

The openings on the other sides of the icons, if there is a complete iconostasis, have doors with icons of angels; they are termed the "Deacon's Doors." Altar boys and others with business behind the altar use these, although no one is to go through any of the doors without an appropriate reason. Altar service—priests, deacons, altar boys—is restricted to males. Females are invited to participate in every other area of church life. Their contribution has been honored equally with men's since the days of the martyrs; you can't look at an Orthodox altar without seeing Mary and other holy women. In most Orthodox churches, women do everything else men do: lead congregational singing, paint icons, teach classes, read the epistle, and serve on the parish council.

12. Where does an American fit in?

Flipping through the Yellow Pages in a large city you might see a multiplicity of Orthodox churches: Greek, Romanian, Carpatho-Russian, Antiochian, Serbian, and on and on. Is Orthodoxy really so tribal? Do these divisions represent theological squabbles and schisms?

Not at all. All these Orthodox churches are one Church. The ethnic designation refers to what is called the parish's "jurisdiction" and identifies which bishops hold authority there. There are about 6 million Orthodox in North America and 250 million in the world, making Orthodoxy the second-largest Christian communion.

The astonishing thing about this ethnic multiplicity is its theological and moral unity. Orthodox throughout the world hold unanimously to the fundamental Christian doctrines taught by the Apostles and handed down by their successors, the bishops, throughout the centuries. One could attribute this unity to historical accident. We would attribute it to the Holy Spirit.

Why then the multiplicity of ethnic churches? These national designations obviously represent geographic realities. Since North America is also a geographic unity, one day we will likewise have a unified national church—an American Orthodox Church. This was the original plan, but due to a number of complicated historical factors, it didn't happen that way. Instead, each ethnic group of Orthodox immigrating to this country developed its own church structure. This multiplication of Orthodox jurisdictions is a temporary aberration, and much prayer and planning is going into breaking through those unneces-sary walls.

Currently the largest American jurisdictions are the Greek Orthodox Archdiocese, the Orthodox Church in America (Russian roots), and the Antiochian Archdiocese (Arabic roots). The Liturgy is substantially the same in all, though there may be variation in lan-guage used and type of music.

I wish it could be said that every local parish eagerly welcomes newcomers, but some are still so close to their immigrant experience that they are mystified as to why outsiders would be interested. Visiting several Orthodox parishes will help you learn where you're most comfortable. You will probably be looking for one that uses plenty of English in its services. Many parishes with high proportions of converts will have services entirely in English.

Orthodoxy seems startlingly different at first, but as the weeks go by it gets to be less so. It will begin to feel more and more like home, and will gradually draw you into your true home, the Kingdom of God. I hope that your first visit to an Orthodox church will be enjoyable, and that it won't be your last.

For Further Reading

Many Orthodox churches will have both a lending library and a book table selling icons, books, recorded liturgical music, incense, and so forth after Sunday services. Browsing at your closest church, and talking with the priest or bookstore manager, will best help you determine which items would be most useful.

Much of the below can also be ordered through standard online bookstores. Specialty Orthodox houses are also good resources:

Conciliar Press puts out several magazines, and offers as well books, pamphlets, icons, music, and other materials. Phone 800-967-7377; www.conciliarpress.com

Light and Life Publishing Company is the largest distributor of Orthodox goods and handles books from many small presses. Phone 612-925-3888; www.light-n-life.com

St. Vladimir's Seminary produces both popular and scholarly books, as well as a full range of recorded liturgical music. Phone 800-204-2665; www.svots.edu

Eighth Day Books offers a comprehensive range of Orthodox books as well as classics of literature, history, philosophy, and religion; the catalogue alone is a delightful read. Phone 800-841-2541; www2.southwind.net/~edb/

FOR ICONS

St. Isaac of Syria Skete: Phone 800-81-ICONS; www.skete.com

Holy Transfiguration Monastery: Phone 800-227-1629

WEBSITES

Theologic (center for Orthodox links): www.theologic.com/links/

Orthodox Christian Resources (center for Orthodox links): www.hrweb.org/orthodox

St. Pachomius (Early Church documents): www.ocf.org/OrthodoxPage/reading/St. Pachomius/

Orchid Land (Orthodox FAQ's): www.ilhawaii.net/~orlapubs/opR72.html

Antiochian Orthodox Archdiocese: www.antiochian.org

Orthodox Church in America: www.oca.org

Greek Orthodox Archdiocese: www.goarch.org

Orthodox Peace Fellowship: www.incommunion.org

Holy Cross Church: www.clark.net/pub/holycros

Frederica Mathewes-Green: www.frederica.com

BIBLES

The Orthodox Study Bible (Thomas Nelson Publishers, Nashville, 1993). A New Testament with interpretive notes from an Orthodox perspective.

The Bible and the Holy Fathers for Orthodox, compiled by Johanna Manley (Monastery Books, Menlo Park, CA, 1990). The assigned readings of the Orthodox liturgical year, each one followed by commentary by ancient Christian writers.

The Message of the Bible: An Orthodox Christian Perspective, by George Cronk (St. Vladimir's Seminary Press, Crestwood, NY, 1982).

POCKET PRAYERBOOKS

A Manual of Eastern Orthodox Prayers (St. Vladimir's Seminary Press, Crestwood, NY, 1983).

A Pocket Prayer Book (Antiochian Orthodox Christian Archdiocese, Englewood, NJ, 1956).

PRAYER

The Way of a Pilgrim. This anonymous nineteenth-century work is available in several translations, and is the most popular "beginner's book" on the Jesus Prayer.

The Art of Prayer, by Igumen Chariton of Valamo (Faber and Faber Ltd, London, 1966). A compilation of Orthodox texts on prayer, chiefly from St. Theophan the Recluse.

Orthodox Spirituality, by "a Monk of the Eastern Church" (St. Vladimir's Seminary Press, Crestwood, NY, 1996).

BASIC ORTHODOXY

The Orthodox Church, by Timothy Ware (Penguin, New York, 1963). This summary of Orthodox history and theology is the most popular introduction to the faith. The author is now Bishop Kallistos Ware.

The Orthodox Faith, by Fr. Thomas Hopko (Orthodox Church in America, New York, 1984). A basic introduction to the faith in four slim volumes: Doctrine, Worship, Bible and Church History, and Spirituality.

The Faith, by Clark Carlton (Regina Press, Salisbury, MA, 1997). A recent Orthodox catechism.

THE EUCHARISTIC LITURGY

The Eucharist, by Alexander Schmemann (St. Vladimir's Seminary Press, Crestwood, NY, 1988).

The Orthodox Liturgy, by Hugh Wybrew (St. Vladimir's Seminary Press, Crestwood, NY, 1990).

Orthodox Worship: Synagogue, Temple, and Early Church, by Benjamin Williams and Harold Anstall (Light and Life Publishing Co., Minneapolis, 1990).

WRITINGS OF THE EARLY CHURCH

The Sayings of the Desert Fathers, translated by Benedicta Ward (Mowbray, London, 1975).

The Apostolic Fathers, edited by J. B. Lightfoot and J. R. Harmer (Baker Book House, Grand Rapids, MI, 1998).

On Marriage and Family Life, by St. John Chrysostom (St. Vladimir's Seminary Press, Crestwood, NY, 1986). This is one example of a series of small paperbacks from this publisher. Others include St. Gregory of Nyssa's *On the Soul and Resurrection,* St. Basil the Great's *On the Holy Spirit,* St. John of Damascus' *On the Divine Images,* and so forth.

CONTEMPORARY ORTHODOXY IN AMERICA

Becoming Orthodox, by Fr. Peter Gillquist (Conciliar Press, Ben Lomond, CA, 1992). How a group of ex-Campus Crusade ministers gradually found their way to Orthodoxy.

The Way, by Clark Carlton (Regina Press, Salisbury, MA, 1997). A young man's journey from Baptist to Orthodox.

Facing East, by Frederica Mathewes-Green (HarperSanFrancisco, San Francisco, 1997). A journal of a year in a small Orthodox parish.

ICONS

Praying with Icons, by Jim Forest (Orbis Books, Maryknoll, NY, 1997).

The Meaning of Icons, by Leonid Ouspensky and Vladimir Lossky (St. Vladimir's Seminary Press, Crestwood, NY, 1997).

MODERN MARTYRS AND PERSECUTION

Father Arseny, translated by Vera Bouteneff (St. Vladimir's Seminary Press, Crestwood, NY, 1998).

Christ Is Calling You!, by Fr. George Calciu (St. Herman of Alaska Brotherhood, Forestville, CA, 1997).

Exploring the Inner Universe, by Archimandrite Roman Braga (HDM Press, Rives Junction, MI, 1996).

SAINTS

The Prologue from Ochrid, by Bp. Nikolai Velimirovic (Lazarica Press, Birmingham, England, 1985). The classic compilation of saints' lives for each day of the year, in four volumes.

A Daily Calendar of Saints, by Lawrence Farley (Light and Life, Minneapolis, 1997).

Marriage as a Path to Holiness: Lives of Married Saints, by David and Mary Ford (St. Tikhon's Seminary Press, South Canaan, PA, 1994).

Portraits of American Saints, by George Gray and Jan Bear (Orthodox Church in America, Syosset, NY, 1994).

The Saints of Anglo-Saxon England, by Vladimir Moss (3 volumes—St. Nectarios Press, Seattle, 1997).

COOKBOOKS FOR FASTING AND FEASTING

A Lenten Cookbook for Orthodox Christians (St. Nectarios Press, Seattle, 1982).

Food for Paradise, compiled by the Church of St. John the Russian, Ipswich, MA.

Holy Cross Orthodox Church Cook Book. Our own homemade cookbook. Order direct from Diane Stammer, c/o Holy Cross Church, 105 N. Camp Meade Road, Linthicum, MD 21090; $12.00.

MUSIC

"First Fruits." Byzantine chant in English, by St. Mary Antiochian Orthodox Church in Cambridge, MA.

"Come Receive the Light." The Orthros (Matins) Service of Holy Pascha, by a chorus of three sisters known as "Eikona of Edmond, OK."

St. Vladimir's Seminary choir offers a series of recordings of the basic hymns of Orthodoxy in the Russian style. For example, "The Divine Liturgy of St. John Chrysostom," "Orthodox Hymns of Christmas," "Pascha: Hymns of the Resurrection."

ABOUT THE AUTHOR

Frederica Mathewes-Green is a commentator for NPR's *All Things Considered* and a columnist for *Christianity Today*. The author of the acclaimed books *Facing East* and *Real Choices*, she lives in Baltimore, Maryland.